The Author
The Book
&
The Reader

In this book Robert Giddings explores the literary nexus - the interdependence always existing between writers and their readers through the production and distribution of books. Drawing upon information and insights from the disciplines of history, sociology and politics, as well as media studies and literary criticism, he illuminates the fascinating variation in the ways in which authors have tackled the challenge of truth and story telling. The eight authors chosen to illustrate this theme range from Samuel Johnson in the 18th century to Le Carré in the 20th and all are studied in the cultural context of their time with an emphasis upon the channels of communication and the available technology of printing and publishing. The topic of the how and the why of writing is here treated in a robust and original way and will be of interest to all those with a love of literature in English.

THE MARCH OF INTELLECT

Cartoon of 1828. Some of the fears about unrestricted popular education and scientific progress - street lighting gives the light-of-day; the fashion business becomes gargantuan; there is salon music on the pavement; coachmen read The Times; *dustmen play chess; armies use steam transport; ships fly; the Channel unites France and the British mainland; footmen smoke Meerschaum pipes. But the rise of civilisation is achieved at terrible cost - streets are not cleaned; passengers have to go on stilts; babies drown in filth. Such is the price of human beings getting above themselves.*

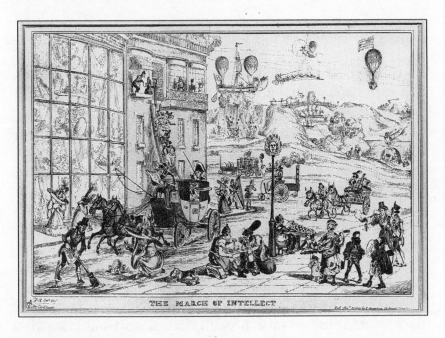

THE MARCH OF INTELLECT

(Author's Collection.)

The Author
The Book
&
The Reader

Robert Giddings

GREENWICH EXCHANGE

LONDON

Published by Greenwich Exchange 1991

ISBN 1 871551 01 3   Pbk.

To the memory of **Arthur Wesley Giddings**, Bathonian and Cabinet Maker, whose copy of Pope's *Works* is ever on my desk.

CONTENTS

ACKNOWLEDGEMENTS

Parts of this book have appeared before as chapters, or sections of chapters, in books written or edited by me (Robert Giddings) or edited by others, as stated below. I am grateful to the Editors and publishers involved in commissioning the items, some now revised for this volume, which first appeared as follows:

Chapter I   was written for this volume.

Chapter II   first appeared as the 'The Fall of Orgilio' in *Samuel Johnson: New Critical Essays* edited by Isobel Grundy (Vision Press 1984).

Chapter III   first appeared as 'Matthew Bramble's Bath' in *Smollet: Author of the First Distinction* edited by Alan Bold (Vision Press 1982).

Chapter IV   first appeared as 'Was the Chevalier Left-Handed?' in *Edgar Allan Poe: The Design of Order* edited by A. Robert Lee (Vision Press 1987)

Chapter V   was written for this volume.

Chapter VI   first appeared in *Mark Twain: A Sumptuous Variety* by Robert Giddings (Vision Press 1985).

Chapter VII   first appeared in *J.R.R. Tolkien: This Far Land* by Robert Giddings (Vision Press 1984).

Chapter VIII first appeared in *F. Scott Fitzgerald: The Promises of Life* edited by A. Robert Lee (Vision Press 1989).

Chapter IX   first appeared in *The Quest for Le Carre* edited by Alan Bold (Vision Press 1989).

I
Lines of communication

Francis Bacon asserted that reading maketh a full man; conference a ready man; and writing an exact man. Language had to be invented. Once we had that we progressed by leaps and bounds. We even began to tell stories and a few began to use their imaginations to make up some fairly elaborate works. The problem was remembering these things. This gave us poetry remembered by rhymes and patterned language. We had then created another dimension to the imagination. Writing created literate man. It turned man into another kind of being altogether, with a vast range of potentialities. Printing was another revolution. Human society would never be the same again. A very serious problem began to be pressing — how are writers to earn a living while they write? Only by negotiating with the means of production, those who have the funds and the machinery. What difference will these arrangements actually make to what writers are able to write? By the middle of the 18th century things had reached crisis point, and Alexander Pope believed he was a member of the generation which would see the end of civilization as he knew it — we would drown in a vast tidal wave of printer's ink.

Books and the man I sing, the first who brings
The Smithfield Muses to the ears of Kings.

1.

Schiller postulated in *Ueber naive und sentimentalische Dichtung* 1796 that there were two types of poets. There are those who are unaware of any division between them and their audience or consumers.

They have something to say, and their assumption is that they may say it directly to those who wish to hear it. Then there are those poets who are acutely aware, to the point of being self-conscious. He distinguishes between the poet for whom poetry is produced spontaneously from personal feelings — this is naive poetry — and the poet whose poetry is the result of reflection — this is sentimental poetry.[1] He aspired to the greatest naivete humanly possible. He wrote to Wilhelm von Humboldt of the conclusion of his *Das Reich der Schatten* that he hoped he would succeed in triumphing by means of:

"sentimental poetry even over naive poetry itself ... Just think ... a poetic representation in which everything that is mortal has been extinguished, nothing but light, perfect freedom, pure potentiality ... I feel really dizzy at the thought of the task and the possibility of its solution ... I am not in complete despair at it, if only my mind can be completely free and washed clean of all the dross of mundane life; I will then concentrate my entire strength and the whole of the ethereal part of my nature for one more great effort, even if I should expend myself completely in the act."
[2]

In Schiller's reckoning Homer, Aeschylus, Shakespeare and (on a good day) Goethe were naive poets. They were not self-conscious. They speak directly to us from the heart. On the other hand there were the sentimental poets — such as Virgil, Ariosto — who stand apart from what they create and express their own feelings. Schiller argues that when man enters the stage of culture, art lays hands on him, and primordial, sensuous unity evaporates:

"... the harmony between sense and thinking, which in the earlier state was **real**, now exists only as an **ideal**. It is not in man, as a fact of his life, but outside him, as an ideal to be realized." [3]

If Schiller is postulating that there was a time when the poet — the writer in the larger sense — could communicate directly with his audience, speak straight from the heart, free from any formal, technical, cultural or commercial restraints at all, then it is hard to imagine when this might have been. Homer (assuming for the sake of the argument that Homer was one, individual poet, the maker of the works we now collectively identify as "Homer") must have been aware that his bardic role as a reciter of epic carried with it certain obligations — cultural, social, political even — as well as the privileges of a poet.

The readiness to qualify Schiller's very interesting assertions in no way denies the validity of his case. Could Schiller be brought back from his grave he could not fail to be impressed at the complexities of the world within which the modern writer must work, and within which the modern writer negotiates creative existence. He could not but marvel at the political and social conventions (not to say laws) which restrict what a writer may say; at the relationships which must be established with agents, editors, publishers, accountants and taxation officials; at the variously arrayed means of production of books, journals, film and broadcasting; and at the wide variety of readership. Yes. He would certainly be compelled to admit that writers are a little less naive than they were in his day in Weimar, even though sentimental is scarcely a word best suited to describe the modern writer.

From the very beginning there has always been a division between the poet, the maker, who imagines, or creates, and the reader who consumes the work. That division, that dividing line, is the line of communication — in the widest sense of the term. Whatever an author wants to say will have to be accommodated within the means of literary production and the socio-economic context of the day. And that will have an impact upon what is said and the way in which it gets said. Willy-nilly the writer will find his/her work shaped, textured and conditioned by a whole set of factors not always subject to the writer's direct wish or control.

This is even to neglect the basic tool of the writer, language. Language itself offers all manner of possibilities and limitations to the nature of utterance. This naturally varies from culture to culture, society to society. Some languages are good at some things, and not at others. As a quantative language with a complex grammar involving accidence, Latin in its very essence was a metric poetic language. French seems supremely suited to elegant rhyme. Lacking strict quantities and having fortunately been subjected to political and cultural influences which involved its collision with Norman French English lost its grammatical inflexions (and a lot more rubbish besides) but rhymes quite well and goes superbly into blank verse. When the only available technology available to the poet was language, then in Schiller's argument, the poet would be at his/her most naive. All the poet needed to worry about was working out the best possible way to say what had been imagined, and then to cast this in a form pleasant to hear and reasonably easy to commit to memory. This gives us some of the initial characteristics of poetry - form and pattern. [4]

There will be serious social consequences, too. We tend to take writing for granted. We should point out to ourselves that the organisation of thought and expression in a society which has not progressed to writing is not "simple" — for it calls for organisation now unfamiliar to us — formulaic, structured in saws and proverbs, patterned in verse and elaborated in narrative. It is aggretative rather than analytic, participatory rather than distanced, and situational rather than abstract.

The coming of writing transforms human consciousness, as well as human society, totally, from top to bottom. The result is the production of thought processes, patterns of thinking, which to the literate have come to seem "natural", even commonplace — part of human nature itself — but which are possible only when the mind has devised and **internalised** the very technology of writing.

The consequences of this line of enquiry are enormous. At the beginning was the word. Oral man. Oral man made the best sense of his world that he could. Society could be organized, but within limits. Seeing was believing. Social organisations were proxemic. Evidence of this survives today in our customs and rituals — witnesses at weddings and the whole business of "Who giveth this woman to be married to this man" etc. Further survivals are found in the debris of folklore, nursery rhymes which seem nonsense to modern children, [5] riddles, mnemonics such as "Thirty days has September". Then came writing. Writing meant that laws could be elaborated, preserved and judgements recorded. Messages could be transmitted over distances and instruction handed on from one generation to another. Property ownership was possible, and could be recorded and proved, entailed and handed on from one person or one generation to another. Sexual relations were altered in societies where this occurred. In Greece during the archaic period which Homer portrayed, heterosexuality was the norm (early twelfth century BC, the age of Mycenaean Greece). After the introduction of writing and the consequent concentration on property and inheritance, human relationships changed. For the aristocracy of this period marriage was concerned with property, inheritance. Upper class women at this time were segregated and consequently could not be seen as the object of romantic attachment. Aristocratic males experienced female company mainly from professional female dinner entertainers, or prostitutes. These were the *hetaerae*, who had certain legal status, but were subject to paying taxes whether they lived privately or collectively in brothels. [6] In such a society homosexuality was encouraged and produced those familiar ingredients of Hellenic aristocratic social living — the all male dinner party, naked exercise in gymnasia, the male comradeship of war (*hieros lochos*) and the cult of male physical beauty.

With writing came new kinds of power — secrets could be written down and kept; those who could write could obtain certain kinds of power. This sense is preserved in the word spell — in a society where just a few could read and write such personal control over language might have connotations of awe. Writing transformed social control. And print revolutionised literacy. The Renaissance was made possible not just by the fall of Constantinople to the Turks and the fleeing westwards of all the learned with their texts which enshrined ancient learning once more to be released upon the world — it also created a revolution to human consciousness because there was in Italy the print technology by means of which knowledge could be made available.

The sacred name in this part of the story is that of Aldo Mannucci (1450-1515) - also known as Aldo Manuzio, who founded the celebrated Aldine press. He studied at Rome and Ferrara, and was patronised by the Pico family. He was funded by Alberto Pico, prince of Carpi, and opened his printing works. He gathered Greek scholars and compositors around him and using Italic print as it was less expensive to reproduce than Gothic or Latin he began to print his famous editions of the classics. His edition of Musaeus' *Hero and Leander* was followed by *Galeomyomachia* and by 1498 he had published five volumes of Aristotle. He then turned to Aristophanes, Thucydides, Sophocles, Herodotus, Xenophon, Euripides, Plutarch and Demosthenes. In 1513 he published Plato. After his death his pioneering work was continued and extended by his brothers-in-law and his youngest son, Paolo Mannucci took it over in 1533 and he concentrated on producing excellent editions of the Latin classics, notably Cicero. A further benefit for mankind fostered, developed and popularized by this remarkable family was the formalization and codification of a system of punctuation we now take for granted. Yet how simple, and how unconnected with anything resembling the technology of the means of literary production and distribution, the Renaissance is made to seem:

"In 1453 Constantinople, the West's umbilical cord to our classical past, was attacked and conquered by Ottoman Turks. Greek scholars emigrated to Western Europe, bringing with them Greek culture, and stimulating an interest in Greek literature ..." [7]

Literate man was not simply oral man plus writing. Literacy made him into quite a different kind of man, with different potential and different ways of looking at the world and ordering the world. Superstition was gradually to yield to science. The struggle informs much of *King Lear*, which is one of the key texts of the period in which this great shift occurred. Much of the dramatic tension is between those who adhere to the old loyalties - such as order, respect, authority, family and social bonds - (Kent, Gloucester, Edgar, Cordelia) and the new, thrusting, rational individualism (Edmund, Regan, Goneril, Cornwall).

When the inextinguishable ferocity of the drama begins, Gloucester, commenting on the conflicts at court and the signs and portents in the sky, remarks:
"These late eclipses in the sun and moon portend no good to us. Though the wisdom of nature can reason it thus and thus, yet nature finds itself scourg'd by the sequent effects: love cools, friendship falls off, brothers divide; in cities, mutinies; in countries, discord; in palaces, treason; and the bond crack'd 'twixt son and father ..." (*King Lear* Act I Scene 2)

Gloucester's world is crumbling, he believes he has seen the best of the times, that bad times are coming. The wisdom of nature he refers to, the new philosophy and endeavours of science, resulting from literacy and the rationalism inspired by print [8] will pull the foundations of feudalism out of the ground. From the collapse will come the new socio-political order which in fact began to piece itself together in England during the mid 17th century. [9] For people of old Gloucester's generation the new rationalism, based on writing and printing, represented the end of civilization as they knew it. His illigitimate son, Edmund, despises the old ways and traditions, and yearns to have his individual ambitions given free rein. He cannot understand why he should be restricted by the plague of custom which would deprive him — born out of wedlock — from the rewards he believes are his.

... Why bastard? Wherefore base?
When my dimensions are as well compact,
My mind as generous, and my shape as true,
As honest madam's issue? Why brand they us
With base? with baseness? bastardy? base? base? (Ibid)

Edmund's is a violent frontal assault on the conventions which
have for generations held traditional society together. The collapse of
those conventions, resulting from literacy and print technology, will lead
to the development of a reading public, the beginnings of representative
democracy, secularism, new property relations, popular education, and
all the dubious blessings of modern times.

The collision between the ideology of Divine Right, in which the
body politic is a natural, organic, God-given system, and the basic ideas
of the new order, in the name of which Charles I was brought to judgement
and which led to the belief that the ancient constitution had broken down
and that the rules of the state could be redrawn in the light of human
reason, can be seen brilliantly contrasted in writings by James I and
Gerrard Winstanley.

In *The True Law of Free Monarchies* 1598 James wrote:
"... The King towards his people is rightly compared to a father of
children, and to a head of a body composed of divers members. For as
fathers the good princes and magistrates of the people of God acknowledged themselves to their subjects ... And the proper office of a King
towards his subjects agrees very well with the offices of the head towards
the body and all members thereof. For from the head, being the seat of
judgement, proceedeth the care and foresight of guiding and preventing
all evil that may come in the body ... The head cares for the body, so doth
the King for his people ..."

By the middle of the next century, after Anglicanism had lost
government support, the Privy Council, Star Chamber and High Commission had been overthrown, printing presses had been liberated and
the propagation of ideas by means of dialogue had been replaced by
publication in pamphlet form, the Bible had been replaced as the supreme
authority by the Common Law [9]. Gerrard Winstanley wrote in 1649:
"In the beginning of time, the great Creator Reason made the earth to
be a common treasury, to preserve beasts, birds, fishes and man, the lord

that was made to govern this creation; for man had domination given to him, over the beasts, birds and fishes; but not one word was spoken in the beginning, that one branch of mankind should rule over another."

The imagery drawn from the body/state analogy has gone for ever. The creative rationality of man has replaced the faith in organic nature — that great and continuing debate as to how we should govern ourselves had been opened up for future generations. [10] Writing, printing and literacy transformed western European society utterly. But the changes were not just external to man, to be found in the environment in which men and women and children had their being. Reading, writing and print were interiorized experiences which transformed the nature of intellectual and imaginative being also.

2.

Modern academic Media Studies may justly be accused of failing to deal historically with the impact of these media developments. Far too much emphasis is placed on contemporary media — on television in particular — and scarcely any scrutiny is given to writing/print/literacy in contributing to what we have become over the previous centuries. It is significant that the work of Marshall McLuhan, and his disciple Walter Ong, has gone so dramatically out of fashion, [11] while all attention gets focused on uses and gratification theory, audience research, and other varieties of occupational therapy devised by the structuralists.

The initiation and proliferation of Media Studies is one of the most remarkable success stories in British education since the 1970s. In no time at all Media Studies had spread across secondary, further and higher education. Several polytechnics were offering Media Studies degrees well before the end of the decade. In 1978 Communication Studies appeared as an A Level subject (although it was not immediately recognised by all universities as a respectable academic subject for university admission purposes) and it was soon afterwards made into a GCE O Level course. In further education Media Studies appeared not only by name (City and Guilds and BTEC offered courses which claimed to combine media skills with media theory) but also appeared in aspects of vocational courses in such areas as Marketing and Advertising. By 1990 it had even reached the primary school curriculum. We have the British Film Institute's word for it: "... a lot of media work being done now in primary schools does derive from, or is analogous to, activities that secondary students do. But this raises questions about progress and continuity in media education. If eight year olds can deconstruct images or storyboard a video, what might fourteen year olds be doing?" asks Cary Bazelgette, the Deputy Head of BFI Education. It raises questions far more fundamental than curiosity about progress and continuity.

If such emphasis is placed on deconstructing images and storyboarding, it compels one further to ask what is actually taught? What is actually taught, what forms the substance, of Media Studies in our schools and colleges?

From my own experience in the field I am compelled to admit that most of the time is spent drumming in a liturgy of the agreed concepts of a sociological or social psychological kind, getting semiology by rote and then progressing to more advanced smartness by developing the ability to quote Althusser, Barthes, Foucault, MacQuail, Hartley, Fiske, Curran and Seaton. These luminaries form Media Studies' Great Tradition. They are to Media Studies what Chaucer, Shakespeare, Donne, Pope, Johnson, Austen, Dickens etc. are to Eng. Lit.

Media Studies have totally failed to deliver their promise. There is little to be had by way of media aesthetics. There is no canon of media classics, as such. The classics of media studies are the Great Names listed above. Knowledge of these masters and their works is what is required in students of Media Studies. Students spend very little of their time exposing themselves to actual media **works** such as dramas, documentaries, films, features, talks, programmes or what have you. This is because the main task has been the acquisition of media studies' metalanguage, the requisite argot for theorizing, analysing and bandying concepts about. This leaves little time for a disciplined attention to media texts.

This is the crux of the entire matter. Most of the time, even at undergraduate level continues to be spent learning to parrot the various approved concepts needed in the search for the media's alleged political indoctrination and social conditioning. Very few media courses are concerned with media aesthetics or developing student skills in creative media practice (writing, scripting, media production). In music, literature, painting, sculpture aspiring practitioners study forms and conventions, and their historical development, absorb the work of the masters and begin practically to develop their own voices. Media Studies in British education have not developed along the same lines. Sociology and aesthetics are essentially irreconcilable. Aesthetics involves judgement. Value judgements are proscribed in sociology. This would fly in the face of the social sciences' righteously asserted disinterest — that oft vaunted detachment which maintains the discipline's only hope of being regarded as a "science".

In a book modestly described by its publishers as "a comprehensive study of media education" putative media teachers are told they "should attempt to make a list of the principal concepts which they wish their students to understand, for it is these concepts which can provide the subject with its continuity and coherence across a wide range of media texts and issues ... Here is my own list ..." [12] Then follows a shopping list of OK terms including "denotation and connotation", "deconstruction", "preferred meaning" and many more. In a work aimed at the students themselves, *The British Media: A Guide for O and A Level Students,* Moyra Grant advises students writing essays to use "the correct terminology — 'dominant ideology' rather than 'main ideas'; 'socialisation' rather than 'brainwashing', etc. Show that you know your subject." [13]

It will be noticed that knowing the subject = being able to reproduce the reified concepts. These concepts are entirely the invention, over the years, of those who play the Media Studies game, and are happily echoed by media sociologists and their fellow travellers, who do their best to drum them into their pupils. Students soon learn that examinations are a game whose rules are made up by examiners. To play the game well according to the rules involves learning to produce the expected terminal behaviour. In Media Studies what is clearly required is the acquisition of the language, and using it to name the parts of society as perceived by the experts. After years spent swotting up their concepts and their semiological terminology the students are merely able to isolate, identify and name the parts which make up the whole. This is perceived as desirable student terminal behaviour. Such are the high-flying parrots of Media Studies. The triumph of the Gradgrindery is breath-taking. Many students begin as Girl Number Twenty, but the system produces its regular output of Bitzers. They are like music students who know their harmony, counterpoint and orchestration, but have little affection (or even acquaintance) with music.

Stated in a million different ways the main message of nearly all currently accepted media textbooks is social conspiracy theory. This can be gleaned from the titles — *Power Without Responsibility*, *Putting Reality Together, The Manufacture of News* — and the chapter headings — "The Political Effects of Mass Communication", "Strategies of Containment", "The Manufacture and Management of Information". Paranoia was the price paid in the late sixties/early seventies when Media Studies was hijacked by Sociology.

The hope probably was that the fledgling discipline might thus achieve some scientific respectability. Yet the Founding Fathers — Marshall MacLuhan, Raymond Williams, Richard Hoggart — had all graduated in traditional English Honours (and at Cambridge, too.) Their interest in media and communication grew out of their general cultural concerns, which had their ultimate origins in the Condition of England debate, stretching back through the life's work of Dr. F.R. Leavis, [14] and back through his predecessors Matthew Arnold and beyond to Coleridge. [15]

What Media Studies seemed to need in its pioneering days was methodological apparatus. This, and this alone, would make it "academic", or — better still — **scientific**. Eng. Lit. had always seemed a bit woolly in this respect. There to hand was all the machinery of Sociology. But Sociology (in its European rather than American version) has ever been a long drawn out dialogue with the ghost of Karl Marx. Tragically Media Studies became reified at a time when British Sociology was exposed to Marxism as elaborated by French intellectuals. Often as not it was imported back to us, having braved the Atlantic crossing and suffered translation into American academic smart aleckery.

This is not to deny the relevance of many sociological insights into the media. But several very serious qualifications must be made. One is that there is much more to the mass media than is dreamed of in your Sociology. Media Studies spends much time in reductive activity. The central concerns are with sex/race/gender; political ideology and bias; cynical manipulation of the innocent public by means of advertising; and identifying and categorizing iconography and signs. There is very little attention paid to the evaluation of television or radio programmes. In other words, there is a complete failure to read media products. The aim of the discipline seems to be to find out how the machine works but not to be aware of what it can do.

The media offer far more than the fulminating version of the world conspiracy theory so regularly rehearsed in Media Studies. As the media seem to have achieved something of a coup d'etat in cultural production and distribution, it could rightly be argued that a proper media education should be enjoyed by all our students. Then there is the very serious point that it is not the teachers' job politically to indoctrinate the students. This is at last being said in Eng. Lit. after years of dalliance with "Radical Literary Theory". [16]

There are two serious faults which run right through Media Studies as a modern academic discipline. One is the continual failure to confront what the media actually produce, to read media texts and attempt serious evaluation of them to produce anything similar to what those in Eng. Lit. might still be tempted to call Practical Criticism. The other is the assumption — if not assertion — that the whole business of the ownership of the means of production and distribution and the relationship which has to be negotiated between the creative imagination, the means of production and the consuming public was a recent phenomenon; that it was, in fact, new and unique to the modern media.

3.

It is only by applying these recently developed interests in the means of production, and their impact on what writers want to say and are eventually able to say and the way in which they will eventually be able to say it, that we can begin to understand literary form and context, and even begin to see how hearers or readers constructed meaning.

Some very serious consequences follow from the assumption, latent in Media Studies as a dogma, that the modern media somehow represent an entirely new and problematic area in social and human communication, unknown to previous generations who did not have (? suffer) media and all the "problems" the media are supposed to bring with them.

The first consequence is the failure to understand the basic snobbery which affects the grammar of our culture. There is always a snobbish preference, or allegiance, to the previous means of cultural production. In a society where literacy is unknown, or not the general norm, poetry — relying as it does for its survival upon rhyme, rhythm and patterned language as aids to human memory — is understandably the major literary means of communication. Ancient literatures provide examples of the consciousness of the society — its history, myths, legends, the totality of the search for value and meaning — preserved in verse or poetry. When writing comes, poetry does not become redundant. On the contrary, the poetic becomes reified, it is perceived and valued as a higher manifestation of literary endeavour than written literature. Although the need for poetic form, pattern rhyme, stress etc., has now been seriously eroded, these poetic forms survive. Poetry has become "literary" — it is a cultural artefact, valued for its own sake. The Poet becomes a recognisable figure in a society's culture. He is patronised, he produces important works, which are read, admired, studied and passed on from one generation to another. Poetry and the idea of the "Poet" survived the impact of print technology on our culture. In 1500 there were three printers in England, by 1600 — the year of *A Midsummer Night's Dream, Henry IV, Henry IV Part Two, Henry V* — there were probably more than ninety.

Drama began manifest development in England during the 1570s, although popular drama had existed long before. But between the last decades of the 16th century and the Puritan closure of the theatres in 1642 the theatre became the first capitalized public entertainment, with professional writers, performers and companies providing entertainment for an audience which paid to get in. During the height of the drama of Shakespeare's time there were six (or more) theatres in London. Yet, such is the snobbery towards the previous mode of cultural production that, in spite of the importance we now attach to Shakespeare and the drama, Elizabethans would have considered the greatness of their literature to have resided in the poetry of Spenser and Sidney.

We now find it very difficult to think of "Elizabethan England" without thinking of Shakespeare. Yet it is a fact that although no edition of Shakespeare's plays was published during his lifetime, he did go to a lot of trouble to ensure that his poems were published. *Venus and Adonis* appeared in 1593, *The Rape of Lucrece* in 1594, The *Phoenix and the Turtle* in 1601 and the *Sonnets* in 1609. He died in 1616 and the plays were not published until 1623. As far as the reputation of our greatest writer is concerned we might well remember, more often than we seem to, that his plays were not performed in anything like the form in which the master actually wrote them until well into Victorian times, and that the birthplace and other trumpery were not bought for the purposes of national self-congratulation until 1847.[17] But let us save our laughter for the amazing fact that it was two hundred and sixty three years after the death of our greatest dramatist that a theatre dedicated to William Shakespeare's works was opened at Stratford-on-Avon.

It took a long time for the novel, to a very large extent made possible by print technology, to be accepted as"literature". Our greatest novelist died in 1870, yet it was not until 1971 that the greatest and most influential academic literary critic, Dr. F.R. Leavis, author of the sacred text, *The Great Tradition*, actually admitted Charles Dickens to his place in the literary Pantheon. Matthew Arnold thought so highly of Dickens that he read his masterpiece, *David Copperfield*, once as a young man and then read it again in later life, having forgotten altogether that he had ever read it before.

The tendency continued into the twentieth century. You have all heard of it. A and B are talking. A says: "Did you see So-and-So on the television last night?" and B will answer: "No. But I read the book." This is because in our culture books are seen as having higher cultural merit than television. To read a book is to engage in a higher cultural/ intellectual activity than in simply watching the television version of a novel. Had B answered: "No. But I heard it when it was on Radio Four" that might not have been quite as good as reading the book, but it would not be quite as bad as just watching it on television. This is because, true to the law of the previous mode of cultural production, radio has more class than television.

Failure to develop a properly informed understanding of the influence of the means of production upon the way the cultural grammar functions distorts our aesthetic perspective and our judgement. It gives the impression that our generation is the first to be "exposed" to the various technologies of communication which may or may not be deployed as part of an ideological conspiracy. In other words, we need to be aware that in attempting to "read" the cultural artefacts and productions of past ages the question of the ownership of the means of production and distribution as well as all the other issues which concern modern Media Studies must be taken fully into account.

The other consequence is that the importance of the complex of negotiations which exist between the creative imagination the author on the one hand and the reader on the other hand is neglected; as is the effect of socio-cultural conventions and technology upon what a writer is able to say and the manner in which the writer is able to say it. The problem is as old as literature itself. The bard, poet, the dramatist, the novelist — the author in any age or any society — does not swim freely in some kind of neutral plasma, unless he has ample independent means. He exists, he makes his existence, by negotiating a place for himself with the means at his disposal. He needs to communicate, but he also needs to eat. Whether with a patron, on a state pension, by royal favour, with a bunch of businessmen who make their living printing and publishing, the writer always has to strike as good a bargain as he can. Homer — whoever he was — was subject to negotiations just as complex for him as those which face a modern writer. His literary form was dictated to a considerable degree by what could be committed to memory. His source materials were the stuff of transmitted memory from one generation to another. The subject matter, form and content were also conditioned by his awareness of his audience. Generations later a poet such as Geoffrey Chaucer had print technology and could assume he was addressing a public who could read, to some extent at least. But he too was restricted as to subject matter and treatment, shown favour as he was by John of Gaunt. *The Book of the Duchesse* was written in honour of Blanche, John of Gaunt's wife. He was patronised by Edward III and Richard II and given an annuity by John of Gaunt, and relied on royal favour for his highly lucrative career in the civil service and various aspects of diplomacy. Henry IV granted him a pension on his accession in October 1399. William Caxton printed Chaucer's masterpieces, *The Canterbury Tales* and *Troilus and Creseide*. Print and patronage combined to serve Chaucer's imagination, offering both opportunities and limitations.

Shakespeare was able to elaborate and display his creative imagination as a dramatic poet, to the extent that he did, in the face of censorship and patronage. Theatre companies were constantly harrassed by the authorities and patronage and protection were needed in order to guarantee survival.[18] Contemporary political events 1599-1601, unrest in Ireland, the Gowrie conspiracy in Scotland and the revolt led by the Earl of Essex, themes of socio-political crises of succession, usurpation, divine right and anarchy, are remarkably paralleled in *Richard II, Henry*

IV Part One and *Henry IV Part Two* and *Henry V*. It is well documented that Queen Elizabeth I found the deposition of Richard II as portrayed by Shakespeare deeply offensive. The scene was published for the first time only in the Fourth Quarto of 1608. These highly disguised treatments were about as far as Shakespeare could go within established liberties.

Shakespeare died a wealthy man. Writing for the theatre, provided that the writer had some control over production costs and remuneration, could be quite a decent way for a writer to earn a living. The Puritans closed the theatres in 1642. When they were reopened at the Restoration there were only two Royal Patent Theatres — Covent Garden and Drury Lane — where there was a monopoly of what came to be known at "legitimate theatre".

John Dryden deployed considerable flexibility in trying to earn his living as a writer by pleasing the shifting tastes of his times. He inherited an estate from his father of about sixty pounds a year, and was able to live in the house of his publisher, Herringman, in London until 1679. His earliest considerable work, published in 1659, was *Heroic Stanzas to the Memory of Oliver Cromwell*, but he found himself able to hail the restoration of Charles II with publication of *Astrea Redux* 1660. Lest there by any mistaking his enthusiasm Dryden followed this with *A Panegyric on the Restoration* in 1661.

His attempts to play to the age's taste for the comedy of what we might generously (? loosely) call intrigue was for a time rewarded, but his zealous application in realizing the trends of the time eventually undid him. He slavishly supplied the needs of the time and produced one success after another — *The Indian Queen* 1664, *The Indian Emperor*, or *The Conquest of Mexico by the Spaniards* 1665 — playing to the contemporary taste for lavish spectacle, scenic accessories, battles, sacrifices, descending gods and off-stage choruses. Much of this seems to prefigure Andrew Lloyd Webber and the shallow musicals of the West End in the 1980s.

While theatres suffered a decline in fortune as the result of plague and fire, Dryden turned to verse again and produced *Annus Mirabilis*. He was glad when the theatres reopened and he was retained as a writer under contract for the King's Theatre, which brought him between three and four hundred pounds a year for rather wretched popular pieces and "restored" versions of classics, including *The Tempest*. He certainly knew how to please the punters, if we may call on Samuel Pepys as witness. He recorded seeing *The Feign Innocence* or *Sir Martin Marrr-all* written by the Duke of Newcastle but "corrected" by Dryden in 1667: "It is the most entire piece of Mirth, a complete Farce from one end to the other, that certainly was ever writ. I never laughed so in all my life; I laughed till my head ached all the evening ... The house full, and in all things of mighty content to me."[19]

Among Dryden's attempts to please contemporary taste for "intrigue" may be mentioned *The Assignation, or Love in a Nunnery* 1673, and *The Kind Keeper, or Mr. Limberham* which was prohibited from the stage after only three performances in 1680.

He than began to work a new seam in popular heroic tragedy. *Tyrannic Love*, or *The Royal Martyr* 1669, which had magic incantations, angelic choirs, a glimpse of Paradise and Nell Gwyn, who after having stabbed herself on stage, was carried off speaking an extraordinary epilogue. The apotheosis of Dryden's heroical extravagance was reached with *Almanazor and Almahide, or The Conquest of Granada* in 1670. It was satirized in *The Rehearsal* 1671 by the Duke of Buckingham, Samuel Butler, Martin Clifford and Thomas Sprat. Dryden is ridiculed in the person of Bayes. This was appropriate enough, as his efforts had just been rewarded by being made Poet Laureate and Historiographer to Charles II, with a pension of three hundred pounds a year and a butt of canary wine. He continued to try to please the taste of the establishment in lavish and spectacular productions, such as *Amboyna* 1673, deliberately composed to coincide with anti-Dutch feelings during the Dutch War, and *Aurenzebe*, his last tragedy in rhymed verse, composed to cater for the public appetite for the Eastern exotic.

With the revival of interest in Shakespeare he climbed aboard the bandwagon with versions of *Antony and Cleopatra (All for Love, or, The World Well Lost* 1678 and *Troilus and Cressida)*. He rightly perceived that the public would be interested in the love motive and focussed all attention on the passionate affair betwixt Antony and Cleopatra, excising all historical and political themes. His partisan spirit was shown to good advantage in his heavy-handed satiric attack on Shaftesbury's efforts to get James, Duke of York, barred from succeeding his brother, Charles II, on the grounds that he was a Roman Catholic. Shaftesbury wanted the

Duke of Monmouth, illegitimate son of Charles II to succeed. Dryden's *Absalom and Achitophel* harmonized well with the sentiments of the court. This was a verse satire, read with joy and pleasure by the political elite. But he knew how to appeal to the tastes of the herd as well, as he demonstrated in the play he wrote at the same time — *The Spanish Friar* — which attacked the Roman Catholic priesthood, a popular target. Further satirical attacks and counter-attacks [20] were followed by his conversion to Roman Catholicism on the accession to James, Duke of York, who became King in 1685. Dryden had clearly demonstrated that if a writer had to earn a living, then in his view, the writer had to provide what the times required. In accord with the trend of the times he now published *The Hind and the Panther* 1687, notorious for its arguments in favour of the old Faith, put into the mouth of "a milk-white hind, immortal and unchanged."[21]

Dryden's loyalty to James was further demonstrated by his reply to the attacks made upon King James by Edward Stillingfleet, the theologian and controversialist. Further Stuart loyalty was brilliantly exhibited in Dryden's flattering farewell to Charles II, *Threnodia Augustalis* 1685 and his poem, *Britannia rediviva* 1688, written in celebration of the birth of James II's heir, James Francis Edward Stuart, Prince of Wales, his only son by Mary of Modena, later known to history as the Chevalier de St. George or the old Pretender.

Consequently Dryden was severly compromised at the Revolution which brought William and Mary to the throne. He lost his office and his pension as Historiographer Royal and Poet Laureate. Thomas Shadwell, his old antagonist, assumed them in his place. He turned to writing plays again and translations of the classics as well as Boccaccio and Chaucer. [22]

In old age Dryden, acknowledged the greatest poet of the age, held court from his chair by the fire at Wills's Coffee House in Bow Street during the winter, and sat on the balcony in the summer months. Here he was seen by the young Alexander Pope, who admired him so much and indeed followed his example. Pope's masterpiece, *The Dunciad*, which is the greatest satire in our language and a massive onslaught on the dangers of print, the publishing industry and all that foreshadowed the mass media we know today, was modelled on Dryden's *MacFlecknoe*. The link between these two poets is even closer. They are connected by the figure of Jacob Tonson, the stationer and publisher. We now enter the age

of the first great commercial printers and publishers who represent a
state of the art which we would recognise as having some close resem-
blance to the modern industry — the age of Tonson, Lintot and Dodsley.

Tonson was apprenticed as a stationer and set up his own business at
the Judge's Head, Chancery Lane, in 1677. He bought the copyright of
Troilus and Cressida in 1679 and obtained half shares in a valuable
property, Milton's *Paradise Lost,* in 1681. He bought the other half in
1690. As Secretary of the Kit-Kat Club he gained the association of such
writers as Pope, Addison, Congreve and Wycherley. It was Tonson who
published many of Dryden's plays, classical translations, Virgil and *The
Fables* in 1699. Tonson published verses by Pope in 1709 and was largely
responsible for the revival of interest in Shakespeare in the early 18th.
century — he published the first edited version of Shakespeare with stage
directions, that by Nicholas Rowe in 1709. He also published, among
other things, Addison's *Cato* 1713 as well as *The Spectator* and in 1725
published Pope's edition of Shakespeare.

These connexions bring us into a new age of authorship and its
relations with the publishing industry. As Lucien Febvre and Henri-Jean
Martin point out in *The Coming of the Book: The Impact of Printing 1450-
1800* (1958) books were for several centuries after the development of
printing and movable type still regarded as precious commodities. They
went out of date very slowly in the 17th. century, they were carefully
preserved, resold and enjoyed a long and useful life. Racine learned his
Greek tragedies from the Aldine editions published one and a half
centuries before his time.[23] But by the time Alexander Pope was approached with the scheme for writing and publishing an English verse
translation of the *Iliad*, books were in the process of being transformed
into quality commercial artefacts. Consider the nature of the arrangement.

Pope's translation was to be published by subscription. One
volume a year was to be issued for six years at a guinea per volume. The
first down payment was to be two guineas. This was to pay the translator's
costs. The succeeding volumes were priced at one guinea each, except the
last, which was "free". The subscribers would get for their money a
handsome six large quarto volume set "printed ... on the finest Paper, and
on a Letter new Cast on purpose, with Ornaments and initial Letters
engraven on Copper."

Subscription edition publication was not itself new — Dryden's Virgil 1697 had been a subscription edition—but this was the first edition of this magnitude given this kind of lavish production and hype. Quality paper was used, and very great care taken with the choice of typeface and page layout. [24] Of equal interest are the payments made to the author/ translator. Alexander Pope was by now an extremely distinguished writer, a commodity a publisher would be glad to have in his stable. Barnaby Bernard Lintot was the lucky man. He was the publisher of Pope, Gay, Farquhar, Parnell, Steele and Rowe. He had published the first version of Pope's *The Rape of the Lock* in 1712. Lintot sold three thousand copies of *The Rape* in just four days. On 23 March 1714 Pope was contracted to Lintot to produce the *Iliad* translation. Pope was to get two hundred guineas a volume and receive seven hundred and fifty copies which he was to distribute to subscribers himself.

Lintot retained the copyright and could therefore produce editions of the work in any style he chose, but not until a month after the subscription edition appeared. It is estimated that Pope made a sum approximate to ninety thousand pounds in today's money. [25] The profession of the writer, the man of letters who had an established and recognisable role as well as the capacity to earn a living, took many years constructing. Christopher Hill believes that Thomas Fuller's *Worthies of England* 1662 was among the earliest serious books aimed at popularity **and** profit, calculated to take advantage of the extension of the domestic reading public and local loyalty and pride. Yet it is important to remember that Thomas Fuller was not a writer, as such. He was an Anglican divine, who regarded his life's work to be the compilation of *The Church History of Britain* — scarcely Book-of-the-Month material. [26]

Pope soon resolved to translate the *Odyssey* into English verse scarcely three months after the last volumes of the *Iliad* appeared in 1720. For Jacob Tonson he also commenced his edition of Shakespeare. The work he did for Tonson was reasonably remunerated, but the *Odyssey* translation brought him in as much as the previous Homer volumes, although he had to pay collaborators a few hundred pounds. The extraordinary financial success of Pope's Homer translations — 1715-1720 and 1725-1726 — had several important consequences. It gave the poet a considerable degree of independence—from patronage and slavery to publishers. It also gave him considerable insight into the industry which created the profits to support writers and their publishers. It also brought him a fair number of enemies. The result was his masterpiece, the most dazzling satire in our language, a brilliant exposition of the possibilities and limitationsof authorship and publishing and an examination of the cultural state of affairs of Augustan England which has proved to be a prediction of the modern dilemma — *The Dunciad*.

4.

The work we now know as *The Dunciad* grew out of Pope's intention to write a continuation of *The Essay on Man*, a series of epistles on the uses of human reason and learning. The last epistle was satirically to treat civilization's misapplication of human abilities and inventiveness. [27] The poet also intended to get his own back by satirizing the enemies he had earned himself — Lewis Theobald, who had attacked Pope's edition of Shakespeare is usually remembered chiefly among them — but there were many who had attacked Pope in print, often out of envy and their names, mostly forgotten today, are preserved in the aspic of Pope's genius. [28]

But the thrust of *The Dunciad* shifted as the themes marinaded in Pope's imagination. The first edition, published in 1724, was superseded, as the work developed. In the final version of 1742 he attacks the corrupt political system of Sir Robert Walpole's Whig jobbery which had dominated British politics for twenty years, buying election after election, stifling protest, buying support and rewarding complaisant mediocrity. His attack goes wider to embrace the philistinism of the court of George II and its impact on the nation. The satirical parallel constantly drawn in Pope's work between the reign of Augustus and that of George II is here at its sharpest. Augustus' reign had removed the empire of Troy to Latium, in *The Dunciad* this is parodied in the removal of the dunces and cretins from Smithfield Fair to the centrality of the court of England — the Empire of Dullness has been realized, the real goals of civilization have been replaced by senseless luxury, materialism and consumption. Everyone has their price, and anyone can be bought — even authors write just for the money. The promise of the intellectual enlightenment, signalled in the work of the scientific and philosophical pioneers of the previous century has been replaced by a wholly materialistic approach to the wonders of the living world. Religion has been toppled by commerce — much of *The Dunciad* actually parodies the Eucharist, and *Paradise Lost*. In such a society dunces are bound to be ennobled. Pope makes the hero of his epic satire Colley Cibber, the mediocrity who had been made Poet Laureate.

Above all *The Dunciad* is an attack on the mass media and mass ignorance. Although he is writing about print, and Grub Street hacks, and rabid semi-literate readers whose banal tastes must be satisfied, it is here that the satire seems aimed at such modern targets. The world of *The Sun, Sunday Sport*, vacuous action-packed and brutally violent films, moronic popular music, shallow West End musical shows, cretinous TV chatshows, quizz-shows and game-shows, situation comedies, junk food, pulp novels, and the whole Coca-colanization of the world is clearly shadowed forth in *The Dunciad's* attack on the mass media industries (printing, publicity, journalism and publishing) and the mass ignorance of the public which lap it all up: [29]

"We shall next declare the occasion and the cause which moved our poet to this particular work. He lived in those days, when (after Providence had permitted the invention of Printing as a scourge for the sins of the learned) Paper also became so cheap, and Printers so numerous, that a deluge of authors covered the land: Whereby not only the Peace of the honest unwriting subject was daily molested, but unmerciful demands were made of his applause, yea of his money, by such as would either not earn the one, nor deserve the other. At the same time the licence of the Press was such, that it grew dangerous to refuse them either: for they would forthwith publish slanders unpunished, the authors being anonymous, and skulking under the wings of publishers, a set of men who never scrupled to vend either Calumny or Blasphemy, as long as the Town would call for it." [30]

These are Pope's own words in explaining how *The Dunciad* came to be written. One of the finest and most perceptive critical analyses of this poem is by the great pioneer of Media Studies, Marshall McLuhan, who points out that the spoof "editor" of *The Dunciad*, invented by Pope, Martinus Scriblerus, author of the footnotes and apparatus which accompanies the text of the poem, reflects on the difficulties of writing an epic about the numerous scribblers and industrious hacks of the press rather than about heroes of ancient days, such as Charlemagne. Scriblerus then goes on to indicate the need for a modern satirist "to dissuade the dull and punish the wicked" as he surveys the appalling state of the nation's culture, brought about by half educating the public, urging them on merely to dull sensual gratifications and providing them with a cheap press.

Scriblerus asserts there are general and economic causes for this state of affairs — cheap paper, modern printing and publishing etc. — as well as the empty ambitions of authors inspired by Dulness, self-opinion and craving self-expression, who have been driven into "setting up this sad and sorry merchandise."

Inexpensive publication and an expanding economy should have brought a golden age of enlightenment, but instead the process has been hijacked by Dulness, and the age of "chaos and old Night" has been removed from the City to the Court, the Polite World: "As the book market expands, the division between intellect and commerce ends. The book trade takes over the functions of wit and spirit and government ... As the book market enlarged and the gathering and reporting of news improved, the nature of authorship and public underwent the great changes that we accept as normal today. The book had retained from manuscript times some of its private and conversationalist character ... But the book was beginning to be merged in the newspaper ... Improved printing technology carried this process all the way by the end of the eighteenth century and the arrival of the steam press." [31]

This presses the question home. Pope is compelled to face — and to make us face — the ultimate catastrophic paradox: language, reading, writing, printing and publishing can be used even more fully to develop our humanity, yet they have it in their power completely to engulf us in a tidal wave of chaotic barbarity. Yet the writer can only fulfil himself by negotiating some kind of relationship with his readership by means of the world of printing and publishing.

The world view put forward in *The Dunciad* is depressing, but recognisably a distortion of the world we know well. Book I opens with the description of the reign of Dulness. Cibber (Bayes) while weighing up the various attractions of going to church, gaming or party-writing, is taken by the goddess to be annointed Poet Laureate. Book II recounts the public games instigated to celebrate his elevation, culminating in a contest to see if critics can stay awake while the works of two authors are read aloud without falling asleep. In Book III, while all lie in a state of deep slumber, Cibber is granted a vision of the ever expanding Empire of Dulness, colonizing court, education, the sciences and the arts. Book IV

represents the triumph of Dulness over all, the growth of indolence and
the relapse of all things back into Chaos and Night. It is a vast, frightening
parody of Creation. In the Beginning Was the Word: in Pope's vision, the
Word returns to destroy the humanity latent in all of us: [32]

> In vain, in vain — the all-composing hour
> Resistless falls: the Muse obeys the power.
> Of Night primeval, and of Chaos old!
> Before her, Fancy's gilded clouds decay,
> And all its varying rainbows die away.
> Wit shoots in vain its momentary fires,
> The meteor drops, and in a flash expires.
> As one by one, at dread Medea's strain,
> The sickening stars fade off the ethereal plain;
> As Argus' eyes by Hermes' wand oppress'd,
> Closed one by one to everlasting rest;
> Thus at her felt approach, and secret might,
> Art after art goes out, and all is night.
> See skulking Truth to her old cavern fled,
> Mountains of casuistry heap'd o'er her head!
> Philosophy that lean'd on Heaven before,
> Shrinks to her second cause, and is no more.
> Physic of Metaphysic begs defence,
> And Metaphysic calls for aid on Sense!
> See Mystery to Mathematics fly!
> In vain! they gaze, turn giddy, rave, and die.
> Religion, blushing, veils her sacred fires,
> And unawares Morality expires.
> Nor public flame, nor private, dares to shine;
> Nor human spark is left, nor glimpse divine!
> Lo! thy dread empire. CHAOS! is restored;
> Light dies before thy uncreating word:
> Thy hand, great anarch! lets the curtain fall,
> And universal darkness buries all. [33]

This depressing vision of the cultural condition of the metropolis
must stand as a portrait — however distorted — of the nation's condition.
It was to this metropolis that the young Samuel Johnson came, less than
ten years after these lines were written, in the hope of achieving literary

fame and fortune. He had an allegiance to the previous means of literary production, too, as he brought with him his drama *Irene*. He hoped to earn a living by literary labours. Looking at his large physical frame the bookseller Thomas Wilcox told him he would stand a better chance of getting his daily bread working as a porter. Johnson soon found there was no hope of getting plays produced unless they were financially backed by patrons. He failed to find any patrons. So he began to negotiate with the new means of literary production — journalism. Like all writers, even Schiller, Johnson had to eat. He offered his services to Edward Cave of the Gentleman's Magazine.

NOTES

1 Bernt von Heisler: *Schiller* translated by John Bednall (London, Eyre and Spottiswood, 1962) pp. 156 ff.

2 Quoted in Heisler op.cit. pp. 157-8.

3 See Isaiah Berlin: 'The Naivete of Verdi' in William Weaver and Martin Chusid (editors) *The Verdi Companion* (London, Gollancz 1980) pp. 2 ff.

4 See William Bright: 'Literature — Written and Oral' in Deborah Tannen (editor) *Georgetown University Round Table on Languages and Linguistics* (Washington DC, Georgetown University Press 1981) pp. 270 ff., and David Baynum: 'The Generic Nature of Oral Epic Poetry' in Dan Ben-Amos (editor) *Folk Lore Genres* (Austin and London, University of Texas Press 1976) pp. 35 ff.

5 Iona and Peter Opie: *The Oxford Book of Nursery Rhymes* (Oxford, University of Oxford Press 1969) pp. 7-9.

6 They were often highly accomplished dancers, singers, musicians. Several became mistresses of the famous — Aspasia, paramour of Pericles; Lais, the lover of Diogenes the Cynic. They were often credited with hearts of gold. See Ray Tannahill: *Sex in History* (New York, Stein and Day 1979) pp. 67 ff.

7 Philip Howard: *The State of the Language: English Observed* (London, Hamish Hamilton 1984) p. 157. See also M. Ferrigni: *Aldo Manuzio* 1925 and G. Fock: *Bibliotecca Aldina* 1930.

8 See Marshall McLuhan: *The Gutenburg Galaxy* (Toronto, University of Toronto Press 1965) pp. 11-15.

9 Christopher Hill: *Reformation and Industrial Revolution* (London, Weidenfeld and Nicolson 1967) pp. 197-9.

10 See Robert Giddings: 'A King and No King — Monarchy and Royalty as Discourse in Elizabethan and Jacobean Drama' in Clive Bloom (editor) *Jacobean Poetry and Prose* (London, Macmillan Press 1988) pp. 182 ff.

11 See, for example, the genial, efficient but breezily dismissive tone of Frank Kermode 'Sic Transit Marshall McLuhan' in *The Uses of Error* (London, Collins 1990) pp. 82-92.

12 Len Masterman: *Teaching the Media* (London, Comedia Publishing 1985) p. 23.

13   Moyra Grant: *The British Media: A Guide for O and A Level Students* (London, Comedia Publishing 1984) p. 45. Since its publication John Fiske *Television Culture* (London, Methuen 1987) has become the Scripture for all those who aspire to seeming expertise in Media Studies. It may well carry on its covers the slogan: "No CNAA Communication/Media Studies Validation Document is Complete Without It." A well-thumbed copy, along with the baseball cap, clip-board and light-metre, is an essential Vade Mecum of all Media students.

14   See Francis Mulhern: *The Moment of Scrutiny* (London, New Left Books 1979) pp. 48 ff. and 115 ff.; Ronald Hayman: *Leavis* (London, Heinemann 1976 pp. 13-18, 21 ff.: and Terry Eagleton: *Criticism and Ideology* (London, New Left Books 1976) pp. 12 ff. and Lesley Johnson: *The Culture Critics—From Matthew Arnold to Raymond Williams* (London, Routledge and Kegan Paul 1979) pp. 93-108.

15   Johnson op.cit. pp. 18-34.

16   Cf Peter Washington: *Fraud—Literary Theory and the End of English* (London, Fontana 1989)

17   See J. O. Halliwell-Phillips: *Outlines of the Life of Shakespeare* 1891; Levi Fox: 'The Heritage of Shakespeare's Birthplace' in *Shakespeare Survey* I (1948) and Graham Holderness: 'Bardolatry: or, The Cultural Materialist's Guide to Stratford on Avon' in Graham Holderness (editor) *The Shakespeare Myth* (Manchester, Manchester University Press 1988) pp. 2-15

18   See A. L. Rowse: *Shakespeare the Man* (London, Macmillan 1973) pp. 63 ff., and *William Shakespeare* (London, Macmillan 1963) pp. 138 ff., B. L. Joseph: *Shakespeare's Eden—The Commonwealth of England 1558-1629* (London, Blandford Press 1971) pp. 48 ff. and David Nicol Smith: 'Authors and Patrons' in *Shakespeare's England* 1916.

19   Robert Latham: *The Shorter Pepys* (Harmondsworth, Penguin 1985) p. 819.

20   *The Medall: a Satyre Against Sedition* was published in March 1682, this was Dryden's attack on the acquittal of Shaftesbury for sedition. The Whigs' satiric supporters then attacked him in return. Thomas Shadwell led with *The Medal of John Bayes*. Dryden answered this with *Mac Flecknoe, Or A true Blew Protestant Poet T.S.*. He attacked Elkanah Settle, Robert Ferguson, Thomas Shadwell and others in the second part of *Absalom and Achitophel* in November 1682. His party zeal seemed devout.

21   This performance was ridiculed by Matthew Prior and Charles Montagu, first Earl of Halifax, in *The Hind and the Panther transversed to the Story of the Country Mouse and the City Mouse*.

22   *The Hind and the Panther* would not appeal to the supporters of the new settlement, opposing as it did, the unifying powers of the Roman Catholicism to what John Lucas calls "the schismatic and sectarian tendencies of other religions" — see John Lucas; *England and Englishness: Ideas of Nationhood in English Poetry 1688-1900* (London, the Hogarth Press 1990) pp. 11 ff. Samuel Johnson's verdict seems brusque but it is probably just. Dryden might have been less lavish with his praise of James II "for James was never said to have much regard for poetry: he was to be more flattered only by adopting his religion". ('Life of Dryden' in *Lives of the English Poets* 1799) Dryden now published translations of Ovid's *Epistles* 1680; Virgil, Horace, Lucretius, Theocritus — work featured in his *Miscellaneous Poems*, 4 volumes, 1693. Juvenal, Persius in 1697; and in 1697 verse translations of *The Works of Virgil; Fables Ancient and Modern* was published in 1700.

23   Lucien Febvre and Henri-Jean Martin; *The Coming of the Book: The*

Impact of Printing 1450-1800 1958 (translated by David Gerrard, London, Verso 1990 pp. 236 ff.) and Robert Durnton: *The Kiss of Lamourette.* (New York, W.W. Nornton 1990) pp. 108 ff.

24 Maynard Mack: *Alexander Pope: A Life* (New Haven, Yale University Press 1985) pp. 266-7.

25 Mack op.cit. p. 268.

26 Christopher Hill op.cit., p. 198; Godfrey *Davies: The Early Stuarts 1603-1660* (Oxford, University of Oxford Press 1985) p. 409. See W. Addison: Thomas Fuller (London, 1985). Fuller was educated at Queens' College, Cambridge, held various provincial livings until taking the curacy of the Savoy Church, the Strand. He was an ardent Royalist and served as Chaplain to Charles I's army during the Civil Wars. He wrote several important works, including *History of the Holy War* 1639; *Holy and Profane State* 1642; a geographical account of the Holy Land, *Palestine and the Confines Thereof* 1650. His major work, *The Church History of Britain From the Birth of Christ Until the Year 1648* was published in 1655. The *Worthies of England,* published in 1662, was a form of early *Dictionary of National Biography,* arranged on a county by county basis, and appeared a year after Fuller's death in 1661.

27 Mack op.cit. pp. 441 ff.

28 The hero of the earlier versions of *The Dunciad* (first edition published 1728) was Lewis Theobald (1688-1744). Pope had ridiculed him in the *Miscellanies* 1727-8. Pope was deeply offended by Theobald's attack on his capacities as an editor of Shakespeare which appeared in Theobald's *Shakespeare Restored, or A Specimen of the many Errors as well committed as unamended by Mr. Pope in his late Edition of this Poet* 1726. This appeared a year after Pope's edition of Shakespeare. Colley Cibber (1671-1757) was made the hero of the revised version 1743. Cibber was a comic actor of some merit and author of several comedies. He was made Poet Laureate in 1730 and was then attacked by Pope as well as other writers. Not only did Pope and his fellow men of letters feel that making so feeble an author as Cibber Poet Laureate demeaned the literary honour of the title. It was widely believed that Cibber had been elevated because he was so energetic and consisten in his flattery of the "great" — especially Sir Robert Walpole, George II's first Minister. Pope also had personal reasons for his assaults on Cibber. Cibber had traduced his reputation in a pamphlet, *A Letter From Mr. Cibber to Mr. Pope, Inquiring into the Motives that might induce him in his Satyrical Works, to be so frequently fond of Mr. Cibber's name* and in his autobiography, *An Apology for the Life of Colley Cibber,* he had maligned Pope, cataloguing his alleged avarice, malice and sensitivity about his short stature and humped back. See Mack op.cit. pp. 777-781. The satire is spattered with squibs and references to writers, critics and poets — Thomas Bentley, Richard Blackmore, John Dennis, Ambrose Philips, Edmund Curll, Charles Gildon, John Henly and many more — who had offended Pope, or of whom Pope disapproved, either personally or as representative types of the kind of time-serving mediocrities rewarded by the depraved tastes of the day.

29 See Marshall McLuhan: `On Pope's *Dunciad*' in Eugene McNamara (editor) *The Interior Landscape: The Literary Criticism of Marshall McLuhan* (New York, McGraw Hill 1971) pp. 169-179.

30 Alexander Pope: `Martinus Scriblerus of the Poem, *The Dunciad,* in *The Works of Alexander Pope,* (London, Printed for A. Millar, J. and R. Tonson, C. Bathurst, H. Woodfall, R. Baldwin, W. Johnston, T. Caslon, T. Longman, B. Law, T. Field, R. Withy and M. Richardson 1744) Volume III p. xliii.

31   McLuhan op.cit. p. 171.

32   See J. Philip Brockbank ' The Book of Genesis and the Genesis of Books: The Creation of Pope's *Dunciad*' in Howard Erskine-Hill and Anne Smith (editors) *The Art of Alexander Pope* (London, Vision Press 1979) pp. 192 ff.

33   See B. L. Reid: 'Ordering Chaos: *The Dunciad*' in Maynard Mack and James A. Winn (editors) *Pope: Recent Essays by Several Hands* (London, Harvester Press 1980) pp. 678 ff.

II
Samuel Johnson as Parliamentary Reporter

Samuel Johnson, one of the most brilliant men of the 18th century and now a national British folk hero came to London bearing a drama no one was prepared to put on the stage. He nearly starved to death but managed to get a job as an illicit parliamentary reporter. Reporting the debates in the Commons, satirically disguised as *Debates in Lilliput*, he was able to record for posterity the last moments of the premiership of Sir Robert Walpole, who had spent his entire political career trying to manipulate the press by bribing supporters and stifling opponents. Johnson laid the very firm foundations on which the edifice of the Fourth Estate was so firmly to rest for generations.

Only a month separates the first publication of Johnson's *London*, which appeared on 12 May 1738, and the reports of the debates in Parliament, to which Johnson so notably contributed, which began to appear in the *Gentleman's Magazine* in June the same year. The figure of Sir Robert Walpole, and his impact on British social, economic and political experience, is a marked feature of both poem and debates. Yet there appears to be a strange tension between the character of Walpole which dominates *London* and the Walpole figure we find in the *Debates in the Senate of Magna Lilliputia*.[1]

London is described by its author as an 'Imitation'. This was a new genre, used to brilliantly ironic effect by Pope.[2] Johnson said of the imitation in his *Life of Pope*: 'This mode... in which the ancients are familiarised by adapting their sentiments to modern topicks... is a kind of middle composition between translation and original design, which pleases when the thoughts are unexpectedly applicable and the parallels lucky.'[3] Pope's imitations of Horace were very much in vogue, and Johnson resolved to imitate Juvenal in comtemporary terms. The *Third Satire* of Juvenal is his model, in which the protagonist is appalled by the corruption he sees around him and resolves to leave Rome. In *London* the protagonist, Thales, is shocked by the squalid materialism and political jobbery of the metropolis, and tries to get away from it all by going to Wales. The core of the poem is in Thales's speech to a friend as he embarks at Greenwich.

Thales feels that he has been treated with indifference by Sir Robert Walpole, and that the civilizing mission of poetry and the arts is being swamped by trade, commerce and materialism. Walpole is perhaps caricatured in the figure of Orgilio, the proud and pompous statesman, who maintains himself and his faction in power by a complex system of bribery, pocket boroughs, manipulating public opinion and a well oiled political machine which involves lies, pensions, vote-buying and various other 'public Crimes'. Those who go along with the system enjoy the benefit: 'Who shares *Orgilio's* Crimes, his Fortunes shares.' *London* is a very hard-hitting satire, and its contemporary relevance is unmistakable. Johnson does everything except name Sir Robert Walpole; even the newspaper he financed to orchestrate public opinion, the *Gazetter*, is mentioned by name.[4]

Johnson's most sustained treatment of Sir Robert Walpole is to be found in the *Debates*, although there are two other political satires of this period - *Marmor Norfolciense* and A *Compleat Vindication of the Licensers of the Stage*.[5] Some of his comments about Walpole made in later life have been preserved. These are of great interest in the light of his treatment of Walpole at the great crisis of his career, which the young Johnson portrayed for readers of Edward Cave's *Gentleman's Magazine*. Both the political satires show Johnson as the spokesman of patriot, Tory, anti-Walpolean views. The debates cover the period of the collapse of confidence in Walpole as Britain was pushed into war with Spain and Walpole was hounded from office. But it would be true to say that the protrayal of Sir Robert in the *Debates* is not altogether unfavourable.

The comments of the mature Johnson on Walpole are also interesting. Boswell records very little evidence of Johnson's views of Walpole, but we have other sources. Sir John Hawkins (1719-89), the lawyer and magistrate, who knew Johnson well, and whose biography of Johnson was published in 1787, four years before Boswell's *Life*, records that Johnson had a high opinion of Walpole: "Of Sir Robert Walpole, notwithstanding that he had written against him in the early part of his life, he had a high opinion: he said of him, that he was a fine fellow, and that his very enemies deemed him so before his death: he honoured his memory for having kept his country in peace many years, as also for the goodness and placibility of his temper."[6]

George Birkbeck Hill has preserved this comment of Johnson's on Walpole: 'He was the best minister this country ever had, as if he would have let him he would have kept the country in perpetual peace.'[7] Is it possible to reconcile these seeming contradictions? It is worth recalling that Johnson publicly affirmed the importance of getting at the truth about politics at the very time he was writing the *Debates*. In January 1739 he wrote: "Political Truth is undoubtedly of very great Importance, and they who honestly endeavour after it, are doubtless engaged in a laudable Pursuit. Nor do the Writers on this Subject ever more deserve the Thanks of their Country, than when they enter upon Examination of the Conduct of their Governors, whether Kings, Senates, or Ministers....."[8]

The *Debates* are of outstanding interest in Johnson's output. They are fascinating evidence of his political thinking, and impressive examples of the political journalist's art at a very early stage of its development. A careful reading of the *Debates* will make inevitable a severe overhaul of the oft repeated assertion of Johnson's unqualified Toryism. Further, the *Debates* reveal themselves as an important staging post in our progress towards parliamentary democracy.

The relationship between the centres of political power and the means of communication which exist within society is invariably tense and complex. It is in the nature of things that this should be so, and indeed it continues to be so.[9] On the one hand the ruler cannot exist unless he or she is seen to rule over us. This implies that rulers must encourage communication of some sort. To enable them to exist as a political fact - they must be seen. On the other hand, if free communication of ideas and information is openly allowed, those ideas will include criticism which may be more than a ruler can stomach. The ideal state of affairs for rulers is 'news' without criticism or analysis. This is very difficult to bring about, as most societies have discovered. The social experiences which immedi-

ately preceded Johnson's appearance as a political journalist are important here. The early Stuart kings had relied on censorship, operated
through the court of the Star Chamber. This was abolished during the
English revolution. Oliver Cromwell then replaced censorship with
licensing, which lasted until 1695. This meant that only publishers likely
to favour the status quo were allowed to print and publish.[10] After the
Licensing Act lapsed in 1695 Britain enjoyed what was probably the freest
press in Europe. Then in 1712 came the Stamp Act, which meant that all
publications paid a duty levied by the government. This made publication
expensive. Not one penny paper survived. This was one method of
attempting to prevent murmuring against the state. It succeeded to some
extent, but unintentionally produced a splendid crop of political satires.
Political debate, like water, has a habit of finding its own level.[11] An acute
interest in political debate, commercial and colonial obsessions, and the
development of print technology and transport would have made the early
development of our newspaper industry possible, but in fact it was a
difficult birth and of sickly growth - thanks very considerably to government restrictions. It was only as the result of the work of a few mavericks
such as Abel Boyer,[12] who began to publish a yearly register of political and
other occurrences between 1703 and 1713, and began the monthly
publication of the *Political State of Great Britain* in 1711, that the trade
was opened up at all. Boyer's journal continued to publish accounts after
his death, until 1737.

Even though the electorate was still a very small section of the
public, the battle for public opinion was clearly being waged as early
as the 1720s. Stamp Duty and Paper Tax were not sufficient to control
public opinion. After a somewhat patchy start to his political career[13]
Robert Walpole unquestionably came to the fore after the sensational
collapse of the South Sea Scheme. He was perceived as the saviour of
the nation and his alleged grasp of economic and fiscal affairs became
part of Whig mythology. By 1721 he was First Lord of the Treasury
and Chancellor of the Exchequer. He was really personally responsible for the government of the country, and under him there soon
occurred a transfer of power to the Commons, in which house he was
able to manage a Whig majority. His major political rival Bolingbroke,
a pardoned Tory Jacobite, was not allowed to resume his seat in the
Lords, and direct political opposition was thus precluded him. But
there was still the press.

Among the group of Tory wits which surrounded Bolinbroke was one Nicholas Amhurst. In 1720 Amhurst began to edit the *Craftsman*, which was to be for ten years a sharp and scathing voice raised against Walpole and his system: 'corruption is a poison', the *Craftsman* opined, 'which will soon spread itself through all ranks and orders of men; especially when it begins at the fountainhead.' During the election of 1727 Bolingbroke wrote in Amhurst's paper an account of Robert Walpole as a bluff villain: "with a Smile, or rather a Sneer, sitting on his Face and an arch Malignity in his eye.... They no sooner saw him, but they all turned their Faces...and fell prostrate before him. He trod on their Backs...and marched directly up to the Throne. He opened his Purse of Gold which he took out in great Handfuls and scattered amongst the Assembly. While the greater Part were engaged in scrambling these Pieces he seized...without the least Fear, upon the sacred Parchment itself. He rumpled it unduly and crammed it in his Pocket. Some of the People began to murmur. He threw more Gold, and they were pacified...." [14]

Walpole was so enraged at this portrait of him that he had Amhurst arrested, though proceedings failed.[15] In the face of opposition such as this, administrations had no recourse but to prosecute the printers and publishers for seditious libel, or buy their silence, or subsidize rival publications to refute them.[16] It was rumoured that Walpole spent some £50,000 from Treasury funds in buying the support of the press, and the Duke of Newcastle spent £4,000 on pensions for journalists. A note in Pope's *Dunciad* has this comment on one such newspaper, the *Daily Gazeteer*: "Into this, as a common sink, was received all the trash, which had been before dispersed in several Journals, and circulated at the public expence of the nation. The authors were the same obscure men; though sometimes relieved by occasional essays from Statesmen, Courtiers, Bishops, Deans, and Doctors. The meaner sort were rewarded with Money; others with Places or Benefices, from an hundred to a thousand a year."

The note goes on to estimate that between 1731 and 1741 'not a Pension at Court, nor Preferment in the Church or Universities, of any Consideration, was bestowed on any man distinguished for his Learning separately from Party-merit, or Pamphlet-writing.'[17]

In 1731 the *Gentleman's Magazine* began to publish parliamentary reports, and this was followed later the same year by the *London Magazine*. Initially both publications relied heavily on Boyer's *Political State of Great Britain*, but gradually they began to print their own versions of parliamentary debates. They were obviously successful in appealing to the appetites of their readership, and they managed to avoid being legally taken to task by feigning only to publish during the parliamentary recess. This was a loophole in the law, which was closed by a resolution passed in the Commons on 13 April 1738. In order to escape the consequences of defiance they had no alternative but to pretend that the debates they recorded were fictions. The *London Magazine* purported to carry the accounts of the debates of a non-existent club. The *Gentleman's Magazine* caried the accounts of the *Debates in the Senate of Magna Lilliputia*. Being a Lilliputian Correspondent was the first well paid job that Samuel Johnson had.[18]

It was an accident of history that Johnson arrived on the scene as an ambitious young writer, willing and ready to bend his skills to political journalism, at the final stages of the career of Sir Robert Walpole. Johnson was to write in his *Preface to Shakespeare* some years later that Elizabethan tragedy was not 'a poem of more general dignity or elevation than comedy; it required only a calamitous conclusion, with which the common criticism of that age was satisfied, whatever lighter pleasure it afforded in its progress.'[19] As a young writer he appeared on the scene opportunely to observe and portray the spectacular and calamitous fall from office of the presiding political genius whose personality undoubtedly dominated the first half of the eighteenth century. The fall of Orgilio was nigh when Edward Cave employed the young Johnson in the offices of the *Gentleman's Magazine* in St. John's Gate.

Walpole's career had not been a glittering or untarnished success, but it had been - until the late 1730s - apparently unstoppable. The deaths of Stanhope in 1721 and Sunderland in 1722, and the despatch of Carteret to Ireland in 1724, removed his most serious rivals.[20] He bought favour in the Commons and exercised sole influence over George I.[21] One obvious measure of his success was the frequency of his decoration. He was made a Knight Bachelor in 1725, a Knight of the Garter in 1726 (the first Commoner Blue Ribbon since 1660),[22] and

1723 his eldest son had been made a peer. The *Craftsman* described parliament as 'a Polyglott with 500 Mouths and as many Tongues... his Mane and his Tail were tied up with *red Ribbons* at vast expence; but he was usually led by the Nose with the *blue one*.'[23] By manipulating the matter of the royal allowances and influencing George II through his wife, Queen Caroline of Ansbach, while others mistakenly sought favour through the new king's mistress, the future Countess of Suffolk,[24] Robert Walpole ensured the survival of his political influence after the sudden death of George I in 1727. As he himself commented: 'I have the right sow by the ear.'

The basic principles of his policies were simple - peace abroad and prosperity at home. These required his maintaining the alliance with France, encouraging colonial trade by removing restriction 1730-35, and aiding the landowning class (his main support) by adjusting the taxes paid on land, while raising revenues from alternative sources. His Excise Bill (1733), Gin Act (1736), Playhouse Act (1737) and unpopular foreign policy made him enemies within his own party (led by William Pulteney, later Earl of Bath) and at court. But he managed to steer a safe course through these stormy waters, at least until the crisis with Spain in 1737. Even George II had to admit his courage: 'He is a brave fellow. He had more spirit than any man I ever knew.'[25]

But there were serious signs of Walpole's growing unpopularity. His attempts to restrict smuggling and regulate trade were interpreted as assaults on British liberties, and there were riots in Edinburgh and London. The city interests in London were disaffected towards him. His attempts to prevent satiric stage attacks on his policies were resented. He lost the support of Frederick Prince of Wales by opposing the increase to his allowances. The death of his great protectress Queen Caroline of Ansbach in November 1737 was a serious blow. Frederick controlled boroughs in the county of Cornwall, and he attracted the support of Pitt and the Greville family.[26] It was the war with Spain which brought Robert Walpole's career to catastrophe. Johnson's account of these final scenes is more moving than his unsuccessful attempt at tragedy, *Irene*.

Public attention now turned to Britain's relations with Spain. The claim was made that English traders to the West Indies were roughly handled by Spanish officials searching for contraband. It was claimed that one Robert Jenkins, master mariner, had his ear cut off by a coastguard. The question raised was whether the Spanish had the right to search our vessels. Sir Robert Walpole's seemed to be the sole voice for peace. The Lords passed resolutions on 2 May 1738 against the Spanish right to search, but Walpole managed to exclude this resolution from the Commons. The clamour for war with Spain continued during the autumn, while Walpole exerted all the diplomatic muscle he could through his minister at Madrid, Sir Benjamin Keene.[27] Keene was able to negotiate a convention with Spain. While this was achieved, Walpole managed to get parliament prorogued, and it did not assemble again until 1 February 1739. The convention provided for a settlement of disputes within eight months, which would be negotiated between specially appointed plenipotentiaries. Walpole feared that war with Spain would precipitate a French invasion and a Jacobite rebellion. One of our major markets - Spanish America - could only be maintained by force. It was known that much of our trading there was illegal. English settlers were beginning to make their claim to Honduras by cutting logwood on the coast, and our colonization of Georgia brought us into conflict with the Spanish in Florida.[28] These attempts at peace with which Walpole hoped to paper over the cracks were described by William Pitt as 'an insecure, unsatisfactory, dishonourable convention'. The popular cry of the day was 'No search!' Although Walpole spoke well in the Commons in defence of his policies, the address of approval was only carried by a majority of twenty eight on 8 March 1739. Some of his enemies combined to form a group, the Patriots, led by Sir William Wyndham,[29] who resolved to secede from the Commons the next day.

Walpole's answer was to push through measures which would gain him support from the commercial interests, granting to molasses and sugar the same principle of free export which applied to rice, and removing duties from Irish wool and woollen yarn and preventing their being exported to anywhere but Great Britain. By these means he hoped to have the powerful of the land behind him when the time came to ratify the Convention in May 1739.

Walpole knew that the British demand for the rejection of the right claimed by the Spanish to search British vessels for contraband would be the core of the discussion. It was. Two of his colleagues-the Duke of Newcastle and the Earl of Hardwicke-both spoke on behalf of the nation in taking a high-handed tone with the Spanish.[30] George II was of the war party. Against his better judgement Walpole instructed Keene to demand the surrender of the right to search. The Spanish refused. On 19 October 1739 war was declared amid popular acclaim. 'They now ring the bells,' he said, 'they will soon ring their hands.' His career in public office now reached its climax.

The catastrophe was worthy the pen of a tragedian. Samuel Johnson rose to the task. His handling of these final moments of Walpole's career is very interesting. The most obvious quality to be noticed in Johnson's account of the debates which brought Walpole's public life to an end is the positon of sympathy in which he is placed. Reading the *Debates* as a drama one would be bound to describe Sir Rub Walelop, as he appears in the Senate of Lilliput, as the tragic hero. In giving Walpole such a good press Johnson was in part yielding to his own instincts as an author, and shaping political material which had come into his hands with the almost unconscious skill of the true artist. But he was also guided by political motives. The fact is that Walpole's career was terminated by a faction of his own party. To paint this group as the goodies in a dramatic version of events would not serve the ends of Johnson's Toryism. I further believe that the curmudgeon in Johnson drove him to give Walpole a fair hearing in the face of all the opposition stacked against him.

Walpole was a sick man. Bad health had dogged him all his days. In the summer of 1710 he had suddenly been taken ill and his life had been feared.[31] He recovered. On 3 May 1715 he was again taken seriously ill for a month. In the spring of 1716 his life was again despaired of and he convalesced in Chelsea. He wrote to his brother Horatio on 11 May, 'I gathered strength daily... from the lowest and weakest condition that ever poor mortal was alive in.' In April 1727 he further showed signs of considerable physical weakness. In June of this year, when living in daily fear of his dismissal by George II, he received a visit from Arthur Onslow,[32] who found him in a very weak condition. Walpole burst into tears and declared: 'he would never leave the court if he could have any office there, and would be content even with the comptroller's staff.'[33] Now, at the very crisis of his career, he was suffering from two terrible ailments-gout and the stone.

Alexander Pope wrote at this time: 'And all agree, Sir Robert cannot live.'[34] He could have resigned. In fact he twice attempted to, but George II begged him to stay in office, broken in health, because he could not resign, and compelled to wage a war he had done his best to avoid. Additionally he was burdened by the sure knowledge that there would be considerable pressure to have him impeached, as he had been the sole advocate for peace. He knew that Newcastle, the greatest borough-monger of them all, was already working against him behind the scenes, and that the Duke of Argyll, his chief adviser in Scotland, had gone over to the opposition.[36] Even the elements, true to the manner of poetic drama, turned against him. From 1715 until 1740 Britain had enjoyed abundant harvests, with only two minor exceptions in 1727 and 1728. But the winter of 1739-40 was a long and cruel one, with severe frost and resulting distress. Bread prices rose, there were public riots, and Sir Robert Walpole got the blame for this as well.[37]

Tory opposition to him was weakened by the divisions which existed between Bolingbroke and Pulteney, rivals for the leadership after the death of Wyndham in 1740. The was was not going well and Britain faced the storm on the continent alone.[38] A scapegoat was clearly called for. The process of Walpole's toppling was put in motion in the House of Lords on 13 February 1741 when Lord Carteret introduced a motion to address the king requesting Walpole's dismissal, and Samuel Sandys, M.P. for Worcester, introduced the same motion in the Commons.[39]

On 25 April 1741 George II's second parliament was dissolved, and the new parliament assembled on 1 December. Walpole's majority had gone. The Pelhams and Hardwicke, his former cronies, came to terms with the opposition Whigs, with the proviso that Sir Robert Walpole was not to be persecuted. On 9 January 1742 he was made Earl of Orford. Two days later he resigned his offices.

Johnson's account of these proceedings achieves dramatic grandeur; it is among the finest things he composed. He was writing within severe restrictions. He was recreating events he had not personally witnessed, handling issues of considerable complexity and attempting dramatic verisimilitude.[40] His version of the debate in the Lords of 13

February 1741 appeared in July and August 1741. He reports eleven of the speeches on the main motion for removing Walpole, and the course of the debate is well balanced. Carteret appears in the Lilliputian version as Hurgo Quadrert and his speech covers twelve pages. His argument is a mixture of national pride as Britain (Lilliput) faces the combined might of France and Spain (Blefuscu and Iberia) and outrage at the folly of the nation's commercial policy: "Nor has our Trade...been only contracted by the Piracies of *Iberia*, but has been suffered to languish and decline at Home, either by criminal Negligence, or by their compliance for *Blefuscu*, which has given rise to other Calamities. The State of our Woollen Manufactures is well known, and those whose Indolence or Love of Pleasure keep them Strangers to the other Misfortunes of their Country, must yet have been acquainted with this, by the daily Accounts of Riots and Insurrections, raised by those who having been employed in that Manufacture, can provide for their Families by no other Business, and are made desperate by the Want of Bread." [41]

The motion was opposed by the Duke of Newcastle, supported by Hardwicke, Cholmondeley, the Bishop of Salisbury and Hervey.[42] In part it might be Johnson's sense of the dramatic which prompted him to portray the attempted support of Walpole in the way that he did, but it is certainly effective. He seems to be true to character. Newcastle's speech is rather heavily elaborated, and Lord Hervey's is passionate, almost shrill-as Hurgo Heryef he concludes: "To condemn a Man unheard is an open and flagrant Violation of the first Law of Justice, but it is still a wider Deviation from it to punish a Man unaccused; no Crime has been charged upon this Gentleman proportioned to the Penalty proposed by the Motion, and the Charge that has been produc'd is destitute of Proof.

Let us therefore....reverence the great Laws of Reason and Justice, let us preserve our high Character and Prerogative of Judges, without descending to the low Province of Accusers and Executioners, let us so far regard our Reputation, our Liberty, and our Posterity, as to reject this motion." [43]

The debate lasted eleven hours. When put to the vote the motion was defeated 108 to 59.

The debate in the House of Commons (Clinabs) on the same day did not appear in The *Gentleman's Magazine* until eighteen months after the report of the debate in the Hurgos[44]: that is to say, a full two years after the events it recounts. It may be that Edward Cave considered the speeches too robust, violent and painful, and that it was not wise to print them while Sir Robert Walpole was still in office. Certainly there was much cut and thrust and plenteous blood was drawn.

Samuel Sandys, introducing the motion, gave a fiery speech which referred to the 'Corrupters of the Country', 'the Enemies of Commerce', 'the Deserters of their Allies' and 'the Corrupter and his Associates, the Lacqueys of his Train'. This was simple and brutal, but we sense a vastly higher level of mentality in the finely honed rhetoric of William Pitt (Ptit): "The minister who neglects any just Opportunity of promoting the Power or increasing the Wealth of his Country is to be considered as an Enemy to his fellow Subjects; but what Censure is to be passed upon him who betrays that Army to a Defeat, by which Victory might be obtained; impoverishes the Nation whose Affairs he is intrusted to transact by those Expeditions which might enrich it, who levies Armies only to be exposed to Pestilence, and compels them to perish in sight of their Enemies without molesting them?

It cannot surely be denied that such conduct may justly produce a Censure more severe than that which is intended by this Motion, and that he who has doomed Thousands to the Grave, who has co-operated with foreign Powers against his Country, who has protected its Enemies and dishonoured its Arms, should be at least stripped of those Riches which he has amassed during a long Series of prosperous Wickedness, and not barely be hindered from making new Acquisitions, and increasing his Wealth by multiplying his Crimes." [45]

The presentation of Sir Robert Walpole's final speech reveals Johnson's genius as a writer of political journalism which, in his hands, becomes the stuff of high drama. It is important to stress that this moment is actually constructed by Johnson. If we compare it with other respectable historical sources, we see immediately that the creative writer in Johnson has taken over entirely. The account given in William Coxe's *Life of Sir Robert Walpole* (1798) is dignified if not indignant, prolix, and packed with an almost paranoid detail.[46] Walpole, really the accused in a trial, is now the focus of attention. What will he say in his own defence? In Johnson's

version he begins by requesting to know the whole accusation before he
addresses himself to his defence. This is a fine stroke, as it prepares us
finally for his great moment, and brings the whole matter into sharp
relief. William Pulteney (Pulnub) summarizes the case against him.[47]
Walpole then answers: "The Gentlemen who have already spoken in my
Favour have indeed freed me from the Necessity of wearying the House
with a long Defence, since their Knowledge and Abilities are so great that
I can hope to add Nothing to their Arguments, and their Zeal and their
Friendship are so ardent, that I shall speak with less Warmth in my own
Cause...."

He goes on to say that if they suffer the terrors of a dream in which the
army is annually established by his authority, in which the disposal of all
posts and honours is his alone, and in which he uses this power only to the
destruction of liberty and of the nation's commerce, then compassion
would compel us to awaken them from these painful delusions, so that by
opening their eyes they would clearly see that "the Prerogative has made
no such Incroachments, that every Supply is granted by the Senate, and
every Question debated with the utmost Freedom, as before that fateful
Period in which they were seized with this political Delirium that so long
harrassed them with the Loss of Trade, the Approach of Slavery, the
Power of the Crown, and the Influence of the Minister."

The irony is masterly, coming as it does after his use of the defence
offered by his supporters. Beneath the seeming breadth and generosity
of his utterance there is the reduction of his enemies' case to the level of
dream and delusion. Beneath calm surface eloquence lurks the monster
of contempt.

The final thrusts come when he replies to Pulnub's charges of personal
corruption, which he apparently fails to understand. How could he be
accused of rapacity? or avarice? or excessive demands upon His Majesty's
liberality? "Since, except the Places which I am known to possess, I have
obtained no Grant from the Crown, or fewer at least than perhaps any
Man who has been supposed to have enjoyed the Confidence of his
Sovereign. All that has been given to me is a little house at a small
Distance from this City, worth about Seven Hundred Pounds, which I
obtained that I might enjoy the Quiet of Retirement without remitting my
Attendance on my Office."

He then gives his attention to the order on his shoulder, for which he had so often been attacked, which, he says, he had almost forgotten to mention: "But this surely cannot be mentioned as a Proof of Avarice; though it may be looked on with Envy and Indignation in another Place, can it be supposed to raise any Resentment in this House, where Many must be pleased to see those Honours which their Ancestors have worn restored again to the Commons."[48]

He then awaits the verdict of the House with a calm arrogance worthy of Coriolanus: "Having now, Sir, with due Submission offered my Defence, I shall wait the Decision of the House without any other Solicitude than for the Honour of their Counsels, which cannot but be impaired if Passion should precipitate, or Interest pervert them. For my Part, that Innocence which has supported me against the Clamour of the Opposition will establish my Happiness in Obscurity, nor shall I lose by the Censure which is now threatened any other Pleasure than that of serving my Country."[49]

When the motion was put to the vote, Walpole was saved. He had a majority of 290 to 106 votes. William Shippen[50] and thirty-four Jacobite Tory MPs walked out of the House, and several Tories took the lead offered by Edward Harley[51] and voted for Walpole.

It was the election of midsummer 1741 which destroyed Walpole. Whig support in Scotland was whittled away, and the influence exerted by the Prince of Wales over boroughs in Cornwall gave Whig seats to Lord Falmouth and Thomas Pitt of Boconnoc. Walpole now saw the end of his political career was inevitable. His son Horace Walpole has left a description of him at this time, sitting 'without speaking, and with his eyes fixed for an hour together'. But he still hoped against hope. He believed that a promised increase of income of £50,000 a year to the Prince of Wales might remove the Prince's support for the opposition, and that the Tories might be unable to form a government. Although conscious that his support in the Commons was diminishing, he defended his war policy against the attacks of Pulteney: 'He exceeded himself; he particularly entered into foreign affairs, and convinced even his enemies that he was thoroughly master of them. He actually dissected Mr. Pulteney.'[52] It was finally his family who persuaded him to resign.[53] On 9 February 1742 he was created Earl of Orford, and on the 11th he resigned. He was awarded a pension of £4,000 a year. George II wept.

It is a deeply enjoyable irony that Walpole's very attempts to restrict satiric atttacks on his policies and limit discussion of his activities should have resulted in his being immortalized in the majestic prose of one of the giants of our literature. Johnson's achievement as a political journalist is indeed a worthy one. By putting these accounts of parliamentary debates in circulation-however craftily disguised and dramatically written up they may be-Johnson contributed generously and characteristically to the further development of our nation's political consciousness. And this achievement must place him in company which would certainly have surprised him, for he therefore belongs with John Wilkes, William Cobbett, William Hazlitt and the other ornaments of our radical tradition. Henry Flood, MP for Winchester, who knew Johnson, once declared that he would not have made a very good parliamentarian, as, 'having been long used to sententious brevity and the short flights of conversation, [he] might have failed in that continued and expanded kind of argument, which is requisite in stating complicated matters in publick speaking.'[54] But Johnson made his own invaluable conbution to that much wider and more significant continuous and expanded kind of argument. Albert Camus asked: 'What is a rebel? A man who says no.' Throughout Mark Twain's discourse with the world there is an implied 'Oh yeah?' Samuel Johnson's contribution was the civilized 'yes but'. It is a just and fitting coincidence that Cobbett inhabited the rooms in Bolt Court once used by Samuel Johnson.[55]

NOTES

1.   See Walter Jackson Bate, *Samuel Johnson* (London: Chatto and Windus, 1978), pp. 175ff.

2.   See Maynard Mack, 'Wit and Poetry and Pope: Some Observations on his Imagery' in *Eighteenth-Century   English Literature: Modern Essays in Criticism*, ed. James L. Clifford (London: Oxford University Press, 1959), pp.   33-4.

3.   *Lives*, Vol. 3, p. 176.

4.   See Yale, Vol. 6, pp. 47-52; for Orgilio as Walpole, see J.P.Hardy, *Reinterpretations: Essays on Poems by Milton, Pope, and Johnson* (London: Routledge and Kegan Paul, 1971), pp. 113ff.

5.   See Yale, Vol. 10.

6.   Sir John Hawkins, *Life of Samuel Johnson* (London, 1787),   p. 514.

7.   *Johnsonian Miscellanies*, ed. G.B. Hill (Oxford: Clarendon, 1897), Vol. 2, p.

309. The comment was made by William Seward (1747-99),man of letters, a friend of Johnson.

8.   Johnson in the *Gentleman's Magazine*, January 1739, p.3.

9.   We must confront the highly centralised, and secretive, power that still characterizes our society under a government that is centralising   every day' (Tony Benn in the *Guardian*, 3 October 1983). See Stuart Gerry Brown, 'Dr. Johnson and the Old Order',*Marxist Quarterly*, 1, October-December 1937, pp. 418-30, reprinted in *Samuel Johnson: A Collection of Critical Essays*, ed. Donald J.Greene (Englewood Cliffs, New Jersey: Prentice Hall, 1965), pp. 158-71

10. See Christopher Hill, *Reformation to Industrial Revolution* (Harmondsworth, Penguin, 1971), pp. 197ff.; Samuel Rawson, *The Constitutional Documents of the Puritan Revolution* 1625-1660 (Oxford: Clarendon, 1906), pp. 374ff.; F.S. Siebert, *Freedom of the Press in England* 1476-1776 (Urbana, University of Illinois Press, 1952), pp. 346-52.

11.   John Arbuthnot, The *John Bull Pamphlets* (1712); Jonathan Swift,*The Drapier's Letters* (1724), and *Gulliver's Travels* (1726); John Gay, *The Beggar's Opera* (1728); Alexander Pope, *The Dunciad*, Books I-III (1728); John Gay, *Polly* (1729); Jonathan Swift, A *Modest Proposal* (1729). Book IV of *The Dunciad* dates from 1742. These works establish a tradition of social and political satirical debate which we tend to think of as characteristic of the eighteenth century, and the tradition continues in the pamphleteering of John Wilkes, *The Letters of Junius*, (1769-71), and Smollet's *Adventures of an Atom* (1769).

12. Abel Boyer (1667-1729) came to England from Upper Languedoc in1689 and was employed as French tutor to William, Duke of Gloucester. He developed a flourishing printing and publishing trade in London.

13. Walpole had been supported early in his career by Sarah, Duchess of Marlborough, and was recognized leader of the Whigs by 1703. By 1711 he was leader of the House of Commons, but was damaged by the fall of Marlborough. He was imprisoned in 1712 on charges of venality in the Navy accounts. His support of the Hanoverian succession and his leading the prosecution of Oxford, Bolingbroke, Stafford and Ormonde in 1715 for intrigue with the Stuarts again established his political authority. The Jacobite rising of 1715 confirmed his status. He was driven from office by the manipulations of Stanhope and Sunderland in 1717 and for a time joined forces with the Tory opposition.

14. Quoted in S.E. Ayling, *The Georgian Century* 1714-1837 (*London*: Harrap, 1966), p. 118.

15. For accounts of the struggles between Walpole, ministerial control and the press, see L. Hanson, *The Government and the Press* (Oxford: Clarendon, 1936), and I.R. Christie, *Myth and Reality: The British Newspaper in the Later Georgian Age* (London: Macmillan, 1970).

16. See Dorothy Marshall, *Eighteenth-Century England* (London: Longmans, 1982), pp. 67-8 and C.B. Really, 'The London Journal', *Bulletin of the University of Kansas Humanistic Studies*, Vol. 5, No. 3 (1935), 10ff.

17. *The Dunciad*, ed. James Sutherland (London: Methuen, 1943, repr. 1965), pp. 311-12. This is a comment on Book II, line 314. See also J.B. Owen, *The Rise of the Pelhams* (London: Methuen, 1957), Ch. 1.

18. J.P. Hardy, *Samuel Johnson: A Critical Study* (London: Routledge and Kegan Paul, 1979), pp. 34-6, 41ff.; W.J. Bate, *Samuel Johnson*, pp. 162-71; John Wain, *Samuel Johnson* (London: Macmillan, 1980), pp. 79-82; James L. Clifford, '*The*

Young Samuel Johnson (London: Heinemann, 1959), p. 148; Boswell, *Life*, Vol. 1, p. 115ff.

19. 1765: Yale, Vol. 7, p.68.

20. Dorothy Marshall, op. cit., p. 130.

21. J.B. Owen, op. cit., pp. 55-7; Lewis Namier, *The Structure of Politics at the Accession of George III* (London: Macmillan, 1960, pp. 28ff.; J.H. Plumb, *Sir Robert Walpole: The Making of a Statesman* (London: Cressett Press, 1956), pp. 353ff.

22. In modern times Sir Winston Churchill and Sir Anthony Eden have been similarly honoured.

23. *The Craftsman*, 22 July 1727.

24. Henrietta Howard (1681-1767), bedchamber woman to Caroline when she was Princess of Wales. A celebrated beauty, she was the original of Pope's Chloe. See Alan Bold and Robert Giddings, *True Characters* (London: Longmans, 1984), p.55. For Walpole's survival after George I's death, see Lord Hervey, *Some Materials Towards Memoirs of the Reign of King George II*, ed. Romney Sedgwick (London: Eyre and Spottiswoode, 1931), Vol. 1, p. 22ff.).

25. For a brief summary of these early years of Walpole's administration see Keith Feiling, *A History of England* (London: Macmillan 1969), pp. 654-59. This period saw the vast influx of wealth to this country as the result of his economic policies. See Robert Giddings, 'Smollett and the West Indian Connexion' in *Smollett: Author of the First Distinction*, ed. Alan Bold (London: Vision Press, 1982), pp. 55-8.

26. For an interesting discussion of the influence exerted by Frederick, see Betty Kemp, 'Frederick Prince of Wales' in *The Silver Renaissance*, ed. A. Natan (London: Macmillan, 1961), pp. 38ff.

27. Keene (1697-1757) was a skilled diplomatist. An agent for the South Sea Company in Spain, Consul at Madrid in 1724, and our Ambassador there in 1727-39 and (after the Spanish war) 1748-57. He died in Madrid.

28. Feiling, op. cit., pp. 658-59; Gerald Graham, *A Concise History of the British Empire* (London: Thames and Hudson, 1972), pp. 62-7.

29. Wyndham (1687-1740), 3rd B2aronet, Tory M.P. for Somerset. A staunch Jacobite, he was implicated in the Jacobite rebellion of 1715: a firm supporter of Bolingbroke.

30. Thomas Pelham-Holles (1693-1768), first Duke of Newcastle. A Whig and initially a supporter of Walpole, and his Secretary of State. He became Premier in 1754 but retired two years later. Philip Yorke (1690-1764), first Duke of Hardwicke, was Lord Chancellor from 1737, later holding office under Newcastle. Remembered for presiding over the trial of the rebel Lords in 1745, and promoting the laws which forbade the wearing of tartan.

31. His clerk, James Taylor, wrote to Walpole's brother, Horatio (16 June 1710) that he was suffering from 'collero morbus'.

32. Arthur Onslow (1691-1768): Whig M.P. for Guildford and later for Surrey 1728-61, Speaker of the House of Commons. Onslow left interesting accounts of contemporary politics and politicians. See the *Onslow MSS in Historical Manuscripts of the House of Commons 1895, 14th Report, Appendix, Part ix.*

33. *Onslow MSS*, p. 517.

34. ' 1740. A Poem' in *Imitations of Horace*, ed. John Butt (London: Methuen, 1939, repr. 1969), p. 334.

35. William Coxe, *Memoirs of the Life and Administration of Sir Robert Walpole, Earl of Orford* (London, 1798), 1, 625.

36. Archibald Campbell (1682-1761): 3rd Duke of Argyll, Keeper of the Privy Seal 1725 and of the Great Seal 1734-61. He later advised the raising of Highland regiments in 1746, after the second Jacobite rebellion. His defection was a serious blow to Walpole's political machinery.

37. See Thomas Tooke, *A History of Prices* (London, 1838), p. 43, and *The Gentleman's Magazine*, IX (January 1739), 7-10.

38. Our victory in Porto Bello in 1739 was eclipsed by the failure of the expeditions in the Main and Cuba in 1741. The catastrophic campaign at Cartagena, portrayed by Smollett in *Roderick Random* (1748), brought great suffering. Smollett served on H.M.S. *Chichester* (see Robert Giddings, *The Tradition of Smollett* (London: Methuen, 1967), pp. 87-91). The death of the Emperor Charles VI at the end of 1740 brought the union of France and Spain with the aims of Frederick II of Prussia to partition Hapsburg lands and place the Elector of Bavaria on the imperial throne (see Johnson's memoirs of Frederick, *Gentleman's Magazine*, 1756). The French occupation of Prague and an additional French army in the Rhineland caused George II to conclude a treaty of neutrality between France and Hanover without consulting Walpole. The alliance with France had been a cornerstone of Walpole's European policy.

39. Sandys (1696-1770) had long opposed Robert Walpole, from the moment of the Excise Bill onwards. He was a member of the Committee of Enquiry into Walpole's conduct in 1742. He was created Baron Sandys in 1743. John Carteret (1690-1763), later first Earl Granville, was the son of Baron Carteret and a long standing rival of Walpole. He had been Secretary of State in Walpole's administration, 1721-24. Carteret was a favourite of George I as a result of his speaking fluent German and supporting pro- Hanoverian policies. Walpole got rid of him by sending him to Ireland as Lord Lieutenant, 1724-30. Although he attempted to prosecute Swift after the publication of the *Drapier's Letters*, the two became warm friends, and intrigued against Walpole in and out of Parliament. Carteret's motion was seconded by Bertie Willoughby (1692-1760), 3rd Earl of Abingdon, and supported by John Campbell (1678-1743), 2nd Duke of Argyll, Henry Howard (1694-1758), 4th Earl of Carlisle, George Montagu Dunk (1716-71), 2nd Earl of Halifax, and John Russell (1710-71), 4th Duke of Bedford.

40. Sir John Hawkins (1719-89), author and student of politics, who knew Johnson well through connections in *The Gentleman's Magazine*, asserted that the style of each speaker was accurately represented. Later critics, such as George Birkbeck Hill (1835-1903), claimed that Johnson's reports displayed an ignorance of debating. See Donald J. Greene, *The Politics of Samuel Johnson* (New Haven: Yale, 1960), pp. 114ff.; Medford Evans, *Johnson's Debates in Parliament*, dissertation, Yale University, 1933; Benjamin B. Hoover, Samuel *Johnson's Parliamentary Reporting* (Berkeley and Los Angeles: University of California Press, 1953), John Butt's review article on Hoover, *R.E.S.*, n.s., VIII (Oct. 1956), 433-35; F.V. Bernard, 'Johnson and the Authorship of the Four Debates', *P.M.L.A.*, LXXXII (1967), 408-19; Donald J. Greene, 'Some Notes of Johnson and The *Gentleman's Magazine*, *P.M.L.A.*, LXXIV (1979), 75-84. The *Debates* which Johnson wrote for *The Gentleman's Magazine* were reprinted several times, almost immediately after they first appeared in Cave's magazine- by John Torbuck (1739-42), Ebeneezer Timberland (1743), and William Sandby (1744). They appeared in *Cobbett's Parliamentary History of England from the Norman Conquest to the Year 1803*, ed. John Wright, Vols. XI and XII, printed by T.C. Hansard in 1812.

41. *The Gentleman's Magazine*, XI (July 1741), 347.

42. See note 30, above. George Cholmondeley (1703-70), 3rd Earl of Cholmondeley, Thomas Sherlock (1678-1761), Bishop of Salisbury and John Hervey (1696-1743), Baron Hervey of Ickworth, a friend of Lady Mary Wortley Montagu. He was several times attacked by Pope, who immortalized him as Lord Fanny, and Sporus in his *Epistle to Dr. Arbuthnot*. *Hervey's Memoirs of the Reign of George II*, an invaluable sourcebook of the period, were edited by J.W. Croker in 1848: see also notes 24 and 47.

43. *The Gentleman's Magazine*, XI (August 1741), 416.

44. *The Gentleman's Magazine*, XIII (March 1743).

45. Ibid., p. 133.

46. Cf. Coxe, op. cit., 1.657-69, and Hoover. op. cit., pp.96-103. Coxe seems to have worked from the account in the *London Magazine*, as well as from private authentic sources.

47. Pulteney (1684-1764) was elected Whig M.P. for Heydon in 1705. Believing that Robert Walpole was deliberately keeping him from the high office he felt he deserved, he developed into one of Walpole's most severe critics, and considerably aided Bolingbroke in *The Craftsman*. He was leading light in the anti-Walpolean group, the Patriots. He was M.P. for Middlesex, 1734-42. A forceful advocate of the war with Spain. In 1731 he fought a duel with Lord Hervey. He was a truly fearsome orator: Walpole once said, 'I fear Pulteney's tongue more than another man's sword.'

48. He refers here to the Order of the Garter. 'Another Place' is a House of Commons term for the House of Lords. See note 22 above.

49. *The Gentleman's Magazine*, XIII (April 1743), 180-83.

50. Shippen (1673-1743):M.P. for Bramber 1707-13 and Newton 1714-43. He declared the motion was a scheme for maintaining the Whigs in power by turning out one minister only to have him replaced by another Whig.

51. Edward Harley (1699-1755), nephew of Robert Harley (1661-1724), first Earl of Oxford (who had been impeached by Walpole in 1717 for his intrigue with James Stuart, the Old Pretender), became Earl of Oxford on the death of the first Earl's son Edward in 1741. His example was followed, according to Nugent, 'by the country gentlemen to a man' *(Memoirs of Robert Earl Nugent* (London, 1898),p. 94).

52. Horace Walpole to Horace Mann, 19 Oct. 1741 *(Correspondence,* ed. W.S. Lewis *et al.* (New Haven: Yale University Press, 1937-82), Vol. 17, p. 171); Coxe, op. cit., Vol.3, p. 588.

53. Horatio Walpole (Sir Robert's brother), *Memoirs of Horatio, Lord Walpole* (London, 1820), Vol. 1, p. 123.

54. Quoted in Boswell's *Life*, Vol. 2, p. 139.

55. Daniel Green, *Great Cobbett: The Noblest Agitator* (London: Hodder and Stoughton, 1983), p. 442.

III

Tobias Smollett
and the
West Indian Connection

Tobias Smollett came to London seeking literary fame and fortune. He too carried a drama which no one would stage. In desperation he joined the Navy and served as Surgeon's Mate in the terrible West Indian campaign fought during the war which had brought Walpole's career to an end. Smollett returned and exposed the horrors of the war in fiction. Failing to find patrons to support him he turned his house into a kind of literary factory. At the end of his life he wrote an extraordinary novel which contains a brilliant portrait from several points of view of a magnificent Georgian city, built from wealth achieved during the very war Smollett had so vigorously protested.

"By a kind of magnetic force England draws to it all that is good in the plantations. It is the centre to which all things tend. Nothing but England can we relish or fancy; our hearts are here, wherever our bodies be. If we get a little money, we remit it to England. They that are able, breed up their children in England. All that we can rap and rend is brought to England ..." Edward Littleton, Agent for the Island of Barbados, in 1689 [1]

"The sickness still continued to increase among the troops, and even infect the sailors to such a degree that they died in great numbers ... In order therefore to prevent the total ruin of the army and fleet, preparations were made to quit this inhospitable climate ... the whole fleet being wooded and watered for the voyage ... they set sail for Jamaica. Thus ended, in damage and disgrace, the ever memorable expedition to Carthagena, undertaken with an armament, which if properly conducted, might have not only ruined the Spanish settlements in America, but even reduced the whole West Indies under the domination of Great Britain ..."
Tobias Smollett: A COMPENDIUM OF AUTHENTIC AND INTERESTING VOYAGES 1756.1.

The life and career of Tobias Smollett, whose writings are among the greatest ornaments of the glorious literature of Scotland, cannot be read without sadness tinged with a wry amusement at its very Jamesian ironies. Younger son of a landowning gentleman hard-pressed for money, Tobias considered a literary career very early in life. At school he loved the classics, but got himself apprenticed to a surgeon in Glasgow. He left for London, determined to make an impression in the metropolis with his tragedy, *The Regicide*. This was based on the assassination of King James I of Scotland he had read in George Buchanan's *Rerum Scoticarum Historia*. The story of his failures in launching this wretched drama and his struggles to make ends meet in London read like the archetypical history of all struggling early 18th. century writers. It is brilliantly portrayed in the opening chapters of his first novel *Roderick Random* 1748. He was saved from an early grave by serving as a surgeon's mate on HMS *Chichester* during the very Spanish war which brought the downfall of Sir Robert Walpole.

He attempted to make a living as a surgeon in London, a few doors away from Sir Robert Walpole's town house, Number Ten, now the home of British Prime Ministers. He continued to place his faith on the drama and hawked his tragedy everywhere to no avail. David Garrick had obviously been importuned, and a letter he wrote to John Hoadley on 14 September 1746 very interestingly outlines the problems posed when artistic judgement has to wrestle with the problems of patronage by the great and the good: "I have now with me a play, sent to me by my Lord Chesterfield, and wrote by our Smollett. It is a Scotch story, but it won't do, and yet recommended by his Lordship and patronised by Ladies of Quality, what can I say or do? Must I belie my judgement, or run the risk of being thought impertinent and disobliging of great folk? Some advice upon that head, if you please ..."[2]

On this occasion Garrick's judgement as a man of the theatre triumphed over pressure from the great, and he declined the play for performance. Smollett was unforgiving, but he worked his resentments up into the stuff of comic fiction, and these episodes feature in the pages of *Roderick Random*. Relations between the two were not good for some time, but by 1756 Smollett had obviously forgiven Garrick, as he praised him in his *Critical Review* and removed some attacks on Garrick in the second edition of his novel, *Peregrine Pickle*. In fact Garrick put on Smollett's farce *The Reprisal*.[3]

Smollett then plagued the pantomimist and theatrical manager John Rich, who likewise declined the opportunity to stage *The Regicide* and was lacerated by Smollett:"Fraught with the spirit of a Gothic monk, Let Rich, with dullness and devotion drunk, Enjoy the peal so barbarous and loud, While his train spews monsters to the crowd." [4]

Smollett then turned his attention upon the literary dilettante George Lyttleton, first Baron Lyttleton, MP for Okehampton and opponent of Sir Robert Walpole. Lyttleton was the friend of Alexander Pope, and had patronised the Scottish writers James Thomson and David Mallet. It seems Lyttleton did not even bother to read Smollett's play. Smollett bided his time. Then when Lyttleton's wife died and the stricken lord wrote his seemingly sincere *Monody* 1747 Smollett responded with his vicious squib *Burlesque Ode* which purported to lament the death of a grandmother. Arthur Murphy, the actor and biographer of Johnson, claimed that Lyttleton was in such mortal fear of Smollett's critical bile that he refused to publish his *The History of the Life of Henry II and of the Age in which he Lived* until 1767-71. Smollett vented his spleen in his first novel *Roderick Random* 1748 where Garrick is caricatured as Marmozet, Lord Chesterfield as Earl Sheerwit and Rich appears as Vandal. This semi-autobiographical novel also contains superb descriptions of life in the British navy during the recent Spanish war and a brilliant account of the appalling fiasco at Cartagena in 1741.

After the publication of *Roderick Random* Smollett published *The Regicide* by means of a five shilling subscription. Although the play itself has little merit, as a piece of evidence in the history of publishing it is extremely interesting as the dramatist takes the opportunity offered in this mode of publication to publish a *Preface*. Here be bemoans the complete failure of the patronage system to recognise and promote literary or dramatic merit. Smollett was unlucky in attempting to achieve success by his pen during the period between the collapse of the system of patronage by the wealthy aristocracy and its replacement by commercial printing and publishing:

"Had I suffered a repulse when I first presented my performance, I should have had cause to complain of my being excluded from that avenue to the public favour, which ought to lie open to all men of genius; and how far I deserve that distinction, I now leave the world to decide, after I have, in justice to myself, declared that my hopes of success were not derived from the partial applause of my friends only, but inspired ... by the approbation of persons of the first note in the republic of taste, whose countenance, I vainly imagined, would have been an effectual introduction to the stage. Be that as it will, I hope the unprejudiced observer will own ... that every disappointment I have endured was an accumulated injury ...Abuse of prerogative, in matters of greater importance, prevails so much at present, and is so generally overlooked, that it is almost ridiculous to lament the situation of authors, who must either at once forego all opportunities of acquiring reputation in dramatic poetry, or humble themselves, so as to sooth the pride, and humour the petulance of a mere Goth, who, by the most preposterous delegation of power, may become the arbiter of this kind of writing." [5]

It is doubtful if Smollett's play could have sustained itself upon the stage by its own dramatic or poetic merits, but the insight into the weaknesses of the patronage system are very well exposed by the entire episode. As Smollett asserts, it is either up to the whim of the titled and the wealthy, or to theatre managers who look after their friends ("If I must entertain the town with variety, it is but natural that I should prefer productions of my friends, or of those who have any friends worth obliging ...") and his case is further supported by the grim experiences of Samuel Johnson at the hands of Lord Chesterfield.

It was Robert Dodsley, who began life as a footman in the service of the Hon. Mrs. Lowther, but became a poet, dramatist and bookseller and publisher, who put the idea of the dictionary to Samuel Johnson. Dodsley had already published Pope, Young and Akenside and was to publish Johnson's *Vanity of Human Wishes, Irene and Rasselas*. He successfully launched several journals and founded *The Publick Register* in 1741 (he originated *The Annual Register* in 1758.) It was alleged that Addison had been offered three thousand pounds to make an English dictionary. Pope had contemplated the task, and Ambrose Philips had published proposals for a two volume dictionary. In 1721 Nathan Bailey, who kept a boarding-school at Stepney, published *Universal Etymological English Dictionary*, which went through thirty editions. Dodsley did not have the financial resources to back the Johnsonian undertaking in 1746 so he formed a consortium of six London booksellers. They offered Johnson one thousand five hundred and seventy five pounds for compiling his dictionary. It was to take three years and Johnson signed up in June 1746. To publicise the undertaking once it had been underway nine months they published *The Plan of a Dictionary*, and it was Dodsley's idea to dedicate this to Lord Chesterfield.

During the early stages Johnson was reasonably received at Chesterfield's house, but although he was give ten pounds Johnson began to feel he was no more than any other of the noble Lord's protégés. He began to be less and less welcome at Chesterfield's house but swallowed his pride and continued to work on the dictionary. At this time Dodsley published Johnson's *Vanity of Human Wishes* in which Johnson poured much of his disappointment. There are four very poignant lines: "There mark what ills the scholar's life assails; Toil, envy, want, the patron and the jail. See nations slowly rise, and meanly just To buried merit raise the tardy bust ..."

Reciting this poem in old age, Johnson wept at these lines. When Chesterfield heard that the day of the dictionary's publication was fast approaching, wishing to ensure his name might be contaminated with some of its glory, he wrote two puffing articles for a fashionable journal, *The World*. He was to bring down upon his head one of the greatest castigations from disappointed author to indifferent patron which the history of authorship and publishing can example:

7 February 1755.

My Lord:

I have been lately informed by the proprietor of *The World* that two Papers in which my Dictionary is recommended to the Public were written by your Lordship. To be so distinguished is an honour which, being very little accustomed to the favours of the Great, I know not how well to receive, or in what terms to acknowledge.

When upon some slight encouragement I first visited your Lordship I was overpowered like the rest of Mankind by the enchantment of your address ... but I found my attendance so little encouraged, that neither pride nor modesty would suffer me to continue it. When I had once addressed your Lordship in public, I had exhausted all the art of pleasing which a retired and uncourtly Scholar can possess. I had done all that I could, and no Man is well pleased to have his all neglected, be it ever so little.

Seven years, my Lord, have now passed since I waited in your outward Rooms or was repulsed from your Door, during which time I have been pushing on my work through difficulties of which it is useless to complain, and have brought it at last to the verge of Publication without one Act of assistance, or one word of encouragement, or one smile of favour. Such treatment I did not expect, for I never had a Patron before ...

Is not a Patron, my Lord, one who looks with unconcern on a man struggling for life in the water, and, when he has reached ground, encumbers him with help? The notice which you have been pleased to take of my labours, had it been early, had been kind; but it has been delayed until I am indifferent, and cannot enjoy it; till I am solitary, and cannot impart it; till I am known, and do not want it. I hope it is no very cynical asperity, not to confess obligations where no benefit has been received, or to be unwilling that the Publick should consider me as owing that to a Patron, which Providence has enabled me to do for myself.

Having carried on my work thus far with so little obligation to any favourer of learning, I shall not be disappointed though I should conclude it, if less be possible, with less; for I have been long wakened from that dream of hope, in which I once boasted myself with so much exultation,

My Lord,
Your Lordship's most humble servant,
SAMUEL JOHNSON. [6]

In the Dictionary Johnson gives this definition of PATRON: "One who countenances, supports or protects. Commonly a wretch, who supports with insolence, and is paid with flattery."[7]

Smollett, just as Johnson had, was suffering in that stage between the collapse of patronage and the birth of publishing. There was neither the reading public nor the publishing industry big enough to offer sufficient support for writers. None could deny the Herculean efforts Smollett made to earn his living by writing.

He did not do well as a surgeon. He moved from Downing Street to less well-to-do quarters in Curzon Street, married and obtained his M.D. His second novel, *Peregrine Pickle*, was published in 1751 and it was a great success. It was followed in 1753 by *Ferdinand Count Fathom*. He tried medical practice in Bath, and then moved back to Chelsea where he embarked on further literary labours and gave support to other striving scribes. One who knew him well wrote of him at this time:

"He was of an intrepid, independent, imprudent disposition, equally incapable of deceit and adulation, and more disposed to cultivate the acquaintance of those he could serve, than of those who could serve him. What wonder that a man of his character was not, what is called, successful in life!"[8]

He gathered round himself a considerable company of medical men and writers, many of them Scotsmen attempting — like himself — to succeed professionally in London. *Peregrine Pickle* gives us some very interesting glimpses of the manners and methods of 18th. century authorship and publishing. Peregrine joins a company of authors and learns the art of **puffing** — which we of the age of *Wogan* will readily recognise:

"The chief end of the society ... was to assist and support each other in their productions, which they mutually recommended to sale, with all their art and influence, not only in private conversations, but also in occasional epigrams, criticisms, and advertisements inserted in the public papers. This science, which is known by the vulgar appellation of **puffing**, they carried to such a pitch of finesse, that an author very often wrote an abusive answer to his own performance, in order to inflame the curiosity of the town ... "[9]

To sustain his household at Monmouth House, Chelsea, he attempted to organise big "successful" publishing enterprises, produced under his guidance by a kind of literary factory at Chelsea, these were standard works offered for contract to various booksellers, which he then farmed out to his various assistants, the works appearing under his name — a version of *Don Quixote*, a new literary journal, *The Critical Review*, a *History of England*, a seven volume compendium of *Voyages*, a *Universal History* and another journal which he began in January 1760, the *British Journal* which has considerable publishing interest as it contained the first English novel to appear in serial form, Smollett's *Adventures of Launcelet Greaves*.

His stage work, *The Reprisal, or the Tars of Old England* earned him two hundred pounds. In 1762 he edited another magazine, *The Briton*, which supported Lord North and George III. The crisis with John Wilkes' attack on Number 45 of this journal and the subsequent political scandals this incurred no doubt caused Bute to consider the journal did his cause more harm than good and publication ceased in February 1763.

Smollett's literary factory now embarked on a universal gazetteer and translation of the works of Voltaire in thirty eight volumes. Domestic troubles now smote him. His fifteen year old daughter died and his health began to show severe signs of strain. He went abroad for two years and the literary result of this was his idiosyncratic *Travels* 1766. He returned to Bath in 1766 in the hope that the spa might aid his recovery, and ironically it was about this city that he was to write his masterpiece, *Humphry Clinker*. Bath was built with wealth achieved in the colonies — particularly in the West Indies. British dominion over this area had been guaranteed by the outcome of the very war which Smollett had served in as a young man. Using the form of a series of letters he gives a many layered portrait of late 18th. century society through the eyes of various members of the Bramble family.

2.

Writing on 5 May 1770 Matthew Bramble describes how Bath has declined in gentility and good taste as the result of the contemporary passion for luxury: "About a dozen years ago," he writes to Dr Lewis, "many decent families, restricted to small fortunes, besides those that came hither on the score of health, were tempted to settle in Bath, where they could then live comfortably, and even make a genteel appearance, at a small expense: but the madness of the times has made the place too hot for them ... Some have already fled to the mountains of Wales, and others have retired to Exeter. Thither, no doubt, they will be followed by the flood of luxury and extravagance, which will drive them from place to place to the very Land's End ..."

He is touching, of course, upon a theme which was becoming a topic of quite general comment by the close of the eighteenth century. On 14 April 1778 James Boswell and Samuel Johnson dined with General James Edward Oglethorpe, the colonist of Georgia. In the course of the conversation, Oglethorpe began to declaim against luxury. Dr. Johnson argued that luxury produced much good, that no nation was ever hurt by luxury, and asserted that 'every state of society is as luxurious as it can be. Men always take the best they can get.' Oglethorpe countered by claiming that '... the best depends much upon ourselves; and if we can be as well satisfied with plain things, we are in the wrong to accustom our palates to what is high-seasoned and expensive.' Typically, Johnson refused to yield the point.

"But hold, Sir; to be merely satisfied is not enough. It is in refinement and elegance that the civilized man differs from the savage. A great part of our industry, and all our ingenuity is exercised in procuring pleasure ...."

In May 1770, the same month and the same year in which Matthew Bramble wrote about the damaging effects of luxury upon the city of Bath, Oliver Goldsmith published *The Deserted Village*, one of the central statements in our literature on the theme of social decay effected by the trade in luxury and opulence. In the dedicatory letter to Sir Joshua Reynolds the poet wrote that in regretting the depopulation of the country he was inveighing 'against the increase of our luxuries' and went on to say that he expected therefore to have the 'shout of modern politicians' against him. 'For twenty or thirty years past' he suggested, ' it has been the fashion to consider luxury as one of the greatest national advantages ....' Goldsmith told Sir Joshua Reynolds that he thought 'those luxuries prejudicial to states by which so many vices are introduced, and so many kingdoms ... undone'.

The disintegration of the old social order in the wake of the rising tide of luxury, mammonism and the mechanization of life develops into one of the dominating themes of western literature (cf. Wordsworth: *The Excursion*, Book VIII, lines 39 and following) but what Smollett puts before us in the sections on the city of Bath in *Humphry Clinker* is not only sharply and accurately observed social comment, but a portrait of society at a particular stage of development, as the nation slowly changed from supporting itself from its own indigenous resources into a country which fed its population and provided for its luxuries by overseas trade. We are looking at the metamorphosis of an agriculturally based economy into a capitalist imperialist nation.

3.

Britain was never really an important province of the Roman empire, valuable mainly for its grain, tin and lead. There were a few small country towns and large estates but most settled life was in the South East and South West. Bath (*Aquae Sulis*) belonged to the settled part of southern England. It was easy to get to and to get from, the Fosseway ran from north-east to south-west, joining the four towns of Lincoln, Leicester, Bath and Exeter. In Roman times Bath drew visitors for its Temple of Sul. People also came for the sake of the hot springs. The area was conquered by Saxon invaders in 577. The baths were silted up, buildings fell in and birds nested in the ruins.

Bath developed in the early middle ages within the economic context of feudalism, it became an episcopal and monastic city with a local and in part national reputation for its healing springs. By the tenth century it was presided over by a Reeve - an official of some importance in the Saxon period. It had been Christianized some time in the seventh century and was the site of a monastery of Black Benedictine monks, whose abbey was built here. Refugee monks from Ghent came here in the tenth century and the Flemish influence remained strong for over a century. *The Domesday Boke* contains this reference to the city:

"The king holds Bath. In the time of king Edward it was taxed at the rate of twenty hides, when the county of Somerset was assessed. Here the king has twenty four burgesses, paying him four pounds by the year, and there are ninety burgesses under the protection of other men, paying their sixty shillings per annum ..."

The city grew into a prosperous medieval town, its importance the result of its becoming a monastic centre and See - Bath and Wells - ordained by Pope Innocent IV in 1245. Bishop John of Tours had a large abbey built here, bigger than that of Winchester or Ely or Norwich. (The present abbey is sixteenth century and in fact covers only the nave of the original church.) Richard I granted Bath its charter in 1189. The wealth of medieval Bath came from its being the centre of the West Country's woollen trade - as Chaucer says:

"Of cloth-making she had such an haunt
She passed them of Ypres and of Gaunt"

The Monks Mills survived until the eighteenth century. Our best source of knowledge about Bath in the middle ages is John Leyland (1506-52), who noted much evidence of Bath's prosperity, a great gate with a stone arch, sundry churches, and the conveying of the hot spring water by 'pipes of lead' to many houses in the city. The baths were frequented by 'people diseased with Leprosy, Pox, Scabs and Great Aches'. There were several baths, the King's Bath being 'very fine and fair and large ...'.

The rebuilding of the abbey during the fifteenth century is evidence of Bath's continuing prosperity. Oliver King, who became Bishop of Bath and Wells in 1495, put the ecclesiastical accounts in order and saved money towards the rebuilding of what is, in fact, the priory church at Bath.

The Reformation had a catastrophic effect on Bath Abbey. The Priory was dissolved in 1540. Thomas Cromwell's commissioners presented their evidence about the wealth of the religious establishments in such a way as to discredit them as a preliminary to taking them over. The details were always presented in such a way as to suggest bankruptcy and moral degeneracy. On the Priory at Bath they had this to say:

"It may please your goodness to understand that we have visited Bath ... we found the Prior a right virtuous man ... a man simple and not of the greatest wit ... his monks worse that I have found yet both in buggery and adultery, some of them having ten women, some eight and the rest fewer. The House well repaired but four hundred pounds in debt ...."

Reading between the lines we may conclude the establishment was a wealthy one.

The well-to-do citizens of Bath tried to buy King Henry's good favours with presents - including Irish hawks and by granting Cromwell an annuity of £5 a year (approximately £3,000 in today's money, this was before Henry VIII debased the coinage and before the great inflations brought about by the influx of gold from South America). It was to no avail. Immediately before the dissolution the monks sold or granted leases on their lands, revenues and benefices. This was an attempt to capitalize their holdings and to create legal ties in the area. When King Henry's commissioners, John Tregonwell and William Petre, came to Bath to claim the monastic wealth and property, they found the bulk of it disposed of and also that they had to honour contracts the monks had given the local gentry. This is the basis of several of the local fortunes which descended through various families in the city and were to fund the great rebuilding of Bath in the eighteenth century. The commissioners offered the abbey to the citizens of Bath for 500 marks (a mark = 13s. 4d., two thirds of a pound). The cautious Bathonians refused, for fear of cozening the king, but they took things into their own hands. The beautiful and magnificent priory church was stripped of all its valuables - glass, lead, gold - the lot was sold off to merchants. Only the shell of Bishop Oliver King's massive church remained, the walls and certain sections of the roof. King Henry had it sold off to one Humphrey Colles, who in turn sold off the precinct and the church as it stood to Matthew Colthurst. Edmond Colthurst, his son, gave what remained standing of the church to the citizens of Bath for their parish church, and the remainder of the premises he sold to Fulk Morley, from whom it descended to the Duke of Kingston (family name, Pierrepoint) and Earl Manvers. North Parade and South Parade (1735-40) were built on land owned by the Duke of Kingston, hence Duke Street and Pierrepoint Street: Manvers Street, which runs from Pierrepoint Street to the site now occupied by the Spa Station, commemorates the other titled beneficiary of Bath's priory lands, and Dorchester Street, which joins Manvers Street, was named for Evelyn Pierrepoint, first Marquis of Dorchester.

During most of Queen Elizabeth I's reign the abbey lay in ruins, although the city was prosperous enough. Gradually local charity and individual benevolence provided for the repair of the east end of the north aisle. During the years 1573-80 the Queen authorized collections to be made nationwide for the restoration of the church. By the time the Armada services could be held in parts of the abbey, which was finally reconstructed and dedicated to saints Peter and Paul while James Montagu was Bishop of Bath and Wells 1608-16. Evidence of the wealth of the city is to be found in the fact that Elizabeth granted Bath a charter in 1590, by which Bath was declared to be a sole city on its own, and the citizens to be a body corporate and politic, by the name of 'Mayor, Aldermen and Citizens' with full powers of government.

Bath was still not a fashionable medicinable place, and it was some years before Bath was to receive the royal touch which made her fashionable. Anne of Denmark, wife of James I, visited the city in 1616. A new bath had been constructed but it was still the done thing to bathe in the Cross Bath. She was about to enter when she had a vision of a great flame shooting out from the cistern of the Cross Bath and was so frightened that she refused to get in. Instead she bathed in the new baths, still called the Queen's Bath today. The well-to-do now began to come to Bath and neglected the continent, with them came the hangers-on, card-sharpers, hucksters, tarts and their pimps, social climbers, although bathing was a still pretty rough affair: 'The baths were like so many Bear Gardens', a contemporary wrote,

"and modesty was entirely shut out of them: people of both sexes bathing by Day and Night naked; and Dogs and Cats and even Human Creatures were hurled over the rails into the Water while People were bathing in it ...."

The visit of Charles II and his court in 1663 put the royal seal of approval on the spa city (one of the best accounts of Bath at this time is to be found in Pepys' diary for June 1668: he noted among other things, 'a pretty good market place, and many good streets, and very fair stone houses ...').

The creation of Bath as the centre of fashion, for which the Georgian city was built, was the result of a combination of factors: Charles II and his circle created the style of court and society life much as we would recognize it today and places of resort for the well-born and well-to-do had to meet the requirements of those used to metropolitan social life; Bath became a fashionable spa; Richard (Beau) Nash arrived on the scene to organize the city and its entertainments; a combination of war and of trade was beginning to create a massive injection of wealth into British social life; and the landowners (Gay, Pierrepoint, Manvers, Pulteney) got together with the builders and architects (Wood, father and son) to create suitable accommodation to house and to entertain the wealthy in the season (Bath had eight thousand visitors in 1715, the first Pump Room was finished in 1706). The essential links in the story of the creation of Georgian Bath are to be found in the association between Ralph Allen and John Wood. Allen was Bath's wealthy postmaster. He married the illegitimate daughter of General Wade, MP for Bath, who left him his fortune and got him a place on the city Council. Allen bought the quarries at Combe Down. John Wood was a surveyor and architect who was inspired by Palladianism. Wealth, ambition, influence, opportunity, ideas - the equation was complete. Nash recognized the potential of Bath and saw that it needed accommodation for the visitors who would flock to spend their wealth during the season at a fashionable resort which combined medical treatment and entertainment. Royal recognition offered the opportunity to men of vision to put Bath on the map. Allen controlled the raw materials. Wood had the imagination to see in Bath the possibility of creating an elegant and imposing city. The landowners and leaseholders were agreeable. Allen was the vital connection with the city Council. Bath became the first city in Britain to make the holiday and the tourist industry its main source of income. 'The eighteenth century in time saw in Bath a swift, sharp break with the town's old traditions', writes Bryan Little in *The Building of Bath* (1947), 'a jump forward from the early slow evolution from clothing town to Spa. It was a conscious, highly artificial transformation, as much of a change as Swindon or Dagenham underwent in their respective phases of our modern industrial age....' Bramble had a less favourable view. He writes to tell Dr. Lewis that he finds

"nothing but disappointment at Bath; which is so altered, that I can scarce believe it is the same place that I frequented about thirty years ago ... this place, which Nature and Providence seem to have intended as a resource from distemper and disquiet, is become the very centre of racket and dissipation..."

The cause of the trouble, Bramble diagnosed, was 'the general tide of luxury, which hath overspread the nation...'. And where did this wealth come from?

4.

On 26 October 1740 Smollett sails as a surgeon's mate on board the *Chichester,* with eighty guns, one of the largest vessels to leave St. Helens, under the command of Sir Chaloner Ogle, to reinforce the fleet of Admiral Edward Vernon at the West Indies. Britain was at war with Spain. (The terrible conditions of service in the navy during this expedition Smollett described in *Roderick Random* and *A Compendium of Authentic and Interesting Voyages.*) Colonial expansion by means of war, and the wealth from the West Indian slave trade - these are the major sources of the wealth and luxury so frequently noted by commentators of the time. Smollett's associations with both are clear - he served in the West Indian campaign and it was at Jamaica that he met and fell in love with the handsome Creole Anne Lascelles, who became his wife in 1747. She was heiress of an estate and slaves valued then at £3,000. He was to experience great difficulties in laying hands on this wealth. While some of the nation wallowed in luxury at the expense of the West Indies, he was writing, 'I have been hedging and lurching these six weeks in expectation of that cursed ship from Jamaica, which is at last arrived without Letter of Remittance ...' (a letter to William Hunter, 1751). Three years later he writes: 'Never was I so harassed ... as now; a persecution which I owe to the detention of that remittance from Jamaica which I have every day expected since last Christmas ...' (a letter to George Macaulay, November 1754). To his printer he wrote in October 1757: 'It is a very hard case that I should be troubled ... when there are actually fifteen hundred pounds ... due to us at Jamaica ...' (letter to William Strahan). While the nation thrived, he fretted and went short. *'Magnas inter opes inops'* - he might well recall his Horace. Commerce grew faster than agriculture in the period 1690-1760. Imports of merchandise rose from 16s. a head of the population in 1690, to £1 12s. a head in 1760, and exports from 18s. to £2 2s. in the same period, growing at the rate of 1.5 % per annum throughout this period. Trade with Europe almost stagnated, imports falling 53% at the beginning of the century to 44% by 1750 and to 31% by the end of the century. By contrast trade with the North American Colonies and the West Indies, Africa, India and the Far East increased by leaps and bounds. Independent planters and traders could get wealthier than the directors of overseas trading companies.

This is how the system worked. The American colonies supplied Britain with some necessities, such as naval stores, iron, in the normal way of trade. Much of it was carried in American shipping, the rest of the trade was lucrative (developed under the Navigation Acts) and the gain went to the British mercantile interests. A large part of the colonial imports were re-exported to Europe, and in the process giving a profit of some fifteen per cent of the trade to British shippers and merchants, as well as encouraging new industries such as tobacco-curing and sugar-refining. In addition, British manufacturers were engaged in making goods to exchange for slaves, as well as engaging in the trade itself. Defoe, writing in 1728, said: 'As slaves are the produce of the British Commerce in their African Factories ... they are so far a branch of the British Exportation, just as if they were first brought to England, landed there, and sent Abroad ...' (*A Plan of the English Commerce*, 1728). The plantation economy of the West Indies and parts of the American colonies was ultimately financed from England and gave its profits to England.

This was also the case with other triangular trade patterns. The wealth created in trade with the West Indies reappeared in Britain in the pockets of returned nabobs, negro-drivers, planters, clerks, factors and hucksters - the wealth they brought back with them was invested in England in titles, in land, or further commercial ventures. This trade in turn created banks, other financial institutions, such as insurance companies, which brought further invisible earnings from abroad. The wealth of the Lascelles family in London, of the Beckford family (William Beckford squandered the family fortune on Fonthill Abbey and Beckford's Tower, in Bath), of the Pinney family in Bristol, of the Pulteney family of Bath, of the Gladstone family in Liverpool - all was based in slave plantations in the West Indies.

Slaving produced wealth not so much because slaves were cheap (they were not) but because there was such a demand for sugar. By the mid-eighteenth century there were two giants among sugar exporting islands, British Jamaica and French Saint-Dominique. A feature of the sugar trade was the habit of the plantocracy to live as absentee landlords in England, leaving estates in the hands of overseers and attorneys, spending income from slaves and sugar at home in England. The essential part of the trick was that slaves made it possible to replace former crops such as coffee, tobacco, indigo, fruit, etc. - all of which could be grown on small acreages for modest or uncertain profits - with a vast monoculture, sugar. It was a rich man's crop, needing huge estates and a massive labour force, based on large investment sunk in the purchase of estate and slaves.

The tonnage figures of British shipping is striking evidence of the growth of Britain as a trading and commercial nation in this period. In 1702 total British tonnage was 323,000, but by 1763, the year in which the Peace of Paris brought to an end the Seven Years' War and gave Britain the best bits of North America and India, total tonnage was 496,000. The tonnage engaged in foreign trade rose from 123,000 in 1702 to 304,000 in 1773. The figures on entries and clearances at British ports show the same staggering increase: from 827,000 tons in 1686 to 1,450,000 in 1765. The new wealth brought expansion in housing in Britain and more city life. For ordinary people wages were higher than before and opportunities for social betterment were increasing. It was this that attracted migration from country areas to the cities, falling food prices and rising wages. Standards were most evidently rising among the merchant and trading

classes. There were more goods to be sold and improved transport led to
an increase of trade internally. Shopkeeping thrived: 'A pastrycook's
shop, which twenty pounds would have furnished at (one) time,' wrote
Defoe, 'could now cost upwards of three hundred pounds' (*Complete
English Tradesman* 1725). War itself was another seemingly inexhaust-
ible source of profit. Trade increased at the end of each war in the century
(War of the Spanish Succession 1701-14, War of Jenkins' Ear 1739-41,
War of the Austrian Succession 1740-48, The Seven Years' War 1756-63
and the struggle in the American colonies lasted from 1775 to 1783). Some
industries thrived in war, such as iron and non-ferrous metal smelting,
coal, animal breeding, the leather trades (James Brydges, first Duke of
Chandos, 1673-1744, MP for Hereford, paymaster of the forces abroad
1707-12, made a fortune from supplying footwear for Marlborough's
armies and became Handel's patron), canvas, woollens, shipbuilding,
chemicals - war created demand and eliminated the need for 'wastage'.

As merchants made it, they moved out to the plusher suburbs. That
the period was one in which suburbia extended outwards from the central
city may be evidenced from the growth of London at this stage which by
1760 had a population of over 1,000,000. The pattern in Bath was
unusual, as the housing need here was not only residential-suburban, but
urban-seasonal. Consumption was the obvious sign of the new affluence
- coffee-and tea-drinking (hence the need for all that sugar!), chocolate-
drinking, the use of china, lacquer, wall-paper (from China), furniture-
making as a delicate art, which relied so heavily on the import of
mahogany from the West Indies (Chippendale's *Gentleman and Cabinet
Maker's Directory*, the first comprehensive trade catalogue of its kind, was
published in 1754). 'An ordinary tradesman now ... shall spend more
money by the year than a gentleman ... and shall increase and lay up every
year too ... a shoemaker in London shall keep a better house, spend more
money, clothe his family better, yet grow rich too', commented Defoe. 'It
is evident where the difference lies: an estate's a pond, but trade's a
spring.' The estimated growth in per capita income between 1688 and
1770 is from £8 a year to £18 a year.

In Charles II's time the well-to-do sipped coffee in the coffee houses of
London, but by quite early in the reign of George III the British were
swilling tea in the comfort and privacy of their own homes. Arthur Young
wrote in *Farmer's Letters* (1767) 'as much superfluous money is expended
on tea and sugar as would maintain four million more subjects on bread.'

Sir Frederick Eden(*The State of the Poor or An History of the Labouring Classes in England*, 1791) records that, 'even in poor families tea is not only the usual beverage in the morning and evening, but is generally drunk in large quantities at dinner ...'. Tea was drunk without milk (which was considered unhealthy) and therefore needed to be sweetened. West Indian sugar was on every table. In 1700 the British consumed 10,000 tons of sugar a year, but by 1800 we managed about 150,000 tons - if the population had doubled during the century, it means that the consumption by each Englishman had risen seven-and-a-half times. 'Your very chambermaids have lost their bloom ... I suppose by sipping tea!' lamented Jonas Hanway (1712-86).

It is tea, with its inescapable need for sugar, which created the West Indian connection and the inevitable economic and social consequences so carefully noted by Smollett. So many had made money by the 1760s that they now wanted to push their way in to the centre of the social scene. People of all classes flocked to Bath. The old caste system seemed to be breaking up. An an anonymous poet commented:

"No seats for peeresses are now appointed But rank and title are all disjointed And every great upstart whom great Nash had humbled, With Dukes and Princes, counts and Lords is jumbled."

5.

Smollett knew Bath well. He visited the city several times in the season and at one time he had entertained the idea of practising here as a physician. He lived variously at South Parade, at the Bear Inn and in Gay Street. In his letters, novels and medical works Bath features quite frequently, and his observations are invariably shrewd and perceptive. By the time he first came to Bath he was a fully qualified physician and had served in the Spanish War of 1739-41 (which provided him with material for some of the most striking scenes in *Roderick Random*, 2 vols., 1748). In 1752 he published a very detailed account of the use of the waters at Bath, *An Essay on the External Use of Water ... with Remarks upon the Present Method of Using the Mineral Waters at Bath in Somersetshire, and a Plan for Rendering them more Safe, Agreeable and Efficacious*. The work is valuable still, not so much on medical grounds, as for its accurate contemporary portrait of how the waters were used. This alone would demonstrate how well Smollett knew the city:

"Diseased persons of all ages, sexes and conditions, are promiscuously admitted into an open bath, which affords little or no shelter from the inclemencies of the weather ...."

He apportions much of the blame for the lack of full and sensible use of the baths to the medical profession (satiric portraits of medical men and comic accounts of the practices are a feature of all his novels); and also blames the mayor and corporation for not fully exploiting the city's most famous natural resource. 'Narrow minds will ever have narrow views', he wrote:

"the Corporation of Bath seems to have forgot that the ease and plenty they now enjoy, and to which their fathers were strangers, are owing to their Waters, and that an improvement upon their Baths, would, by bringing a great concourse of company to their town, perpetuate these blessings to them and their posterity. How little is to be expected from them ... might have been guessed by their conduct to Mr. Wood ... to whose extraordinary genius they are indebted for a great part of the trade and beauty of the place; yet they have industriously opposed his best designs, which ... would have rendered Bath, in point of elegant architecture, the admiration of the whole world ..."

He is clearly well acquainted, from this evidence alone, with Bath in its hey-day, when its social life was so strictly organized by Nash. (This was Nash's great achievement, his regimen made Bath an entertaining and a safe place for people to come and bring their families: he aimed to free Bath from 'rustic' associations, to replace its primitive amenities and to draw up a code of conduct - he stamped out duelling, laid down rules for dress, created orchestras, waits, card salons, dances, assemblies.) This was Bath before the invasion of the *nouveau riche,* which could boast the architectural glories of the Chandos Building, Ralph Allen's town house, North and South Parades, the Grammar School, houses in the Vineyards, Trim Street, Queen Square, Kingsmead Square, Gay Street, Widcombe House and Prior Park. It is Bath at this period which he describes in several scenes in *Peregrine Pickle* (4 vols., 1751). The satire here is mild, he mocks the idle and empty world of fashion in the spa, the quacks, the gamblers, the social climbers and rogues of all degree. Many passages in the first edition were cut out from the second and all subsequent editions, among them are passages concerned with Bath doctors who, Smollett says, were scandalmongers:

"... among the secret agents of scandal, none were so busy as the physicians, a class of animals who live in this place like so many ravens hovering about a carcase, and even ply for hire, like scullers at Hungerford-stairs ..."

Another section describes how Bathonians rely on stray dogs to act as turnspits to roast their Sunday dinners and Peregrine and his mates nab all the dogs one day and the citizens have recourse to various shifts both comic and dramatic to get their dinners cooked:

"One master of a family ... was obliged to undertake the office of turnspit ... to the destruction of his appetite and the danger of his health: another being driven to the necessity of cutting the roast into steaks, fell sick of mortification and well nigh lost his wits: and a third, having contrived to suspend the sirloin above the fire ... the pack thread gave way towards the end of the operation, and the meat falling down, discharged the contents of the dripping pan upon his leg, which was scalded in a miserable manner ...."

What comes through here is the unspoiled and suburban nature of Bath at the time. There is none of that sense of the hectic and the dislocated which is so characteristic of the Bath scenes in *Humphry Clinker* (3 vols., 1771).

An often (and justly) praised quality in *Humphry Clinker* is Smollett's brilliant exploitation of the multidimensionality offered in the very structure of an epistolary novel. It is worth pondering the effects achieved from seeing reality through the various eyes of Matthew, Jerry, Lydia, Tabitha and Win. The result is not simply that we gradually build up an objective construct of reality from this variety of sources, but that through this necessarily and essentially fragmented texture of perceptions a subjective view almost imperceptively dominates. This is especially (and strikingly) true of the sections on Bath, although I would also urge that a similar case could just as well be based on the sections on London or on Scotland - other areas which we know Smollett felt deeply about.

What comes through in the Bath scenes in *Humphry Clinker* is the sense of collapse, confusion and social disintegration which the rising tide of luxury and its effects on social harmony have clearly started. Consumption and display have become the only human goals; tolerance, compassion and ordinary humanity (such as Matthew himself shows when he rescues young Clinker) have sunk without trace. The dominating view is that of Bramble and it is his insight into what is happening at Bath with is the enduring impression we take from those pages of *Humphry Clinker*. The mature view is dominant, Jerry and Lydia marvel at the wonders and opulence they see around them, but their view is immature and unsound.

"Bath to me is a new world. All is gaiety, good humour and diversion. The eye is continually entertained with the splendour of dress and equipage, and the ear with the sound of coaches ... The Squares, the Circus, and the Parades put you in mind of the sumptuous palaces, represented in prints and pictures, and th new buildings ... look like so many enchanted castles..."

But Lydia's gushing commendations stand little chance against Bramble's collective impression of a city brought by folly, luxury, greed and shallowness to the brink of disintegration:

"Every upstart of fortune, harnessed in the trappings of the mode, presents himself at Bath, as in the very focus of observation. Clerks and factors from the East Indies, loaded with the spoil of plundered provinces; planters, negro-drivers and hucksters from our American plantations, enriched they know not how; agents, commissaries and contractors, who have fattened in two successive wars ... usurers, brokers and jobbers of every kind.... Knowing no other criterion of greatness, but the ostentation of wealth ... all of them hurry to Bath ...."

It is no accident that he associates the social decay with the stink of physical rottenness. At the Assembly Bramble faints at the smell:

"It was indeed a compound of villainous smells .... Imagine to yourself a high exalted essence of mingled odours arising from putrid gums, imposthumated lungs, sour flatulencies, rank armpits, sweating feet, running sores ... plaster, ointments and embrocations ...."

The architecture is given in terms of meretricious flamboyance, high consumerism: 'The Circus is a pretty bauble, contrived for shew' and he comments on 'the affected ornaments of the architrave, which are both childish and misplaced' and talks of the 'want of beauty and proportion' in the new architecture. The city has become 'the very centre of racket and dissipation' inhabited by 'lunatics'. Two impressions are particularly strong here, the emphasis on dirt and disease, and the sense of chaos. No reader may easily forget Bramble's words about 'scrophulous ulcers' and 'sweat and dirt, and dandriff, and the abominable discharges of various kinds, from twenty different diseased bodies' and the awful suggestion of the source of the taste and smell of the waters:

"I find that the Roman baths ... were found covered by an old burying ground, belonging to the Abbey; through which, in all probability, the water drains in its passage; so that as we drink the decoction of living bodies at the Pump Room, we swallow the strainings of brotten bones and carcases at the private bath ...."

The pathological element is indelibly strong: '... we know not what sores may be running into the water while we are bathing, and what sort of matter we may thus imbibe; the king's evil, the scurvy, the cancer, and the pox ....' The sense of physical decay is carried over onto the very structure and anatomy of Bath, which he says are liable to blow down in the wind as they are built of soft crumbling stone, while their appearance is suggestive of deformity - 'the wreck of streets and squares disjointed by an earthquake'.

West Indian associations run throughout. Bramble is distressed in the morning to hear 'two negroes, belonging to a Creole gentleman, who lodged in the same house' practising the French-horn, and there are the inevitable West Indian heiresses: 'The ball was opened by a Scotch Lord, with a mulatto heiress from St. Christophers ....' Bath was in the process of being taken over by the West Indian traders, who formed their own social circle with all the other West Indian families to whom they were linked by marriage, by business association or neighbourhood. The same names crop up in island social circles and at Bath - Akerse, Bannister, Douglas, Ottley, Skerrett, Tuite, Kirwan, Phipps, Oliver, Manning. Bath Abbey contains the memorials of numerous members of the West Indian community who found Bath to their liking, and possibly stayed longer than they had at first intended. The family and friends, their children and black servants, together might form a seasonal booking of some hundred and fifty people. It was to accommodate such parties as this from Barbados, Antigua, Jamaica that Sir William Pulteney, himself a wealthy plantation owner in the West Indies, bought and developed the Bathwick Estate. The city of Bath which Smollett captures in *Humphry Clinker* is clearly responding to that significant West Indian connection.. It is a paradigm of western European economic development, a city which in a microcosm embodies that series of changes from the primitive and the savage, through feudalism, mercantilism and colonial capitalism.

"Thus the number of people, and the number of houses continue to increase; and this will ever be the case, till the streams that swell this irresistible torrent of folly and extravagence, shall either be exhausted, or turned into other channels, by incidents and events which I do not pretend to foresee ...."

We know now that what Smollett saw was only the beginning; imperialism then had hardly flexed its muscles.

In fact an examination of Smollett's treatment of Bath and the West Indian connection reveals the complex materiality of *Humphry Clinker* as a literary text. Working within an accepted literary convention of the day - the epistolary novel perfected by Richardson, with the denouement of recognition and marriage forming the 'happy ending' - Smollett has symptomatically demonstrated the essential contradiction in the novel as a *genre* - that it was essentially the product of bourgeois capitalism, and yet is quintessentially antagonistic to its very means of production. How extraordinarily apt is that accidental image of the corrupting bodies from the ancient burial ground whose very dissolution created the capital investment in real estate which made the industrial revolution of Bath possible, and whose very corruption seeps through to infect the contemporary world, literally bodying forth Marx's concept of the system's carrying within itself the seeds of its own destruction.

NOTES

1. Edward Littleton was educated at Westminster and St. Mary Hall, Oxford, and was Fellow of All Souls College, Oxford 1647. He was a barrister at Lincoln's Inn before going to Barbados as Secretary to Lord Willoughby of Parham in 1666. He was a judge 1670-1683 and Agent for the Island of Barbados 1683. He wrote on the colonies, finance and general politics 1664-94.
2. Lewis Melville: *The Life and Letters of Tobias Smollett* (London, Faber and Gwyer 1926) p.25.
3. Alan Kendall: *David Garrick* (London, Harrap 1985) p.80.
4. Smollett: *Reproof*. Rich was also lampooned by Pope in *The Dunciad*.
5. Smollett: *Preface* to *The Regicide*, London 1749.
6. See Christopher Hibbert: *The Personal History of Samuel Johnson* (Harmondsworth, Penguin 1984) pp.60-72 and 91-3; also James Boswell: *The Life of*

Samuel Johnson (London, Dent 1923) Volume I pp. 155-157.

7. E.L. McAdam and George Milne (editors) *Johnson's Dictionary: A Modern Selection* (London, Macmillan 1982) p.285.

8. Dr. John Moore, quoted in Melville op.cit. p.33.

9. Smollett: *Peregrine Pickle* (London, Oxford University Press 1964) Chapter CI, p.641.

IV

Edgar Allan Poe
meets Inspector Morse

Writing gave us fiction. Printing gave us the detective story. The detective story gave the world the genius of Edgar Allan Poe, but his fiction provides one of the finest treatments of the prototypical right hand/left hand relationship we find in Sancho Panza/Don Quixote, James Boswell/Samuel Johnson, Sam Weller/Mr. Pickwick, Dr. Watson/ Sherlock Holmes, Tinker/Sexton Blake, Terry McCann/Arthur Daly, Sergeant Martin/Adam Dalgleish — and is still with us in the persons of Sergeant Lewis and Inspector Morse.

1.

Edgar Allan Poe prefaces 'The Murders in the Rue Morgue' with the following sentence from Sir Thomas Browne: 'What song the Syrens sang, or what name Achilles assumed when he hid himself among women, although puzzling questions are not beyond **all conjecture.**' [1] The emphasis on **all conjecture** is significant, and the whole quotation is an apposite text for the Dupin stories. It signals not only the leading theme of these fictions - that conjecture in the hands of an expert may be a key which unlocks the most baffling mysteries - but also evokes associations with the author of *Pseudodoxia Epidemica* (1646) and *Hydriotaphia, Urn-Burial* (1658).

Browne's first volume was a demolition of the silly things which thousands of people believed - vulgar errors, travellers' tales, superstitions, fabulous animals, false opinions, common fallacies, pious myths, hoaxes, hexes and a gallimaufry of widely credited nonsense - while the second was a treatise on human mortality and ancient burial customs. Sir Thomas Browne was a successful and distinguished physician but also an eclectic scholar whose intellect was drawn as to the magnetic North towards all that was mysterious, arcane, the unthinkable and the semi-morbid. Browne thrived on paradox. He was intoxicated by unanswer-able questions, fascinated by hieroglyphs, puzzles, cryptograms and the riddles of antiquity. But behind all his energetic ratiocination there was a rockbed of firm belief that a simple, clear and direct solution exists for each and every one of the mysteries we turn our minds to, could we but see it. His *Garden of Cyrus* (1658), for example, is a study of the quincunx and the appearance of the number five in a wide variety of phenomena; he believed that five was one of the mysterious numbers which held the universe together, that it pervades all the horticulture of antiquity and recurs throughout all plant life and the figurations of animals.

The emphasis on all conjecture in the sentence is Poe's, but it draws attention to the eneluctable seduction of the curious-minded by seemingly imponderable questions. Sir Thomas Browne himself is here echoing Suetonius, who recorded that Tiberius was devoted to Greek and Latin literature, and had a particular bent for mythology:

"... and carried his researches in it to such a ,ridiculous point that he would test professors of, Greek literature - whose society-he cultivated above all others - by asking them questions like: 'Who was Hecuba's mother?'-'What name did Achilles assume when he disguised himself as a girl at the court of King Lycomedes?'-'What song did the Sirens sing?' " [2]

Suetonius is celebrated for his gift of supplying curious biographical details, and he records of Tiberius that he was strong and heavily built and of more than average height: "His shoulders and chest were broad, and his body perfectly proportioned from top to toe. His left hand was more agile than his right, and so strong that he could poke a finger through a sound, newly-plucked apple or into the skull of a boy or young man." [3]

The combination of left-handedness and the interrogation of the mysteries of the world is both striking and to the point.

It urges us further in our enquiries about the nature of Edgar Allan Poe in so far as it is revealed in the Dupin stories, further than the breezy dismissal of Poe's juvenile interests so famously made by his fellow

American, T.S. Eliot. In *The Sacred Wood: Essays on Poetry and Criticism* (1920) Eliot writes:

"That Poe had a powerful intellect is undeniable: but it seems to me the intellect of a highly gifted young person before puberty. The forms which his lively curiosity takes are those in which a pre-adolescent mentality delights: wonders of nature and of mechanics and of the supernatural, cryptograms and cyphers, puzzles and labyrinths, mechanical chessplayers and wild flights of speculation."[4]

This has been a highly influential description of Poe's mind, and as for his art, Eliot did not leave it there. For in his essay 'Wilkie Collins and Dickens' (1927) he took occasion to comment on Edgar Allan Poe's contribution to the 'detective story' as a **genre:**

"The detective story, as created by Poe, is something as specialized and as intellectual as a chess problem; whereas the best English detective fiction has relied less on the beauty of the mathematical problem and much more on the intangible human element. In detective fiction England probably excels other countries; but in a genre invented by Collins and not by Poe ..."[5]

But a careful reading of 'The Murders in the Rue Morgue', 'The Purloined Letter' and 'The Mystery of Marie Roget' can demonstrate quickly enough that Poe was engaged in far more than simply unravelling puzzles, cryptograms and labyrinths, and that these stories are steeped in an intangible human element. The fascination with questions which need answers, with riddles and mysteries - the very basis of Poe's Dupin stories - is never to be underrated. Mankind has a record of obsession with all manner of 'mystery', from the high-flown to the most humble. It is a fascination which appears fundamental in human narrative.[6]

Ancient examples of 'mystery' such as the story of Oedipus, thus continue to hold our interest and, it is claimed, hold essential clues to the explanation of human behaviour. [7] More modern examples, not least Shakespeare's Hamlet, are full of similar probes and attempts at detection. It is this irreducible human curiosity which unites Oedipus, Hamlet and Dupin, and places Poe's Chevalier in company to which Eliot (at least) thought he was scarcely suited.

When Oedipus solves the riddle of the Sphinx, he saves Thebes from a dreadful tyranny long endured. When Thebes is afflicted by a terrible plague, he attempts to seek out the cause, only to discover that Thebes is being punished for the crime of its King - unknowingly Oedipus has killed his father and married his mother. In Sophocles' drama the Chorus assure us that none can be called happy until that day arrives when we carry our happiness with us down into the grave in peace.[8] It is my guess that the tragedy of Oedipus fascinates us not because of its gloomy moral precepts, but because it involves the unravelling of a great mystery. Human beings have always loved riddles,[9] and Sophocles' great tragedy opens at the moment when King Oedipus, who seems so all-powerful and so secure, is asked the question: why is this happening? He is bound to seek the cause of the distress endured by Thebes in order to bring it to an end. The unravelling of this mystery constitutes the tragedy of Oedipus.

Hamlet further demonstrates how fascinating a really complex mystery can be. Sadly familiarity and the distortions of post-romantic criticism have dampened the sense of mystery, focusing far too much attention on the 'psychology' of the Prince of Denmark, but if we read the play properly we can see that essentially it is constructed on the basis of a mystery (the death of Hamlet's father in strange circumstances), a hypothesis which would explain the mystery (the revelations of the Ghost), and the testing of the hypothesis (the play scene and all which follows from it). This will all be plain enough if we consider *Hamlet* as a tragic drama, in terms of dramatic action, rather than in the light of a Coleridgean/Bradleyan character study of Hamlet himself. As the tragedy unfolds we learn, as Hamlet learns, that God did not abandon Creation after the Fall, that Providence is there to help good to triumph over evil, offering opportunities through the agency of Fortune. Man must exercise judgement, his right under free Will, to help the workings of Providence. Horatio, always prosaic and down-to-earth, urges Hamlet not to go through with the duel with Laertes if he has any misgivings. Hamlet answers:

"Not a whit, we defy augury: there is a special providence in the fall of a sparrow. If it be now, 'tis not to come; if it be not to come, it will be now; if it be not now, yet it will come - the readiness is all. Since no man owes of aught he leaves, what is't to leave betimes? Let be."[10]

Hamlet's resigned 'Let be' answers his previous 'To be, or not to be'. He now knows that provided he exercises his judgement, that faculty in which man is superior to the beasts, and is ready to choose a course of action when Fortune offers it, he may trust to divine Providence, which is omnipresent to oversee the will of Almighty God. At the end of *Hamlet* Providence has prevailed - evil has been exposed and punished, social order has been restored, and those who nobly died shall rest in peace. The riddle, the mystery and the numerous questions posed have all been answered.

2.

Oedipus, Hamlet and Dupin each epitomize an ideological moment. Oedipus is quintessentially Hellenic. Hamlet truly Elizabethan. Dupin is very American, despite his Parisian location, or it may well be, because of it. In the Hellenic conception of the tragic, man was pitted against the remorseless and capricious gods. Tragedy here had little to do with reward or retribution; it was concerned - on the contrary - with the spectacle of man pitted against an unreasonable destiny which destroyed him. As George Steiner has written:

"the *Iliad* is the primer of tragic art. In it are set forth the motifs and images around which the sense of the tragic has crystallized ... the shortness of heroic life, the exposure of man to the murderousness and caprice of the inhuman, the fall of the City ... the fall of Troy is the first great metaphor of tragedy ... Fate is given a name, and the elements are shown in the frivolous and reassuring mask of the gods. But mythology is only a fable to help us endure. The Homeric warrior knows that he can neither comprehend nor master the workings of destiny ... Call for justice or explanation, and the sea will thunder back with its mute clamour. Men's accounts with the gods do not balance."[11]

Hamlet enshrines the Elizabethan world-view. It portrays man created in the form of an angel, but fallen from the state of grace. Grace is always attainable through the intervention of the Saviour. Providence is there to see that good triumphs over evil. The tragic sense is presented in the manner in which men must endure in the context of the resolution of tragic circumstance. In Shakespeare's world man is not alone in his predicament. The hand of God may reach out to help him, can he but see it. We are not as flies to wanton boys, who kill us for their sport; but we must endure our going hence, even as our coming hither. This is what such fellows as Hamlet should do, crawling between earth and heaven.

The basic assumptions on which the world of Dupin is constructed are quite different, and different in fundamental and revealing ways. In moving from the world view of the Oedipus dramas to *Hamlet* we shift from a conception of humanity as sport for the gods, to that of a benevolent and loving creator who seeks to help mankind save itself and regain a state of grace, offering his creatures providential warnings and stimulation to their divine reason so that they might seek solutions by exercising judgement. On 6 April 1580 there was an earthquake sensed quite strongly in England. The Queen and her council interpreted this as a sign that divine punishment was at hand for the nation's sins. A catalogue of fast days and prayers, including special prayers to be recited by the heads of households when families retired to bed, was proclaimed. [12] The defeat of the Spanish armada would seem to the Elizabethans fully to justify the measures prescribed after such portentous warnings.

The world of Dupin, significantly located by Poe in Paris, the centre of the Enlightenment, is one based on the divinity of human reason. Dupin solves mysteries in his own room. He works at night. He bases his solutions on evidence he reads in newspapers. His activities personify the free play of individual intellect. It is important to note that the narrator first meets him in a library; books are a powerful emblem of human knowledge. Dupin manifests that *hubris* which sadly is such a part of the legacy of the scientific enlightenment [13] and which Europeans take to be such a typical quality of modern North Americans. America itself was a product of the enlightenment, constructed, put together after the war with Britain in 1776, by human effort: it was not a nation organically developed over the years in the course of various accidents of history. In Anthony Burgess's words:

"When Europe, after millennia of war, rapine, slavery, famine, intolerance, had sunk to the level of a sewer, America became the golden dream, the Eden where innocence could be recovered ... in America man could glow in an aura of natural goodness, driven along his shining path by divine reason. The Declaration of Independence itself is a monument to reason. Progress was possible, and the wrongs committed against the Indians, the wildlife, the land itself, could be explained away in terms of the rational control of the environment necessary for the building of a New Jerusalem. " [14]

Dupin is the natural heir of that unmistakably Newtonian confidence we find in such comments as that which Newton wrote in a letter to Rober Hooke on 5 February 1675: "If I have seen further than you and Descartes, it is by standing upon the shoulders of Giants ... I frame no hypothesis; for whatever is not deduced from the phenomena is to be called an hypothesis; and hypotheses, whether metaphysical or physical, whether of occult qualities or mechanical, have no place in experimental philosophy. " [15]

Dupin's individualism is wholly American. He is also, be it noted, a young man.

3.

Writing in *The Atlantic Monthly* in December 1899 Hamilton Wright Mabie asserted: 'Poe stands alone in our literature, unrelated to his environment and detached from his time.' [15] Lewis Mumford believed that Poe escaped into:' a phantasmal world which registers a complete divorce from his environment'. [16] An examination of the character of C. Auguste Dupin and the relationship between Poe-as-narrator and the Chevalier Dupin will reveal that these opinions require considerable qualification, if not rejection.

To begin with an absolutely basic condition - the means of literary production and their effect on the nature of that which is produced - Dupin is essentially a creature of the age of print. The kind of narrative which gave us Dupin was only possible in an age which had interiorized literacy. And the technology of paper manufacture, printing and transport had combined in creating an extended mass literacy, producing a new kind of narrative, which involves the temporal sequence of events, in which the situation at the end is subsequent to that which pertained at the beginning. [17] Economic and technical factors contributed considerably to the thought-processes which mark Dupin out as the first modern detective, the prototype of all those intellectual sleuths from Sherlock Holmes to Adam Dalgleish. The very ratiocination which is Dupin's hallmark, was also the product of a stage in the history of human culture, being, as it was, the effect of the impact of writing and printing on the way the human mind worked. [18] Walter Ong asks:

"Why is it that lengthy climactic plot comes into being only with writing, comes into being first in the drama, where there is no narrator, and does not make its way into lengthy narrative until more than two thousand years later with the novels of Jane Austen? Earlier so-called 'novels' were all more or less episodic ... The climactic linear plot reaches a plenary form in the detective story - relentlessly rising tension, exquisitely tidy discovery and reversal, perfectly resolved denouement. The detective story is generally considered to have begun in 1841 with Edgar Allan Poe's ' The Murders in the Rue Morgue' ... "[19]

Walter Ong's discussion of the various answers to these questions is satisfactory at most levels, but leaves one or two important points unmade. He is surely correct in his interesting proposition that all lengthy narrative before the early 1800s was episodic, and that this was universally the case, and that no one had written a 'detective' story before 1841. Berkley Peabody's book *The Winged Word: A Study in the Technique of Ancient Greek Oral Composition as Seen Principally Through Hesiod's Works and Days* (1975) offers some useful pointers, and what he has to say about ancient Greek narrative song has a wide if not universal application, namely that there is a basic incompatibility between linear plot and oral memory, and what was communicated in ancient Greek epos drew its strengths from the remembered (often formulaic and traditional) stanzaic patterns, rather than in the singer's attempts individually to organize 'plot' in a particular way or fashion. In Peabody's words: 'A singer effects, not a transfer of his own intentions, but a conventional realization of traditional thoughts for his listeners, including himself.' [20]

The poet, the singer - call him what you will - did not directly convey to his audience a story-line, with characters, plot, situations, climax, etc. of his own imagining, but recalling, and embroidering as he recalls them, all the previous treatments of the same subject matter that he has ever heard, and the audience respond to his offering because their understanding, likewise, is conditioned hugely by what they have all heard and remembered before. The very word for this kind of performance - a rhapsody - means something stitched together.[21] The obvious parallels are to be found in modern popular culture, in the Westerns - say, of John Ford - where Ford draws on the situations, characters and iconography of all the Westerns he has seen, and the audience respond in large part by drawing on their collective experience of cinema Westerns. [22] The bard,

singing epic material to the tribe, takes part in an act of public recollection
or memory; he is in a situation which is not entirely under his own control.
The resulting 'Work' is the final product of interaction between the singer,
the tradition on which he draws, and the audience to whom he sings.

Literacy and print allow the 'author' to organize plot as never before,
and to construct a sequence of events under his own conscious control. The
'text' is composed to be consumed by a distanced reader, often in solitude.
Narrative develops tighter climactic structures:

"Print ... mechanically as well as psychologically locked words into
space and thereby established a firmer sense of closure than writing
could. The print world gave birth to the novel, which eventually made the
definitive break with episodic structure. "[23]

The detective story is a fine example of the heavily structured plot,
which builds up to a finely graded tension, climaxing in recognition, or
explanation, or reversal of fortune, and in the denouement of which all the
fine details - clues, observations, pieces of evidence - are shown to be
totally relevant. Such narrative was only possible in print. Print provided
the immediacy of text in which the plot was presented. Print also plays
another important part in the riveting success of Poe's Dupin tales; Poe
obtained his basic material from the daily newspapers he read, [24] but also
Dupin bases his investigations and hypotheses on evidence of cases that
he reads in newspapers. He solves the mystery of the murders in the Rue
Morgue by reading accounts of the crimes and the depositions of witnesses
in the papers. Not only does this make the case much more of a 'closed-
door' mystery, but it supports the credibility of the story. Newspapers are
part of the daily and weekly ebb and flow of modern life, and having
newspapers play such an important part in Dupin's expertise gives the
story a contemporary vraisemblance. Even though the genius of C.
Auguste Dupin is rare, eccentric and poetic, he clearly inhabits the same
world as we do. In three important respects then, print technology
influenced the very nature of these fictions: the technology created the
means of literary production and distribution which Poe was able to
exploit - 'The Murders in the Rue Morgue' appeared in *Graham's Magazine* in 1841, 'The Mystery of Marie Roget' was serialized in the *Ladies'
Companion* in November and December 1842 and February 1843, and
'The Purloined Letter' appeared in *The Gift* in 1845 - the very nature of

the prose narrative itself, with its concentration of a sequence of events, accumulation of detail, unravelling of mysteries and the climax of denouement - all this was made possible only by the impact of print on literacy, which meant that certain habits of reading become interiorized; and finally, the believable quality of the stories themselves, the manner in which Poe is able to insinuate the credibility of Dupin's genius, is the result of his being presented to us as a reader of newspapers.

4.

Dupin is an epic character in so far as he epitomizes the spirit of his time and the character of his nation. He is very American, and very much a man of his period. The quoted passage at the opening of 'The Murders in the Rue Morgue', the story which introduces Dupin to us, is from Sir Thomas Browne's *Urn-Burial*, and associates Dupin immediately with Achilles. His mental characteristics are given us as emphatically analytical, rational and reflective. But these qualities are harnessed to **usefulness.** This is a very American quality. [25] 'The Murders in the Rue Morgue' opens:

"The mental features discoursed of as analytical, are, in themselves, but little susceptible of analysis; We appreciate them only in their effects. We know of them ... that they are always to their possessor ... a source of the liveliest enjoyment. As the strong man exults in his physical ability ... so glories the analyst in that moral activity which **disentangles** ...the higher powers of the reflective intellect are more decidedly and more usefully tasked by the unostentatious game of draughts than by all the elaborate frivolity of chess. In this latter, where the pieces have different and **bizarre** motions ... what is only complex is mistaken (a not unusual error) for what is profound." [26]

Monsieur C. Auguste Dupin, though he may reside in Paris, presents some very American qualities. He is young, and though of good old family stock, the family fortunes have declined and he has to shift for himself in the world. He cares only for the basic necessities of life. His individualism shows itself in the way he abjures most social contacts. Although, no less than Oedipus and Hamlet, Dupin finds himself entangled in the resolution of mysteries, there are several important qualities which mark Dupin out as a new departure. Each of the three tales which feature Poe's analytic hero is unique unto itself, but there are some common features which are very important in qualifying the essence of Dupin, and establishing that there is much more to be yielded by examining them than simply demonstrable Freudianism. [27] One obvious difference is that Dupin is not personally involved in the problems he solves. They are not a matter of life and death to him. Nor does he set out - as Oedipus had - to solve a problem which affected the whole community. Nor, as was the case with Hamlet, does he wrestle with problems of kingship, succession, conscience, heaven and hell. The importance of the mysteries lies in the very fact that he is the one who solves them by exercising his particular gifts. This is one of the first points Poe makes about him.

The Dupin stories are studies of what Poe terms analytic mental features. They are not susceptible to analysis themselves; he tells us this at the opening of the first one, 'The Murders in the Rue Morgue' (1841). We can only appreciate them in their effects. To those who possess them they are a source of 'the liveliest enjoyment'. They seem to consist in the ability to assemble all the known and verifiable factual elements of a puzzling situation, and then almost by a process of intuition infer a hypothesis from them, which explains that which is otherwise inexplicable. All three mysteries present a factual surface quality which seemingly cannot logically be explained.

In 'The Murders in the Rue Morgue' a young woman and her mother are foully done to death in a locked room, with the key inside the room. Who could have committed such a crime when there was not apparent means of entry or exit? 'The Mystery of Marie Roget' presents a murder case which baffles the Prefect G- of the Paris police; it seems an 'ordinary' murder and yet appears unsolvable. A young girl's body appears in the Seine. On the face of it, she had been violated and murdered by a gang of ruffians, who then disposed of her corpse in the river. But in the search for the gang, all the clues peter out. In the last Dupin story, 'The Purloined Letter', a vital document disappears. The police have every reason to suspect its having been taken by a particular individual, yet all attempts to find the letter come to nothing. It is correctly assumed that the letter can only be valuable to him who stole it if it can be produced at a moment's notice, and therefore he must have it near him - yet no one can find it.

In each case a baffling question is answered in the same way: Dupin, completely removed from the crime, assembles the circumstances of the mystery and sorts through all the facts which can be verified; from these, and from these alone, a hypothetical explanation **presents itself.** The moment between the final assembly of the evidence and the production of the solution is rather like the moment when an electric current arcs between terminals. The analyst, such a man as Dupin, rejoices in the ability to 'disentangle', yet, as Poe describes it, this power is at root the ability to assemble and then to conclude. The kind of person Poe presents is fond of enigmas, conundrums and hieroglyphics: 'exhibiting in his solutions of each a degree of acumen which appears to the ordinary apprehension preternatural. His results, have, in truth, the whole air of intuition.'

This admirable faculty possessed by Dupin is 'much invigorated' by the study of the highest branches of mathematics, yet Poe goes to a lot of trouble to assert difference between **calculation** and **analysis:**

"I will ... take occasion to assert that the higher powers of the reflective intellect are more decidedly and usefully tasked by the unostentatious game of draughts than by all the elaborate frivolity of chess. In this latter, where the pieces have different and **bizarre** motions, with various and variable values, what is only complex is mistaken (a not unusual error) for what is profound. The **attention** is here called powerfully into play ... in nine cases out of ten it is the more concentrative rather than the more acute player who conquers. In draughts, on the contrary, where the moves are **unique** and have but little variation, the probabilities of inadvertence are diminished, and the mere attention being left comparatively unemployed, what advantages are obtained by either party are obtained by superior **acumen.**"[29]

Dupin has the mystic's or the seer's ability to perceive those things clearly and obviously which are obscured from normal viewers by the film of custom and familiarity. Dupin can see what would be obvious to all if only they would learn to look. He makes no astounding 'discoveries'. What he observes and what he reports would be visible to all those who would attempt to solve the mysteries on which he is engaged. This is brilliantly demonstrated in 'The Purloined Letter', although it is the basic principle in all the Dupin stories, where the stolen letter has been hidden by being deposited 'beneath the nose of the whole world'. [30]

Wordsworth believed that the task of the poet was to take ordinary and familiar subjects and throw over them a certain colouring of the imagination, so that ordinary things 'should be presented to the mind in an unusual aspect'.[31] Dupin is, in fact, a true poet. He looks at the world in an unusual way. Poe establishes the link between poetry and mathematics in 'The Purloined Letter'. The Prefect believes that the guilty Minister

"is a fool, because he has acquired renown as a poet. All fools are poets; this the Prefect **feels**; and he is merely guilty of a *non distributio medii* in then inferring that all poets are fools. [32]

It is in this discussion that a very interesting aspect of the relationship between Dupin and Poe-as-narrator is put to the reader. Poe doubts that the Minister is a poet: 'The Minister I believe has written learnedly on the Differential Calculus. He is a mathematician, and no poet.' [33] Dupin disagrees; he says that the Minister is **both** a mathematician **and** a poet; 'As poet **and** mathematician, he would reason well; as mere mathematician, he could not have reasoned at all, and thus would have been at the mercy of the Prefect.' Dupin's interlocutor answers:

"You surprise me ... by these opinions, which have been contradicted by the voice of the world. You do not mean to set at naught the well-digested ideas of centuries. The mathematical reason has long been regarded as **the** reason *par excellence.*"

Dupin replies, quoting Nicolas Chamfort's comment: *'Il y a à parier ... que toute idée publique, toute convention reçue, est une sottise, car elle a convenu au plus grand nombre.'* [34]

Dupin then deals with the common fallacy that mathematics, being in essence logic pure and simple, and poetry, the reckless flight of the imagination, are contradictory and irreconcilable aspects of human endeavour:

"The mathematicians ... have done their best to promulgate the popular error to which you allude, and which is none the less an error for its promulgation as truth. With an art worthy of a better cause ... they have insinuated the term 'analysis' into application to algebra. The French are the originators of this particular deception; but if a term is of any importance ... then 'analysis' conveys 'algebra' about as much as, in Latin, *'ambitus'* implies 'ambition', *'religio'* 'religion', or *'homines honesti'* a set of 'honourable men' ..."

" ... I dispute the availability, and thus the value, of that reason which is cultivated in any especial form other than the abstractly logical. I dispute, in particular, the reason educed by mathematical study. The mathematics are the science of form and quantity; mathematical reasoning is merely logic applied to observation upon form and quantity. The great error lies in supposing that even the truths of what is called **pure** algebra, are abstract or general truths. And this error is so egregious that I am confounded at the universality with which it has been received. Mathematical axioms are **not** axioms of general truth. [35]

It is Dupin's awareness of the relationship between poetry and mathematics, and that the combination of the two skills may produce that acumen which is the result of the exercise of the analytical powers of the mind, which causes him to respect the Minister D- so much as an **opponent:** '... if the Minister had been no more than a mathematician, the Prefect would have been under no necessity of giving me this check. I knew him ... as both mathematician and poet, and my measures were adapted to his capacity.'[36] There are several concepts in this discussion to be noted. Above all there is the undeniable admiration called for in the contemplation of poetry when combined with logic; and equally striking, there is the acknowledgement that these qualities are rarely found in human kind. This is bound to be the case; the humdrum majority are mundane, men of genius are rare. But the opposition between orthodox opinions ('You surprise me by these opinions, which have been contradicted by the voice of the world; You do not mean to set at naught the well-digested idea of centuries ...') and unorthodox (*Il y a à parier ... que toute idée publique, toute convention reçue, est une sottise, car elle a convenu au plus grand nombre ...*') is very powerfully made.

5.

The relationship between Dupin and the narrator of these tales is one which figures frequently in western literature from the late sixteenth century. It is one we seem to find satisfying and indeed revealing as to the nature of our humanity. Poe gives us a clue when he talks of the old philosophy of the Bi-Part soul in 'The Murders in the Rue Morgue'. Dupin is the intellectual genius of the partnership - the narrator is the admiring, regular guy. The narrator is 'astonished' at the 'vast extent' of Dupin's reading, and feels his 'soul enkindled' within him by 'the wild fervor, and the vivid freshness of his imagination'. He is soon convinced that 'the society of such a man' would be a treasure 'beyond price'. Typically in this type of relationship, the regular guy 'frankly confides' these feelings to the superior partner, and is happy to give himself up 'to his wild whims with a perfect abandon.' [37] There is a hint that Dupin's eccentric genius almost topples into madness, 'the result of an excited, or perhaps of a diseased intelligence'. [38]

The Dupin/Narrator relationship is one of the several reasons which makes the reading of these three so-called 'detective' stories so satisfying, for here Poe has delineated the classic Don Quixote/Sancho Panza partnership. Dupin is the detached genius, whose ice-cold racing intellect can solve crimes and unravel mysteries simply by basing his investigations on evidence brought to him by agents or which he garners by reading the newspapers; the role in which Poe seems to cast himself is that of the admiring, rather modest but carefully observing companion of the lofty genius. This is the relationship we find in Quixote/Panza, in Dr. Johnson/ James Boswell, in Samuel Pickwick/Sam Weller, Sherlock Holmes/Dr. Watson and in modern times that between P.D. James's Detective-Inspector Adam Dalgleish and Detective-Sergeant Martin. The theorizing genius in these relationships is often a poet, and the companion either a countryman or man of lowly occupation who has seen much of the world. Don Quixote has his head turned by reading romances; Sancho Panza is an earthy realist. Dr. Johnson was a eccentric intellectual who did strange thins with orange peel, but was an outstanding scholar and poet; Boswell was a man of the senses and a worldly realist. Samuel Pickwick has all the unworldly perceptions of an innocent child; Sam Weller is worldly-wise and hard-boiled. Sherlock Holmes solves crimes which baffled Scotland Yard, plays the violin and takes drugs; Dr. Watson is an amiable old buffer who has seen much of the world. Adam Dalgleish is an intellectual and a published poet, but his Sergeant is 'a countryman by birth and inclination and was often heard to complain of the proclivity of murderers to commit their crimes in overcrowded cities and unsalubrious tenements'. [39] In recent months a similar partnership has fascinated the public in the shape of Sergeant Lewis and Inspector Morse. This superb drama series made by Central Television, based on fiction by former Oxford classics don Colin Dexter, has earned considerable ratings (the repeats during the spring of 1991 gained up to sixteen million viewers which brings the series into the same class as *Coronation Street*) and puts forward a carefully created version of this same, classic relationship. Lewis is a quiet, bright, hard-working family-man, who loves fish-and-chips and the ordinary things of life. Inspector Morse (code — puzzles, intellectual dexterity, gedditt ??) is an eccentric bachelor who loves Wagner, classical music, real ale, *The Times* crossword, *The Archers*. Very early in our lives we grow accustomed to this partnership, for it is unquestionably established for us in that of Ratty and Mole. As well as being a master of the river and the skills of sailing and a master strategist, Rat is a poet and singer. After being treated to several verses of Rat's *Duck's Ditty*, Mole says: 'I don't know that I think so very much of that little song, Rat.' He says this cautiously: 'He was no poet himself, and didn't care who knew it, and he had a candid nature.' Indeed, this is the very same relationship we find between the idealistic and ruminating Hamlet, and the down-to-earth Horatio. Hamlet asks him in the grave-yard:

"To what base uses we may return, Horatio! Why may not imagination trace the noble dust of Alexander till 'a find it stopping a bung-hole? ... Alexander died, Alexander was buried, Alexander returneth to dust; the dust is earth; of earth we make loam; and why of that loam whereto he was converted might they not stop a beer-barrel?"

Horatio's answer is as mundane as Mole's: "Twer to consider too curiously to consider so.' [40] Its comic counterpart is to be found in the equally satisfying relationship between Arthur Daly and Terry McCann in *Minder*. It is the would-be tycoon and con-man with his head in the clouds, Arthur Daly, who talks poetically of being a 'small chip in the computer of life' and is given to philosophical musings on the state of the world; and it is the earthy Terry, ex-boxer and former resident of one of Her Majesty's prisons, who thinks of money, food and 'pulling the chicks'. [41]

These relationships seem to involve two opposing value systems, the intellectual and the worldly, the spiritual and the corporeal, mind and body; and they seem to become obsessive in western literature at approximately the time when Descartes put into circulation his cardinal point about the essential difference between spirit and the matter and rejected scholastic tradition and theological dogma. Few things are as powerful as an idea which occurs at the right time, and western civilization seemed ready to accept Descartes' ideas, which led to the concepts of consciousness and existence and the mind/body dichotomy. Renaissance theology had placed great emphasis on the human mind as the seat of the rational soul which differentiated us from animals - in that brilliant phrase of Robert Henriques: 'a man was an animal with a mind added; the way that you added an auxiliary motor to a sailing boat.' [43] As Claudius says of Ophelia's insanity: '... poor Ophelia/Divided from herself and her fair judgement/Without the which we are but pictures, or mere beasts ...' [44] Significantly our fascination with the contemplation of animals in zoological gardens dates from the same period.

We have bestowed these values on our hands. The right hand is taken to stand for logic, virility, consciousness, rationality and harmony. The Latin *dexter*, which gives us dexterous, meant to the right-handed side, and dexterous, originally meant right-handed. In heraldry the dexter applied to the right side of the shield of the person holding it (the left side of the one viewing it). It carried all the associations of order, stability, **right.** The left hand is taken to stand for the opposite qualities. Its Latin name, *sinister*, carries all the associations of disorder and disruption. It was considered unlucky to enter a room or a house with the left foot first. In ancient Rome wealthy citizens employed a boy to stand at doorways to remind guests to enter right foot foremost. In heraldry the bend-sinister (running across the shield from right to left) was an indication of bastardy. In augury the left side of anything was considered an unlucky sign. In politics the right stands for tradition, the left for radicalism and change. In the French National Assembly 1789 the reactionaries sat on the right, the democrats on the left. In many a social context today those who buck 'the system' and become labelled trouble-makers are said to be 'bolshie'. [45] The right-hand view of the world is the conservative and orderly one, personified in literature in the prosaic philosophy of Sancho Panza, worldly-wise and forever pulling his master back from the excesses of his own romantic imagination; Sancho finds his successors in Boswell, Weller, Watson, Sergeant Martin and Terry McCann. The left-hand view is bodied forth in the eccentric, wayward, ambitious figures who cause such a stir in the world, classically personified in Don Quixote and powerfully echoed in Samuel Johnson, Samuel Pickwick, Sherlock Holmes, Adam Dalgleish and Arthur Daly. These are the poets of politics; we should recall that Shelley called poets 'the unacknowledged legislators of the world'. Eccentric geniuses are frequently found to be left-handed.

The man of the left in these tales is the Chevalier C. Auguste Dupin, who looks at everything from an unusual point of view and refuses to take things on face value. We are several times given evidence of this, and he comments on it himself. In 'The Murders in the Rue Morgue' he compares the orthodox methods of police search with his own:

"The Parisian police, so much extolled for **acumen,** are cunning, but no more. There is no method in their proceedings, beyond the method of the moment ... The results attained by them are not unfrequently surprising, but, for the most part, are brought about by simple diligence and activity. When these qualities are unavailing their schemes fail. Vidocq, for example, was a good guesser, and a persevering man. But, without educated thought, he erred continually by the very intensity of his investigations. He impaired his vision by holding the object too close. He might see, perhaps, one or two points with unusual clearness, but in so doing he, necessarily, lost sight of the matter as a whole. Thus there is such a thing as being too profound. Truth is not always in a well. In fact, as regards the more important knowledge, I do believe that she is invariably superficial. The depths lies in the valleys where we seek her, and not upon the montain-tops where she is found. The modes and sources of this kind of error are well typified in the contemplation of the heavenly bodies. To look at a star by glances - to view it in a side-long way, by turning toward it the exterior portions of the *retina* (more susceptible of feeble impressions of light than the interior,) is to behold the star distinctly - is to have the best appreciation of its lustre - a lustre which grows dim in just proportion as we turn our vision fully upon it. A greater number of rays actually fall upon the eye in the latter case, but, in the former, there is the more refined capacity for comprehension. By undue profundity we perplex and enfeeble thought... "[46]

Dupin is able to solve the vexing case of the stolen letter by his ability clearly to see the obvious, not to seek the truth in the infinitesimal. This is a technique acquired only after serving a long apprenticeship, not revealed by a sudden accidental glance. He explains this to the admiring narrator:

"There is a game of puzzles ... which is played upon a map. One party requires another party to find a given word - the name of town, river, state or empire - any word, in short, upon the motley and perplexed surface of the chart. A novice in the game generally seeks to embarrass his opponents by giving them the most minutely lettered names; but the adept selects such words as stretch, in large characters, from one end of the chart to the other. These, like the over-largely lettered signs and placards of the street, escape observation by dint of being excessively obvious. "[47]

Dupin's penetration of the mystery of the case of Marie Roget similarly is the result of his trained ability to concentrate his attention on the wholeness and completeness of the situation:

"In that which I now propose, we will discard the interior points of this tragedy, and concentrate our attention upon its outskirts. Not the least usual error in investigations such as this is the limiting of enquiry to the immediate, with total disregard of the collateral or circumstantial events. It is the malpractice of the courts to confine evidence and discussion to the bounds of apparent relevancy. Yet experience has shown, and a true philosophy will always show, that a vast, perhaps the larger, portion sof truth arises from the seemingly irrelevant ... "[48]

This independence of Dupin's, this willingness to do things in a new way and thus to achieve practical results, is very American. He may be seen in some ways as a representative figure not so much of the French *ancien régime* as of a society the very founding of which was an attempt on a national scale to create something new, by applying human reason to the task of constructing a Great Society, applying theory to practice. Dupin does, in fact, frequently declare his independence from the traditional way of doing things.

The Dupin/Narrator stories exemplify the union of the left-hand/right-hand aspects of the human personality, which is a leading theme of Poe's *Eureka: A Prose Poem* (1848). Here Poe argues that the universe was a work of art, and there is no such thing as mathematical demonstration, that intuition alone is valid: 'All Things and All Thoughts of Things, with their ineffable Multiplicity of Relation, sprang at once into being from the primordial and irrelative One' - this is the opening thesis of *Eureka*. Poe dismissed all those who would place reason above intuition - such as Aristotle (Aries Tottle) among other, who are held in discredit because their sluggish logic and their rejection of 'the Soul which loves nothing so well as to soar in ... regions of illimitable intuition'.

Eureka proposes that a pre-existing Godhead, created a 'primordial Particle' of absolute Unity combined with capacity to divide infinitely, irradiating spherically vast numbers of infinitely minute atoms. These atoms tend to unite, and this gives us the principle of gravity. They also have the power to repel, which is the quality scientists have termed heat, magnetism, electricity. In Poe's theory gravitation and electricity, attraction and repulsion, are the two principles of the created universe, the material and the spiritual. Attraction is the body, repulsion is the soul. [49] The duality of personality is an obsessive theme in Poe's work. It is the basis of that deeply disturbing story 'William Wilson' (1839). In 'The Fall of the House of Usher' a logical and reasonable narrator collides with the bizarre world of the Usher household and is repelled by it - body and soul, consciousness and the unconscious, reality and dream come into direct conflict. In the right-hand/left-hand, duality we get the partnership of attraction (right) and repulsion (left) - the body (earthy, realistic, mundane) and the soul (ineffable, flighty, other-worldly). It is classically embodied in the Narrator/Dupin. The narrator is the ordinary guy, Dupin the wayward genius. Significantly Dupin can only function at night, the time when the soul is freed from the prison of the body, when the censoring powers of reason relax and the sub-conscious is given free rein. But was Dupin left-handed?

NOTES

1. The lines Poe quotes at the opening of 'The Murders in the Rue Morgue' are from Chapter V of *Hydiotaphia, Urn-Burial* (1658) by Sir Thomas Browne (1605-82). Browne attended the University of Oxford and various continental medical schools at Montpellier, Padua and Leyden, preparatory to his career as a physician in Norfolk. He visited a site in this county where some workmen had discovered several burial-urns containing mortal remains possibly thousands of years old. He was moved to write *Hydriotaphia, Urn-Burial*, a resonant meditation on death and mortality and funeral habits. In the passage Poe quotes Browne asserts that there are some things which may seem deeply and mysteriously unknowable which may yet be revealed by conjecture, but there are some questions forever obscure: 'What time the persons of these ossuaries entered the famous nations of the dead, and slept with princes and counselors, might admit a wide solution. But who were the proprietaries of these bones, or what bodies these ashes made up, were a question above antiquarism: not to be resolved by man ...'

2. Suetonius, *The Twelve Caesars*, translated by Robert Graves (Harmondsworth: Penguin Books, 1957), p. 144.

3. Ibid., p. 143.

4. This is considered a sufficiently worthwhile comment on Edgar Allan Poe to be quoted in Justin Wintle and Richard Kenin (eds.), *The Dictionary of Biographical Quotation* (London: Routledge and Kegan Paul, 1978), p. 602.

5. T.S. Eliot, 'Wilkie Collins and Dickens' in *Selected Essays* (London: Faber and Faber, 1953), p. 464.

6. See Alexander H. Krappe, *The Science of Folklore* (New York: W.W. Norton and Co., 1964), pp. 79, 201 ff; Erich Fromm, *The Forgotten Language* (New York: Grove Press, 1957), pp. 198ff.

7. Ernest Jones, *The Life and Work of Sigmund Freud* (Harmondsworth: Penguin Books, 1961), pp. 39-40, 302-3,367, 373-74 and 526.

8. Sophocles, *King Oedipus*, in *The Theban Plays*, translated by E.F. Watling (Harmondsworth: Penguin Books, 1947), pp. 73ff. See also Homer, *Odyssey*, II, 271-80 and Aeschylus, *Seven Against Thebes*, 742-1084. The Oedipus legend was also the subject of a tragedy by Seneca. See Richmond Y. Hathorn, *Tragedy, Myth and Mystery* (Bloomington: Indiana University Press, 1966), pp. 33ff.

9. Flavius Josephus, the great Jewish historian (A.D. 37-98), records in his *Jewish Antiquities* that Hiram, King of Tyre, and Solomon once had a contest in riddling, in which Solomon won a large fortune, later lost to Abdemon, one of Hiram's subjects. According to Plutarch, Homer died of chagrin because he was unable to answer a particular riddle.

10. *Hamlet*, V, 2, 208-17. Cf *Matthew* X. 29: 'Are not two sparrows sold for a farthing? And one of them shall not fall on the ground without your Father.'

11. George Steiner, *The Death of Tragedy* (London: Faber and Faber, 1961), pp.5-6.

12. *Calendar of State Papers 1579-80*, edited A.J. Butler, Public Record Office (1904), pp. 227ff.

13. Cf. Erich Heller, *The Disinherited Mind* (Harmondsworth: Penguin, 1961), pp. 14-19.

14. Anthony Burgess, *Is America Falling Apart?* in *New York Times Magazine*, 7 November 1971, reprinted in Arthur M. Eastman *et al.* (eds.), *The Norton Reader: An Anthology of Expository Prose*, 3rd edition (New York: W.W. Norton), 1973 p. 427.

15. Cf. Max Weber: '... principally there are no mysterious incalculable forces that come into play ... one can, in principle, master all things by calculation. This means that the world is disenchanted. One need no longer have recourse to magical means in order to master or implore the spirits ... Technical means and calculations perform the service ...', *Science as a Vocation* (1919), in *From Max Weber*, edited by H.H. Gerth and C. Wright Mills (London: Routledge and Kegan Paul, 1970), p. 139; see also Julien Freund, *The Sociology of Max Weber* (Harmondsworth: Penguin, 1972), pp. 24ff.

16. Lewis Mumford, *Literary Review*, 5 April 1924, p. 642.

17. Walter Ong, *Orality and Literacy: The Technologizing of the Word* (London: Methuen, 1982), p. 147, cf. ibid., 142ff.

18. See Marshall McLuhan, *The Gutenberg Galaxy* (University of Toronto Press, 1968), pp. 18ff. and 24-8.

19. Walter Ong, op. cit., p. 144.

20. Berkley Peabody, *The Winged Word: A Study in the Technique of Ancient Greek Oral Composition as Seen Principally Through Hesiod's Works and Days* (State University of New York Press, 1975), pp. 172-79.

21. Latin *rhapsodia*, from the Greek *rhapsoidia*.

22. See Andrew Sinclair, *John Ford* (London: George Allen and Unwin, 1979), pp. 129-33 and Douglas Pye, 'Genre and the Movies: The Western' in Barry K. Grant (ed.), *Film Genre: Theory and Criticism* (New Jersey: Scarecrow Press, 1977), pp. 206ff., and Peter Wollen, *Signs and Meaning in the Cinema* (London: Secker and Warburg, 1972), pp. 94ff.

23. Walter Ong, op. cit., pp. 148-49.

24. See Killis Campbell, *The Mind of Poe and Other Studies* (New York: Russell and Russell, 1962) pp. 165-66. Poe got the basic idea of 'The Murders in the Rue Morgue' from the account of the murder of the Parisian prostitute, Rose Deacourt (see *Washington Post*, 3 October 1912); the role of the orang-outan, probably came from Poe's reading in the *Shrewsbury Chronicle* of July 1834 the account of the apprehension of an orang-outan, trained by its owner to climb buildings and to rob apartments - see *Notes and Queries*, 17 May 1894. 'The Mystery of Marie Roget' was based on the murder of the New York cigar store assistant, Mary Rogers, which Poe read in the newspapers of the day - see Julian Symons, *The Tell-Tale Heart: The Life and Works of Edgar Allan Poe* (London: Faber and Faber, 1978), pp. 224-25; Alan Bold and Robert Giddings, *True Characters: Real People in Fiction* (London: Longman, 1984), p. 231; and John Walsh, *Poe the Detective: The Curious Circumstances Behind 'The Mystery of Marie Roget'* (New Brunswick: Rutgers University Press, 1968), pp. 5-21.

25. On the coin-operated hot-drinks machines at the college where I was once employed was the motto: 'If it's useful, it was invented by an American.'

26. *The Murders in the Rue Morgue*, In *Selected Writings of Edgar Allan Poe*, edited by David Galloway (Harmondsworth: Penguin, 1970), pp. 189-90.

27. See Marie Bonaparte, *The Life and Works of Edgar Allan Poe: A Psycho-Analytical Interpretattion* (London: Imago, 1949), pp. 427-57.

28. 'The Murders in the Rue Morgue', op. cit., p. 189.

29. Ibid., 189-90.

30. 'The Purloined Letter', *Selected Writings of Edgar Allan Poe*, op. cit., p. 345.

31. Wordsworth, *Preface to the Lyrical Ballads* 1800; cf. Robert Giddings and Elizabeth Holland, *J.R.R. Tolkien: The Shores of Middle-earth* (Junction Books, 1981), pp. 254-55.

32. 'The Purloined Letter', op. cit., p. 342.

33. Ibid.

34. 'The odds are that all ideas held by the public at large, every received convention, are stupid, for the very reason that they suit the masses.' Nicolas Sebastian de Chamfort (1741-94), French *literateur*, renowned wit and aphorist, committed suicide during the Jacobin terror.

35. 'The Purloined Letter', op. cit., pp. 342-43.

36. Ibid., p. 343.

37. 'The Murders in the Rue Morgue', op. cit., pp. 192-3.

38. Ibid., p. 194.

39. P.D. James, *Cover Her Face* (London: Faber and Faber, 1962), p. 48.

40. Kenneth Grahame, *The Wind in the Willows* (1908; London: Methuen, 1977), pp. 27-8.

41. *Hamlet*, V, 1, 197-206. This is the earliest recorded version I have been able to trace of that familiar plaint of those who nominate themselves the voice of the 'common-sense' view of the world, checking all tendency to question and examine the world's multifarious experiences with their restraining caution: 'But you are reading too much into it!' The relationship between Hamlet and Horatio is the collision between poetry and prose. Cf. Antonio Gramsci, *Selections From the Prison Notebooks* (London: Lawrence and Wishart, 1971), pp. 326ff.

42. *Minder*, a Thames Television drama series, had become a national institution by the early 1980s and gave several new phrases to the language, including 'her indoors' (a term of semi-endearment used by Arthur Daly to refer to Mrs. Daly). In May 1981 *Minder* was given the Ivor Novello Award for Best T.V. Theme Music. Arthur is generally acknowledged one of George Cole's best creations, and the basis of the situation is invariably Arthur's setting up some shady deal involving stolen property or some racket, and then managing to disappear when the going gets tough, leaving his minder, Terry McCann, to fend for himself. The Arthur/Terry relationship is mirrored in the duo from the law who are set to bring them to justice, the righteous and clear-thinking Chisholm, and the bluff, jocular and easy-going Jones.

43. Robert Henriques, *No Arms, No Armour* (1939: London: Collins, 1951), p. 326.

44. *Hamlet*, IV, 5, 81-3.

45. Carl Gustav Jung, *The Psychology of the Transference*, in *The Practice of Psychotherapy*, translated by R.F.C. Hull, in *Collected Works of Carl Gustav Jung*, edited by Read, Fordham and Adler (London: Routledge and Kegan Paul, 1954), Vol. 16.

46. 'The Murders in the Rue Morgue', op. cit., pp. 204-5.

47. 'The Purloined Letter', op. cit., p. 345.

48. 'The Mystery of Marie Roget' in Edgar Allan Poe: *Tales of Mystery and Imagination* (New Jersey: Castle, Secaucus, 1983), p. 244.

49. I am greatly indebted to Julian Symons's elucidation of the complexities of *Eureka* - see *The Tell-Tale Heart*, op. cit., pp. 200

V

Charles Dickens:
Print, Public and the
Shape of Fiction

Boz took a few years to find the vocation he was so obviously born for. He always wanted to be an actor, tried work as a lawyer's clerk, like Samuel Johnson he served his time as a parliamentary reporter and then hit the big time writing serial fiction to satisfy the huge appetite revealed by the beginnings of mass literacy, itself the accidental by-product of Christian evangelism. His fiction had to accommodate itself within serial parts which carried advertisements. It was the advertisements for consumer goods which actually generated the income which paid the author.

1. Print and Public.

Charles Dickens was born in 1812 and he died in 1870. His life spanned a period of massive developments in printing technology and in the means of transport - factors which, combined with government legislation which lowered paper costs and reduced the tax paid on advertising revenue, were to create the popular press and mass produced journalism - as well as a period which saw the foundation of popular education and the creation of the mass reading public. It was no accident that as a youth he was an avid reader of popular crime magazines [1] as crime was one of the major ingredients of the new mass publications and has remained a staple of the popular press ever since the early Victorian period (the *News of the World* was founded in 1842). Also, Dickens was a devout reader of the early English periodic literature - of Addison, of Steele and Goldsmith in particular. [2] These experiences early introduced him to violence and melodrama as subjects for writing, and to the idea of literature as a popular, periodically published artifact. Popular journalism of the sensational sort - with its obsession with "human interest", with crime, with the unexpected, with sudden reversals of fortune, with wealth and snobbish fantasies and with sensationalism - and the mechanics of periodic publication are, in fact, among the major considerations which shape, texture and condition his fiction. [3] The intrusion of violence and crime into the very texture of domestic life is given to us in *Dombey and Son* in that section which describes how the *Dombey* mansion goes into its own idiosyncratic mourning after the funeral: "Mr. Dombey ordered the furniture to be covered up ... Accordingly, mysterious shapes were made of tables and chairs ... covered over with great winding sheets. Bell-handles, window-blinds, and looking glasses, being papered up in journals ... obtruding fragmentary accounts of deaths and dreadful murders ..."

Writing in the *Preface to the Lyrical Ballads* at the opening of the nineteenth century, Wordsworth spoke of the fact that the shoving together of people in large numbers in cities and the fact that they were expected to do such boring and unfulfilling work, made people want to read about exciting things, about out of the way places, of horrors and excesses - and he comments on the fact that **this was a new human experience.** The human mind, Wordsworth asserted, was capable of being excited "without the application of gross and violent stimulants..." One being, he believed, was elevated above another in proportion as he possesses the capacity to be stimulated without the excitement provided by extremes of passion and sensationalism - and he saw his duty as a poet lay in the direction of enlarging this capacity among readers of poetry. It is very important in this case to pay particular attention to the fact that Wordsworth believed the situation he saw around him was new and recent and that his service, as a poet, was particularly relevant at that time: "For a multitude of causes, unknown to former times, are now acting with a combined force to blunt the discriminating powers of the mind, and, unfitting it for all voluntary exertion, to reduce it almost to a state of torpor. The most effective of these causes are the great national events which are daily taking place, and the increasing accumulation of men in cities, where the uniformity of their occupations produces a craving for extraordinary incident, which the rapid communication of intelligence hourly gratifies. To this tendency of life and manners the literature and theatrical exhibitions of the country have conformed themselves..." [4] People lived dull lives and did dull work, they craved excitement, and newspapers which contained reports of war, revolution and murder provided it. Wordsworth's case has, indeed, become a familiar one: "Have you noticed that life, real honest-to-goodness life, with murders and catastrophes and fabulous inheritances, happens almost exclusively in newspapers?" asks a character in Jean Anouilh's *The Rehearsal*. When Dr. Johnson wrote in his *Life of Gray* that he rejoiced to agree "with the common reader" in his opinion of Gray's *Elegy,* he did not mean that he was happy to have the same opinion as the man in the street. He was referring to those sophisticated, educated, cultivated readers of taste and discrimination who read the best poetry of the day. Now a quarter of a century later we find the poet of the *Lyrical Ballads* deploring the public's appetite for newsprint. At the same time Coleridge begins that long series of pronouncements on the deplorable influence of the circulating libraries and other cheap publishing agents which, he believed, only provided idle pastimes and reinforced prejudices, and the modern reader of popular works he characterizes as saying: "I take up a book as a Companion, with whom I can have an easy cheerful chit-chat on what we both know beforehand ... In our leisure hours we have a right to relaxation and amusement."[5] The reading public, that modern phenomenon whose taste Dickens was to satisfy and from whom he made a fortune (and an even bigger fortune for his publishers) is here deplored.

The creation of this new, mass reading public was the result of the reforming zeal of various religious bodies and evangelical reformers. William Cobbett, it is often claimed, was the first man deliberately to try to reach the new reading public, and his weekly *Political Register* dates from 1802, but the complex of causes which achieved this popular reading public go well back in to the preceding century. Religious reformers and philanthropists wanted the public to be able to read the scriptures for themselves and it is one of the strangest quirks in the history of communications that it was the religious philanthropists who taught the public to read, and that the public then went out and bought the *Daily Mail.* Lord Northcliffe's fortune was made possible by the Sunday School movement. Adam Smith, Thomas Robert Malthus, Robert Owen, Jeremy Bentham and James Mill all saw popular education as an important element in the reform of state and society. The Sunday School reformers saw reading as the path to perfection in life everlasting.

The founders were people such as Robert Nelson (1655-1715) and Hannah Moore (died 1833). Hannah Moore was moved by pity at the terrible poverty she saw round her at Cheddar that she started Sunday Schools for the poor in the 1780s. When she died she left £30,000 to found further schools. Dr. Andrew Bell founded the National Society for the

Education of the Poor in the Principles of the Established Church in 1811. Hannah Ball had founded a Sunday School at High Wycombe in 1769 and in 1780 the Nailsworth Dissenters Sunday School was founded in Gloucestershire. Robert Raikes (1735-1811) was a printer at Gloucester and opened his first Sunday School there in 1780. He spread the knowledge of a plan for cheap schools for the poor. These schemes got the support of John Wesley who campaigned to educate the poor. Some Dissenters complained that this was a campaign to break the Sabbath, but the idea spread.

In 1803 the Interdenominational Sunday School Union was founded. Thus were established the main links between the charity schools and the (rather tardy) intervention of the state in matters educational in 1870 (The Forster Act). It is depressing to record that the Lords Spiritual opposed the miniscule government grant proposed towards education in 1830 as the Anglican church regarded the education of the poor as their affair (and reserved the right to do very little about it). In 1833 the Whig government under Lord Grey awarded the first government grant "for the purposes of education". The sum involved was £20,000. The approximate importance of education in the national budget may, perhaps, be gauged from the fact that in the same year parliament granted £50,000 for the improvement of the Royal stables. In 1839 the education grant was increased to £30,000 and a special committee of the Privy Council was formed to supervise the spending of this sum, including the appointment of inspectors to visit schools. By 1858 the government grant was increased to £900,000, but inspectors' reports indicate that only one tenth of the children in the schools visited were proficient in reading, writing and arithmetic. Throughout this period which leads up to the direct involvement of the state in the passing of the Forster Act, the religious and charity schools flourished. By the seventeen fifties it is estimated that they had 30,000 children in their care. Methodism was a very important factor in this development, with meetings, group instruction and the production of cheap literature. By 1830 the schools had between 800,000 and 1,500,000 children. This was clearly a revolution in literacy. [6]

The beginnings of the primary school educated public whose taste in fiction Dickens was so professionally to realize are to be found in the schools set up by Andrew Bell, an Anglican clergyman, in 1798 and by Joseph Lancaster, a Quaker in 1801. Unfortunately the religious division between the Church of England and the various Non-conformist organisations was to persist and was to characterize the development of our popular education throughout the nineteenth century, but both Bell and Lancaster used the older children as monitors to teach the younger ones. Bell himself said, "Give me twentyfour pupils today, and I will give you twentyfour teachers tomorrow". This economic view of educational strategy is a vital element in their success. The monitorial system had the clear merit of economising in teachers and in money, as one teacher could manage several hundred children at a cost of seven shillings a year per child. The followers of Joseph Lancaster founded the British and Foreign Society in 1808 to spread education by the use of his methods and in 1810 Lancaster himself published *Report of Joseph Lancaster's Progress from 1798*. Financial problems drove him from Britain in 1818 and he went to Canada and founded a school in Montreal. Considerable interest was sustained in his work in Britain and was fanned by the publication in 1833 of his last pamphlet *Epitome of Some of Chief Events and Transactions in the Life of Joseph Lancaster, Containing an Account of the Rise and Progress of the Lancastrian System of Education*. His rivals in the Anglican camp were mobilised by the bishops who backed Andrew Bell and organised the National Society for the Education of the Poor in the Principles of the Established Church. It was much the richer of the two rival outfits and in its first twenty years the Society founded three thousand schools.

There is little doubt that the doctrinal animosity between the two groups, the Anglicans and the Non-conformists, was a considerable handicap in the growth and development of popular education as the partisans of each group would prefer to see children not educated at all rather than fall into the clutches of their rivals, and every step which was proposed by the state for making any increase in the provision of education for the poor was resisted by one faction or the other, nevertheless, the *Parliamentary Select Committee Report on Education in England and Wales* in 1835 estimated that one million and seventy thousand children were being schooled.

Other no less important developments were the Ragged Schools and the beginnings of adult education. The Voluntary Schools for the Education of Destitute Children - the Ragged Schools - were founded by John Pounds, a Plymouth shoemaker, about 1818 and the 7th. Earl of Shaftesbury became a noted benefactor. Adult education was started in

Merionethshire, Bala in 1811, and evening schools for adult learners have been a feature of our education system ever since, to the extent that we may too easily take them for granted. To contemporaries they seemed a miracle, and Thomas Cooper, the apprentice shoemaker who was to open his own school in 1827 and became a Chartist and successful radical journalist, is only one of the few who have described the revelation experienced in learning to read (his autobiography, *The Life of Thomas Cooper*, was published in 1872). By the mid-eighteen-fifties an estimated three thousand five hundred adult poor were learning to read. The movement was given impetus by Societies of Odd-Fellows, Mutual Aid Societies (interestingly commented on by William Lovett, the founder of the London Working Men's Society and later Chartist leader, and George Henry Lewes when they came to London - Lovett's autobiography, *The Life and Struggles of William Lovett in Search of Bread, Knowledge and Freedom*, is full of fascinating information about the state of the people and of popular education in the early nineteenth century) and by the Mechanics Institutes, from 1823, as well as by the Athanaeums, the Polytechnics, the Peoples Instruction Societies, the Society for the Diffusion of Useful Knowledge, which published *The Penny Magazine*. Much of this was generated and geared up by the Utilitarian movement, but one really impressive thing is the genuine enthusiasm it created, learning is described as an exciting experience, a new experience, even when the working day was fourteen hours or more, people made the time to learn. Christopher North wrote in *Blackwood's Magazine* in 1832 "Nowadays reading is placed on the list of necessaries before eating". William Lovett reported that on first going to a literary study group his "mind seemed to be awakened to a new mental existence: new feelings, hopes and aspirations sprang up within me ..." [8] and Christopher Thompson wrote in his *Autobiography* (1847) "A new era was opening up to us; the prejudiced mists, amongst which we had been groping for ages, were gathering, and as the blessed morning broke, the rusty bolts of ignorance fell down ..." By the eighteen-thirties then, a vast new reading public existed, and what were they to read?

One major source of reading material was to be found in libraries. Before William Ewart (1798-1869) carried the Bill in the Commons which established free public libraries in 1850, there were libraries in working men's clubs and groups and in Trade Unions, in Mechanics Institutes, in factories, in army barracks and police stations, in linen drapers, in

Ragged Schools and Sunday Schools. Subscription libraries for the poor charged a penny or so per volume and the Religious Tract Society had many libraries. In 1778 Fanny Burney wrote: "They are open to every butcher and baker, cobbler, tinker ... throughout the three kingdoms". Churches had libraries too - St. Martin's in the Fields actually ceased to stock fiction after it was found that certain parishioners preferred reading Sir Walter Scott instead of going to Sunday School. The variety of stock held was considerable - trashy romances, Gothic horror, silver fork novels, historical fiction and the expected "improving" literature. A new great source of supply was the appearance in the mid-eighteen-thirties of penny-issue-fiction.

Public houses and coffee houses were additional places which provided reading matter - newspapers and journals - and somewhere to read it. The reduction of duty paid on coffee brought the price of a cup of coffee down from a shilling to three pence or less and coffee houses proliferated as it was easier for working people to eat and drink there than it was for them to travel to and fro: they were allowed to bring their own food in and sit and eat and read journals and periodic publications on the premises which were made as attractive as possible. By 1840 London had one thousand eight hundred coffee houses. They were often used as centres for political organisations among working people, and the early Chartist movement owed a great deal to reduction of import duty on coffee. Angus Reach, in an article called *The Coffee Houses of London*, published in 1845, wrote that the coffee houses were schools of instruction "where instruction is meted out as well as coffee sold ... You go in through a facade of playbills to find yourself in an air of stillness and repose, yet perhaps a hundred people are seated in different boxes, conning over books and newspapers, and sipping their coffee at the same time. You can see at a glance that the majority of the guests are working men ..." [9] This new public was there, waiting for the genius of Charles Dickens to satisfy. In the northern parts of Britain beer was drunk in public houses of repose instead of coffee where they had penny reading rooms, Heywoods in Manchester, for example, opened at six in the morning and closed at ten at night. This was the ideal public for the new periodic serial publication market. [10]

Serial publication opened up a whole new range of possibilities for the small printer (as well as massive opportunities for the well capitalized major publishing operator). Eight pages could be printed on one sheet on a hand press and even quite lengthy volumes could be printed with almost no capital as the income of one issue paid for the next, unsold weekly parts could be stitched and sold as monthly parts and then bound and sold as a normal volume - in effect, all pockets were appealed to. In order to keep costs down, initially there was a particular interest in publishing works which carried no copyright, or works were pirated - Dickens himself was to become one of the most frequent victims of this practice - *Pixwick Papers*, as well as *The Post-humorous Notes of the Pickwickian Club*, edited by 'Bos', *The Memoirs of Nicholas Nicklebery, Dombey and Daughter* etc. [11]

Illustration is important here, as woodcuts on the cover of an issue in monthly or weekly parts made it more attractive to the buyer, in much the same way as the commercial artist's skill is lavished on LP covers today. How many of us have felt that the contents of a modern paperback failed to live up to the promise of its covers? John Harrison, for example, published tons of popular fiction *The Novelist's Magazine* between seventeen eighty and seventeen eighty eight, and each part had a woodcut on the cover. This eighteenth century model was superseded by the nineteenth century periodic fiction publishing industry which had the added advantage of improved technology. Paper is one example. During the Napoleonic Wars the publishing and printing trade had been crippled by the shortage of paper - it earned a very high price. Supplies were uncertain. Books were very costly. Paper cost as much as thirty four shillings a ream, and to this must be added three pence a pound tax and a very high wastage because of imperfect sheets. In 1801 John Gamble patented his paper making machine. This development was held up for a time by trade rivals but it had clearly begun to make its impact by the eighteen twenties, when factory made paper begins to appear on the market and the cost of production was cut by half. Also, the paper made by these methods was of much better quality, and larger in size and this made possible the rotary steam press. Charles, third Earl Stanhope had made a completely iron printing press by eighteen hundred. The next stage was the application of steam power to the printing process made by Friedrich Koenig in 1811-1814 and the superseding of the screw press by the cylinder press by William Nicholson which enabled *The Times* to print four thousand impressions an hour. Another important element is the reduction of government duty on publications. In the early nineteenth century the annual sale of newspapers was twenty four million with about five hundred and fifty published books, in ordinary editions of about one thousand copies. The government had attempted to control and restrict what was published at the turn of the eighteenth and nineteenth century. Direct bribery of journalists was supplemented by the subsidy of newspapers and journals which printed what the establishment wanted. [12] Direct government control of publishing was replaced by various forms of market taxation - Stamp Duty on every newspaper page, and Advertising Duty. These were imposed, not to raise revenue, but to suppress publication. Stamp Duty had been a half penny in the early eighteenth century, but by eighteen fifteen it had risen to fourpence. After the Reform Bill of eighteen thirty two the tax on advertisements was reduced and finally abolished in eighteen fifty three, Stamp Duty was abolished in eighteen fifty five. The role played by the massive development of transport systems in encouraging the expansion of publishing should not be in any way underestimated: from canals, through road transport through to the triumph of steam, this meant not only that publications could be marketed in areas some way from the place of their publication, but that a whole new market was created - the railway bookstall. The figures are impressive: sales of newspapers rose by 33% between eighteen sixteen and eighteen thirty six, and by 70% between eighteen thirty six and eighteen fifty six. [13] The same period saw the publication in period parts of Limbird's *British Novelists* between eighteen twenty three and eighteen forty six, and the *Standard Works of Fiction of All Countries* between eighteen thirty one and eighteen thirty two, *Pattie's Pocket Library, The Novelist, The Novel Newspaper*, all date from this period. One great personal success story here is George Routledge (1812-1888) who started in Soho Square in eighteen forty three and had branches in New York; by eighteen fifty four his *Routledge's Railway Library* had over one thousand and six titles on offer, at one shilling each. He was born in the same year as Dickens. What a coincidence! As John William Palmer (1792-1870), printer to Cambridge University, who sold his London business to Longmans commented: "At the present time books are plentiful, and books are cheap. Formerly books were written for the privileged few; now they are printed for the million. Books of every description, and at almost any price ... All tastes are catered for; all opinions find their peculiar expository organ ... Everything for a penny.

Penny Pulpit - Penny Magazine - Penny Shakespeare - Penny Novelist - Penny Medical Adviser - Penny Educator - Penny Cyclopaedia ..."[14]

2. Serial Parts and Advertising Revenue.

Dickens seems well aware of the need in the world he lived in to advertise what one had to offer. In his fiction there are superb examples of the copywriter's art. There is some interesting dialogue in the scene in Nicholas Nickleby where Squeers meets a prospective client for his dreadful school. Mr. Snawley asks if it is the same Mr. Squeers who advertises in *The Times*? *"Morning Chronicle, Morning Post, Herald* and *Advertiser* - "answers Squeers. Dickens reproduces the advertisement which Snawley would have seen: EDUCATION: At Mr. Wackford Squeers Academy, Dotheboys Hall, at the delightful village of Dotheboys, near Greta Bridge in Yorkshire. Youth are boarded, clothed, booked, furnished with pocket-money, provided with all necessaries, instructed in all languages, living and dead, mathematics, orthography, geometry, astronomy, trigonometry, the use of the globes, algebra, single stick (if required), writing, arithmetic, fortification, and every other branch of classical literature. Terms, twenty guineas per annum. No extras, no vacations, and diet unparalleled ...[1]

Another character we meet in Dickens' early fiction who knows the value of commercial advertising is Mrs. Jarley, the wax-works exhibiter in *The Old Curiosity Shop*. She unrolls a vast canvas on the floor of her caravan for Nell to read, it was about a yard in width and it reached from one end of the caravan to the other. Nell walks down it and reads, in enormous black letters, the inscription: "JARLEY'S WAX-WORK". Another scroll is then unrolled which reads: "One hundred figures the full size of life". And another: "The only stupendous collection of real wax-work in the world". There are smaller scrolls which read: "Now exhibiting within", and "The genuine and only Jarley", "Jarley's unrivalled collection", "Jarley is the delight of the Nobility and Gentry", "The Royal Family are the patrons of Jarley".

Not only does Mrs. Jarley employ snob appeal, novelty and overstatement to yoke in customers, in the manner of so many of her modern brothers and sisters in the selling trade today, she employs the muse of poetry, and there are several gems "couched in the form of parodies on popular melodies". They are very droll - for example there is one which begins "Believe me if all Jarley's wax-work so rare" and "I saw thy show in youthful prime" and "Over the water to Jarley".

These are imitations of the romantic verses of Tom Moore and the imitators of Byron. Mrs. Jarley knows how to saturate the market as these are in the form of printed handbills. Another fashionable kind of advertisement much favoured by the early Victorians was the dialogue, and Mrs. Jarley, sure enough, has some of these too: "... purporting to be dialogues between the Emperor of China and an oyster, or the Archbishop of Canterbury and a Dissenter on the subject of church-rates, but all having the same moral, namely, that the readers must make haste to Jarley's, and that children and servants were admitted at half-price ..."[2]

Mrs. Jarley cunningly employs the angelic Nell to sell the quality of her show and teaches her the patter: "It's not a common offer, bear in mind," she tells her "in the tone and manner in which she was accustomed to address her audiences" and she goes on to tell the child, "the exhibition takes place in assembly rooms, town halls, large rooms at inns ... There is none of your open-air vagrancy at Jarley's remember ... Every expectation held out in handbills is realised to the utmost, and the whole forms an effect of imposing brilliancy hitherto unrivalled in this kingdom. Remember that the price of admission is only sixpence, and that this is an opportunity which may never occur again ..."[3]

She employs the services of the hack poet, Mr. Slum, who claims that several of the leading propriety brand manufacturers in the country have found his services extremely useful and he refers to "the perfumers ... the blacking-makers ... the hatters ...the old-lottery-office-keepers ..."[4] Mrs. Jarley manages to beat this impoverished bard down from five shillings to three and sixpence for a set of commercial verses. She also exploits Nell's young beauty and charm, and she is paraded about the town in a cart, where she is "decorated with artificial flowers" and she disperses handbills from a basket "to the sound of drum and trumpet." The beauty of the child, coupled with her gentle and timid bearing, produced quite a sensation in the little country place ..."[5] Dickens shows us every quality being pressed into commercial service in the need to sell a product, he is well aware of the advertiser's art and artifice - we have additional evidence in *Martin Chuzzlewit* in Mr. Pecksniff's advertisement for new pupils and in the advertisements put about to further the ends of the Anglo-Bengalee insurance swindle.

All Dickens' novels were initially published as serials, and with the exception of *Hard Times* and *A Tale of Two Cities* and *Great Expectations* they were published as monthly serial parts. The relationship between Dickens, his publishers and his public was therefore vital. In order to help the publisher make ends meet and make a profit to share with the author, which could only be done provided the publishers were able to offer advertisers useful space to push their goods, Dickens had continually to appeal to wide readership. He had continually to strive for popularity, for sales. In the eighteenth century novels usually appeared in five volumes, sometimes as many as seven. By the time of Scott and Jane Austen the usual number of volumes was cut down to three or four. Novel reading was expensive as each volume might cost as much as half a guinea. Those who could not afford to buy books might read them by getting them from a circulating library. *Pickwick Papers* was published in 1836 in monthly parts at one shilling each.

Each 'number' consisted of three or four chapters, of about thirty to forty pages of print, with (usually) two plates, several pages of advertisements, with green covers and an engraving on the front cover. Each 'number' appeared on the first day of the month. The usual plan was for a novel to be serialised in nineteen monthly 'numbers' and the last part appeared as a double number, costing two shillings. This last number contained forty-eight pages of text and four plates, with the title page, frontispiece, preface (if any) and other preliminaries. It is worth noting that in many cases the frontispiece could not be published before the last issue as the design might well have given the story away, and the "cliff-hanger" is an essential part of the success of any serial. (The obvious comparison today would be with television serials.) For example, the frontispiece of *Dombey and Son* would have betrayed the fact that young Paul was to die, and the shock of this episode would have been lost.

*Frontispiece of Dombey and Son - published when the
novel was published in book form in April 1848.*

The wrapper to the original serial parts of *Dombey* could shadow forth
the main narrative and thematic material of the novel without giving too
much of the story away - here we have it, the rise and decline of a great
businessman and his household, the tale of Walter Gay, of Florence and
the group at the wooden midshipman's etc. etc. but nothing too concrete
is, in fact, given away.

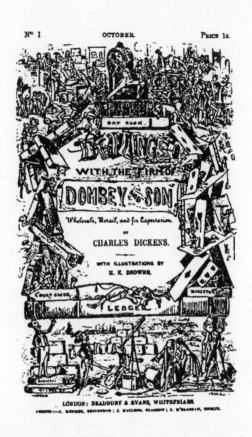

*The original wrapper design of **Dombey and Son**, serialised from 30th. September 1846. An interesting shadowing forth of the substance of the novel, although some incidents (Dombey in Parliament, for example, top right, were not ultimately incorporated in the complete performance).*

The front cover of the serial episode would have an engraving on the wrapper, this was usually retained for the whole of the particular novel's serialisation, inside the cover there would be an illustration which showed some particularly dramatic part of the action that month. The back cover was particularly coveted by advertisers - it was a favourite of the celebrated Mr. Moses, a tailor. Between these two there was a section called "The Advertiser" and between that was the group of chapters containing that month's fiction episode. The *Pickwick Advertiser*, for example, carried commercials for toothache cure and shaving soap:

TOOTH-ACHE.

MR. LOCK continues to CURE the TOOTH-ACHE by fumigation or steam from foreign herbs, which has the effect of destroying the nerve without causing any pain to the patient. The cure is effected in three seconds, the tooth remains firm in the socket, and will not decay any further. The patient will, after this operation, be able to draw into the mouth the external air, strike the teeth together, or hold cold water in the mouth, without any pain. The advertiser has a tooth cured 15 years, therefore he can warrant the cure this length of time.—362, Oxford-street, three doors below the Pantheon. Letters post paid. Reference given if required. Charges moderate, according to the circumstances of the patients. This method is not injurious to the health or teeth.

Recommended by the Faculty.

PEARS'
TRANSPARENT SHAVING SOAP

(The most agreeable and economical extant) produces at once, with either hot or cold water, a profuse creamy lather of exquisite fragrance, without causing redness or irritation. Its convenience particularly recommends it to Tourists, Sportsmen, &c.

Price ONE SHILLING, in a neat case.
Sufficient for twelve months' average consumption.
Sold by Chemists, Hairdressers, and the Inventors,

A. & F. PEARS, 91, Great Russell Street, London, W.C.

Samples sent free by post for Thirteen Stamps.

In fact *Pickwick Papers* may always be cited as an example of the extremely important relationship between author, publisher, public and advertiser. As is well known the sales of *Pickwick* were initially rather slack. This might well have disappointed Dickens' publishers, Chapman and Hall. The publishers had, in fact, pounced on Dickens after the success of his first book, the collected short pieces collectively published as the *Sketches by Boz*, which had made him very well known. [6] The chronology is very revealing - *Sketches by Boz* appeared on February 6th. 1836, and on February 10th. Chapman and Hall made Dickens the offer to write the book which was eventually to become *Pickwick Papers*.[7] He was to provide the letterpress (e.g. the copy) to accompany a series of sporting plates to be drawn by Seymour. The publishers, and this again will demonstrate the significance of market factors in this matter, wanted Dickens to provide something in the nature of the then very fashionable and popular "sporting" stories (cf. *Jorrocks's Jaunts* and its imitators:) in other words, they wanted to cash in on something which they knew would sell well. Dickens was contracted by them to write a monthly instalment of about twelve thousand words, for which he was to be paid £14. He said the offer was "too tempting to resist"[8] although cautioned by his friends that "it was a low, cheap form of publication ..."[9]

The first few issues only sold about five hundred copies a month, but after the appearance of Sam Weller, and in Chapter Twelve (the fifth number) Sam is engaged as Pickwick's servant and the success of *Pickwick* seemed assured. By issue number fourteen Chapman and Hall could offer advertisers the promise of reaching a readership of some twenty thousand. All tried to cash in on the success of *Pickwick*, there were Pickwick canes, toasting forks, gaiters, hats, cigars, chintz, there were Mr. Pickwick's Old Fashioned Candies and Boz cabs as well as Weller corduroys. The advertisers had found Dickens.

The advertisement which appeared in *Pickwick* for Madame Tussaud's waxworks shows us how accurately Dickens' satire of the trade in the person of Mrs. Jarley really is, as it reads like something out of *The Old Curiosity Shop*: "Her Majesty Victoria the first, Her August Mother, the Duchess of Kent, His Late Majesty King William IV, the Dowager Queen Adelaide, the King of Hanover, the Duke of Sussex ... with All the Leading Characters of the Day ... the Whole Taken from Life ... are now added to Madame Tussaud's and Son's Exhibition and Bazaar, Baker Street, Portman Square. Admittance 1s. Second Room 6d - Brilliantly Illuminated ..." Is the advertised "second room" the chamber of horrors?

These advertisements are a fascinating and sometimes amusing aspect of Dickens' serialised parts. The appearance sometimes varies - some are illustrated, some are in bold print, and some in print so small that one can hardly read it. In an age when we are constantly bombarded by advertisers skilled in the latest techniques of psychology and communications, it is curious to look back at the efforts of a more naive era. In some ways the Victorian 'commercial' had a kind of potential which would be unthinkable today. We are used to hearing and seeing that such-and-such a film star, TV personality or other "top" person smarms their hair down with such-and-such, but no doubt we would be shocked to read testimonials given by crowned heads and by ministers of state. An issue of *Nicholas Nickleby* contains a long dialogue supposedly between Queen Victoria and Lord Melbourne (then Prime Minister) on the Penny

Post proposals of Rowland Hill. It is in the form of a short play, and Her Majesty is discovered sitting at a large table, studying *Post Office Reform* by Rowland Hill. Lord Melbourne is at the Queen's right, "watching her Majesty's countenance".

"The Queen: (exclaiming aloud)'Mothers pawning their clothes to pay the postage of a child's letter! Every subject studying how to evade postage, without caring for the law ... such things must not last! (To Lord Melbourne) I trust, my lord, you have commanded the attendance of the Post Master General and Mr. Rowland Hill, as I directed ... Are you, my lord, yourself unable to say anything about this postage plan, which all the country seems to be talking about? ... I wish to learn what your lordship thinks of it ...'

Lord Melbourne (Aside:) ' I really think nothing because I know nothing - may it please your majesty, the Post Master General tells me the plan will not do, and that, to confess the truth, is all I know about the matter ... ' "

The Anti-Corn Law League used advertising space in *Martin Chuzzlewit,* which was serialised between January 1843 and July 1844. The dialogue is used here too in order to explore and to justify a cause. A gentleman and a farmer engage in conversation during a journey on a steamboat. Their unuttterably boring talk is fortunately brought to an end "by the termination of the voyage".

A great deal of advertising space is taken up in these pages by advertisements for clothes. We are offered the "Caspiato, or Folding Bonnet" or "The Gentleman's Invisible Peruke" as well as the "Versatio or Reversible Coat - worthy the Attention of the Nobleman, Merchant or Tradesman" in which item, it is asserted, "the Public must Recognise an Union of Novelty and Usefulness not hitherto Accomplished". There was also, for good measure, the "Patented Royal Prince Albert Elastic Cravat".

For the ladies, *Our Mutual Friend* (1862) offered the "Ondina or
Waved Jupon Crinoline" in which the wearer "may ascend a steep stair,
lean against a table, throw herself into an arm-chair, pass to her stall at
the opera or occupy a fourth seat in a carriage, without inconvenience to
others or provoking the rude remarks of the observers". Thus garbed she
will be free, the makers claimed, "in an important degree," from "all those
peculiarities tending to destroy the modesty of Englishwomen ..." E.
Philpott, of 37 Piccadilly, certainly seemed to have the answer to the
maiden's prayer, in being able to save the embarassment which brought
a blush to the cheek of a young person ... It is indeed strange that this
advertisement should have appeared in the pages of the very novel, *Our
Mutual Friend*, where that celebrated blush is so often invoked.

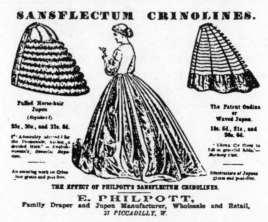

There are innumerable kinds of footwear and even "newly invented **swimming gloves.**" (My emphasis.) Several of the advertisers, taking the hint from Mrs. Jarley's exploitation of the Muse of Mr. Slum, use verse to pursuade purchasers to spend their money. The Laureate of these sartorial sirens is without doubt the hack who wrote for Mr. Moses. His masterpiece, *What is a Gentleman?* appeared with a quiet appropriateness in *Dombey and Son*:

> Manners and learning, you will all confess,
> Are nought without the supplement of dress;
> Good dress, in fact, will cover sore defects,
> While credit on the wearer it reflects.
> The Beau Ideal which the mind supposes,
> Is one who dresses in the clothes of Moses ....

One of the most frequent advertisers of clothes was the versatile company of Edmiston and Son, of 69 The Strand, who offered reversible overcoats, waterproof overcoats and - during the serialisation of *Little Dorrit* (December 1855 to June 1857.) his really tempting complete "Crimean Outfit" - an absolute snip at eighteen guineas!

Nowadays we read occasionally the fairly cautiously worded claims made on behalf of patent medicines of one kind or another. The spread of information and the availability of medication through welfare services in the United Kingdom since 1948 has caused a decline in the popularity of the once all-pervading pill. But to the Victorians it really did seem a cure-all. The most well known pill manufacturers of the time, Morison and Holloway, advertised very often in the pages of Dickens' fiction. James Morison was born in 1770 and claimed to have cured himself of serious diseases solely by means of his own vegetable pills and styled himself "The Hygenist" when he started to vend his own pills in 1825. He called his shop "the British College of Health".

THE

MORISONIAN MONUMENT

ERECTED IN FRONT OF THE

BRITISH COLLEGE OF HEALTH, NEW ROAD,

LONDON,

ON THE 31st OF MARCH, (DAY OF PEACE,)

A. D. 1856.

THIS MEMORIAL,

RAISED BY A PENNY SUBSCRIPTION,

HAS BEEN ERECTED A.D. 1856.

TO

JAMES MORISON,

THE HYGEIST.

MORISON

**Was the first to Protest against Bleeding, and
the Use of Poisons in Medicine.**

Thomas Holloway was born in 1800 in Devonport, the son of an inn-keeper. He came to London at the age of twenty eight where he met an Italian, named Felix Albinolo, from whom he got the idea of an ointment which was to carry the name of Holloway all over the world. The secret of his enormous success, it is acknowledged, was his skilled use of advertising and he soon added the manufacture of pills to his stock in trade for which he also made extravagant claims. He made a vast fortune and endowed the Sanatorium and the College for Women at Egham, the Royal Holloway College (founded 1885) for which he set aside more than a million sterling.

The claims these medicine merchants sometimes made in their advertising copies read like the melodramatic fiction in which they were sandwiched. One Harriet Beacham, subsequently a Morison agent, testifies as follows to the efficacy of Morison's "vegetable universal medicine" - "All my sisters, six in number, had, after equal suffering with myself, been laid in their tomb in the bloom of life." She was saved - of course - by Morison's pills. Then there was the case of the Reverend Mr. Hewlett who cured his large family with Morison's pills, ignoring the alternative suggestions for treatment offered by physicians. "Surely there is a God?" thundered the advertisement, "And as surely there will be a Day of Judgement?" The latter was reserved for Morison's enemies in the orthodox medical profession.

A dosage of six or eight pills was recommended in cases of "smallpox, epilepsy or apoplexy" but there is an account in an issue of *Bleak House* of a patient with unequalled fortitude who began with five pills a day and worked his way up to twenty a day. Finding no sign of relief, he took ten more, and was "suddenly" cured. One lady enjoyed a miraculous recovery after a course of Kaye's Pills and her husband testified to being "Better pleased than if he had received a present of twenty pounds."

Advertisers tried to be topical and the general election of 1852, when free trade and protection were in the air as political issues between the Peelite Conservatives, the Liberals, the Whigs and the Tories under Derby and Disraeli, brought out a rash of punning advertising copy. One pill manufacturer had advice for all party allegiances: "Ministerialists" - who should "minister to their own comfort" - "Protectionists" - "protect themselves from the numerous liabilities of disease" - "Free Traders" - who should "keep open the grand human passage ..."

Sometimes Mr. Holloway's advertisements seemed truly hysterical: "Amputation again saved by Holloway's Ointment". But why, after all, should we feel superior, who cannot tell - it seems - the difference between Butter and Stork Margarine?

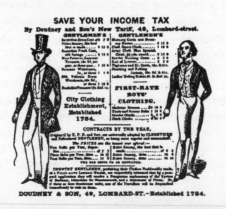

3.The Meat between the Sandwich - the Fiction in the Commercial Break: Dickens' Art - the Publishers - and the Public.

Dickens' art then was very largely conditioned by the fact that he was writing - and knew that he was writing - for a new, "mass" reading public, and that the cheap publication of his novels in serial form was seriously dependent on the sale of advertisement space in the serial parts. He had to satisfy his publishers that what he wrote would appeal to the public. Public taste then, became an appetite which Dickens as a creative artist had constantly and continually to satisfy. I believe that there is evidence to establish the case that his art was fundamentally shaped by the economic and technological context in which it appeared. For some time now critical enquiry into the nature and quality of Dickens' work, the evaluation of his art, has been directed down the avenues of psychological exploration - what was his relationship with his mother and father? How was he affected by the Blacking Factory experience? In what ways did the sudden death of Mary Hogarth, his young sister-in-law, intensify his understanding of the plight of children in early Victorian England? [1] But this is to leave some very significant factors from the equation, and - I believe - this is why we have not yet worked out anything which approximates to a correct answer in assessing Dickens' unusual genius.

Dickens regarded his relationships with publishers as very important. He agreed with Macrone, his first publisher, that he should put together a volume of short pieces to form a book to be published early in 1836. This was *The Sketches by Boz*, for which the young author got £150 for the copyright of the first edition. *Pickwick* was to follow the fair success of *The Sketches*. Another publishing firm, Chapman and Hall, believed they saw potential in the young Dickens, and offered him a contract to write a serial work in twenty installments. He was to get nine guineas a sheet and this would add a clear £14 a month to his income as a reporter. *Pickwick* was advertised for March 31st. 1836 in *Bell's Life in London*, the *Observer, John Bull*, the *Weekly Dispatch*, the *Satirist*, the *News and Sunday Herald* and *The Times*. It was not until Sam Weller made his appearance that sales really peaked - and by August 1836 his publishers had decided he was well worth £25 a month. [2] He was contracted to Macrone to write another novel, and was approached by Bentley to write a further novel. The terms were not very good, as Bentley offered £400 each for the entire copyright of two new novels. Dickens managed to get the offer increased to £500 for each novel, in view "of the rapid sale of

everything I have yet touched." [3] The troubles he had with publishers and contracts and payments over the next two novels, *Oliver Twist* and *Nicholas Nickleby* are complicated and beyond the scope of this study, but they do show us Dickens gradually learning how best to market his talents. He finally broke with Bentley in 1840 and put himself in the hands of Chapman and Hall's firm.

In 1840 appeared *Master Humphrey's Clock*, a new weekly periodical by Dickens which was to contain various new stories and sketches, in the manner of Addison and Steele's periodic literature (which we know Dickens greatly admired.) It was while staying with Walter Savage Landor in his house in St. James's Square, Bath, that Dickens thought of one of the stories - that of the little girl and the old antique dealer - which is known to the world as *The Old Curiosity Shop*. He expanded it into a full length novel because of public pressure - there was considerable public disappointment when it was realized that *Master Humphrey* was not going to be a full length work of fiction, but a weekly miscellany. The first issue came out on April 4th. 1840, but sales soon fell disastrously and after the third issue there was a crisis conference in Chapman and Hall's offices in the Strand, at which Dickens offered to expand the tale of Little Nell into a full length novel. For better or worse, for richer for poorer, he was married to public and publisher alike. The death of Nell was a great success. The great actor Macready felt a chill run through his blood when he saw the print of her lying dead on the couch: " I have never read printed word which gave me such pain, " he wrote in his journal. [4] And Carlyle, Daniel O'Connell, Lord Jeffrey, Landor were all over-come. Lord Jeffrey was found in tears, and when asked if someone had died that he should show such deep grief he replied, "Yes, indeed... You'll be sorry to hear that little Nelly, Boz's Little Nelly, is dead..." [5] Dickens surely knew the effect that this had on his public? He had proved he could do it-and he knew that he would have to go on doing it, although it might make one uneasy actually to claim that those ailing children of Dickens' fiction were slaughtered for the market (the phrase has been used) there is no doubt that there is evidence enough in surviving plans and intentions to show that the effects were aimed at and contrived.

The eighteen forties give us good evidence of Dickens being fully aware of the quality of his genius and constantly striving to contract and market it to the best financial advantage. "I feel my power now more than ever I did. That I know, if I have health, I could sustain my place in the minds of thinking men, though fifty writers started up tomorrow," he wrote to

John Forster on November 2nd. 1843. Copy-right laws and the proper reward of authors was a constant theme of his discourse both private and public during his visit to the United States in 1842.

The sale of his next novel, *Martin Chuzzlewit*, began its serialisation in January 1843. It was a novel its author thought very, very highly of - he called it "in a hundred points immeasurably the best" of his novels - yet it did not sell well. This is vital evidence: Dickens thought the novel had merit, but the public did not buy it. *Pickwick* and *Nickleby* had sold forty and fifty thousand, but the sales of *Chuzzlewit* were hardly over twenty thousand. This was a sad blow, to Dickens and to his publishers, who had expected sales of the kind reached by *The Old Curiosity Shop*, which had peaked at a hundred thousand. [6] There was a council of war at Chapman and Hall's offices. Something had to be done. We know from John Forster's biography of Dickens what was discussed in this meeting. One suggestion was that the public had got used to Dickens in **weekly** installments. Another comment was that since he had been in America the public had lost interest in him. The public had taken to Dickens' book about his visit to America - *American Notes* - and it was decided to exploit their topicality by incorporating some American scenes into *Martin Chuzzlewit*. This intention was announced in the fifth number. We also know from Forster that these bad sales put a great strain on Dickens' relations with his publishers.

He was now approached by Bradbury and Evans who wanted to put a cheap edition on the market of all the books he had written so far and also at the same time to make him editor of a new magazine. Dickens felt that the time was not ripe for such a venture and that he was being exploited. He told Forster that he was afraid of a magazine "just now" and that he was afraid of putting himself before the town as writing tooth and nail for bread ..." (Letter to Forster, 1st. November, 1843.) Instead, he decided to leave England and live cheaply in Italy for some months. He expected great things from his next book, *A Christmas Carol* which, it should be noted, was to be published by Chapman and Hall **on commission**. Six thousand copies of the first edition were sold the day it came out in January 1844, and two thousand copies of the second edition were taken by the trade. The author anticipated that he would make at least £1,000. On February 10th. Chapman's sent him the accounts which revealed that Dickens was to get only £230 on the first edition. He believed that he had been tricked by these publishers: "I have not the least doubt that they have run the expenses up anyhow to bring me back and disgust me with the charges ..." He noted that the various charges for plates, engraving, printing, colouring etc. cut into the profit. (Note - the book was sold to the public at 5s. a copy.) Dickens had now learned some fundamental lessons for an author engaged in earning his living by his pen - that it was essential to shape the tale to the taste established in the audience, and that it was essential to have a sound contractual arrangement with the publishers. He was to continue to shape his fiction to the requirements of his public, for example he deliberately changed the ending of *Great Expectations* to satisfy the public's taste for a "happy ending", and he was always to struggle to get the best he could out of his publishers. I believe that he went on to concentrate more and more on public readings of his work not because he wanted to gain a better "contact" with his audience (as Dr. Leavis asserts in *Dickens the Novelist* 1971) but because it was much easier to earn vast sums of money as a performer of his own fiction than as a writer who continually had to create new stories for serialization and sale to the general public. Also, let it be noted, as a public performer Dickens had cut out the middle-man - the publisher's role disappeared.

Let us consider Dickens' next novel, *Dombey and Son*, in some detail. It is a novel whose construction, planning and serialization we know a fair amount about. First of all, this is the story with which we are today familiar: When the story opens Mr. Dombey is a rich, proud merchant. He is the head of the firm which bears his name. He has just become the proud father of a son who - he hopes - will take on the family business. His wife dies in childbirth, and the man's hopes now centre on his son, Paul. He has a daughter, Florence, who is about ten when the story opens but whom he regards as totally unimportant. He wants the child to be "brought on" as well as possible and to have his abilities fully extended and Paul is sent to Dr. Blimber's school in Brighton. He is a frail and thoughtful child and under the strenuous discipline of home and school he sickens and dies. Dombey's neglect of his daughter is intensified after the death of Paul. Walter Gay, a frank and hearty young man who is employed in Dombey's firm, falls in love with her, but he is sent off to the West Indies, as Dombey disapproves of their relationship. He is shipwrecked on the voyage and presumed lost. Dombey marries again - the proud and haughty Edith Granger, a young widow. He treats her arrogantly and she seems to be driven into the arms of his manager, Mr. Carker, and they run away together to France. They are pursued and Carker is killed in a railway accident. Dombey's business, long undermined by Carker's financial fecklessness, now collapses. Dombey has lost everthing - his fortune, his son, his business, his wife - and his daughter Florence has been driven away from home by his harsh treatment. She has married Walter Gay, who miraculously survives the shipwreck. Dombey lives in desolation but Florence returns and finds the way to his heart. The family is reconciled. Among other important characters in the book are Solomon Gills, a nautical instrument maker (and Walter's uncle) and his friend, the old sea-dog, Captain Cuttle; Susan Nipper, Florence's devoted servant; Toots, the innocent and eccentric admirer of Florence (who marries Susan); Joe Bagstock, the gouty ex-Indian Major who befriends Dombey but deserts him when his fortunes collapse; Mrs. Skewton, the faded old gold-digger who is Edith's mother, and "Cousin Feenix" the faded good-natured aristocrat. That is the shape which *Dombey and Son* now takes, but this was not how the novel was first conceived by Dickens. We have some very significant evidence to support this view.

In July 1846 Dickens wrote a long letter to John Forster, telling him about his plans for *Dombey* in some detail: "I design to show Mr. Dombey with that one idea of the Son taking firmer and firmer possession of him, and swelling and bloating his pride to a prodigious extent. As the boy begins to grow up, I shall show him quite impatient for his getting on, and urging his masters to set him great tasks ... But the natural affection of the boy will turn towards the despised sister; and I propose showing her learning all sorts of things ... to assist him in his lessons ... When the boy is about ten years old (in the fourth number) he will be taken ill, and will die; and when he is ill, and when he is dying, I mean to make him turn always for refuge to the sister still, and keep the stern affection of the father at a distance. So Mr. Dombey ... will find himself at arm's length from him even then ... The death of the boy is death blow, of course, to all the father's schemes and cherished hopes ... From that time I propose, changing his feelings of indifference ... towards his daughter into a positive hatred. For he will always remember how the boy had his arm around her neck when he was dying ... At the same time I shall change her feelings for him for one of a greater desire to love him, and to be loved by him; engendered in her compassion for his loss, and for her love for the dead boy whom, in his way, he loved so well too ..." He goes on to say that Dombey will lose everything, and that he and Florence will be finally reconciled. He ends with some very interesting words about Walter Gay: "About the boy, who appears in the last chapter of the first number, I thing it would be a good thing to disappoint all the expectations that chapter seems to raise of his happy connection with the story and the heroine, and to show him gradually and naturally trailing away, from that love of adventure and boyish lightheartedness into negligence, idleness, dissipation, dishonesty and ruin. To show, in short, that common, every-day, miserable declension of which we know so much in our ordinary life; to exhibit something of the philosophy of it, in great temptations and an easy nature; and to show good turns to bad, by degrees ..."

Another important piece of evidence we have got is the very detailed design for the frontispiece, which we know was very carefully specified by Dickens in written instructions to his artist, Hablot Browne ("Phiz".) This design will shadow forth what was originally in Dickens' mind when he started to write *Dombey*. At the apex of the design sits Mr. Dombey, on a massive throne-like armchair. His dais is a large cash-box and the throne and box are supported on a flowing structure of cash-boxes, ledgers, court guides, directories and playing cards. It is the kind of memory chain we have seen before in Marley in *A Christmas Carol*, of course. These are the emblems of Dombey's world, and the shakiness of that world is shown in the sense of the whole structure's being in constant state of collapse - and there is a superb hidden pun in the cards - "Dealings with the Firm of Dombey and Son" - which also suggests the idea of speculative risk (the business fails because Carker gambles on the stock-market). There seems to be a line of prosperity which flows upward from the left, down through the tumbling cards on the right - on the left we see Dombey triumphant, on the right, humbled. Present also are those recurring emblems of *Dombey*, symbols of time, mortality and immortality, clocks, watches and the sea. It is an interesting piece of evidence which shows how much Dickens could give away, and yet how much he had to keep hidden - there is no evidence here, for example, that Paul is to die, yet we can see that Walter Gay, is a Dick Whittington figure. Also, there are aspects here which do not, in the end, come out in the novel. Dombey is shown in the Houses of Parliament and although we have an MP character in *Dombey* (Skettles) Mr. Dombey does not himself make it to the Commons. The second marriage is shown but not the railway - which has since become significantly associated with this novel. Neither Carker nor Alice (Edith's fated cousin) appears, nor Joe Bagstock nor Mrs. Skewton.

Much had to change as the novel actually began to appear, partly because of market pressures, partly because of moral objections and partly because the fiction seemed to take on and grow as Dickens began to write it. The first episode appeared on 30th. September 1846 and it ran in monthly parts through to the final double number in February 1848. This is a brief summary of how the novel shaped up in its initial serialization:

1. September 1846

This contained the first four chapters and introduced Dombey, Florence and baby Paul and showed the death of the first Mrs. Dombey. We meet Paul's wet-nurse, Polly and the estrangement of Dombey and his daughter is clearly established.

Dickens suggests the gloom of the Dombey mansion and although the exposition is excellent, it is very slow moving and ponderous. Gills and Walter are introduced and placed in a sympathetic light.

The household at the Wooden Midshipman is given to us as a direct and perfect contrast to the Dombey mansion, and Dickens early draws the symbolic contrast between the gloomy, dark and chilly qualities of Dombey's household with the warm loyal and human feeling so characteristic of the Midshipman's place. This is vital in the exposition, and is explored in the second monthly issue.

Sol Gills and Captain Cuttle.

2. October 1846.
This issue contained chapters five to seven and developed the interest of Paul. He is christened and wet-nursed by Polly who loves him in a very warm and human way in spite of the relationship Dombey hoped he had established by "contract".

Polly Toodle,
Paul's Wet-nurse

3. November 1846.
This issue contained chapters eight to ten and continued the focus of attention on Paul, his further progress, growth and character. In this issue we see him sent to Mrs. Pipchin's establishment. Sol Gills gets into financial difficulties.

young Paul and Mrs. Pipchin.

4. December 1846.

Here we have chapters eleven to thirteen, and the emphasis is still on Paul. He is now old enough to be sent to Dr. Blimber's academy.

The illustration is not accurate. The chapter tells us that the Doctor takes only ten boys at a time (it is a "hothouse" of education). As a parallel to this, the last chapter in this issue shows how important Mr. Carker the manager is in Dombey's business concerns, and how the feelings of unease about Walter Gay are gradually developed. He is chosen to go to the West Indies - this will keep him out of the company of Florence Dombey. The exposition is shaping up well, but Dickens is lagging behind in his plans for Paul. The pace of the novel is slower than he had intended. Sales were still good.

Mr. Dombey and
Mr. Carker, the Manager

5. January 1847.

This issue included chapters fourteen to sixteen. Paul continues to be "old fashioned" and is sent home for the holidays. Walter Gay prepares to leave for Barbados. It is in this episode that Paul dies.

This was a stunning success. Dickens brought it off. He had already triumphed with the death of Smike and the death of Little Nell, but the death of Paul Dombey really stunned his readers. Thackeray's *Vanity Fair* was being serialized at the same time, but William Makepeace had to admit defeat - the death of Paul clobbered him. He wrote to his mother a year later that he was "all but at the top of the tree: indeed, there, if the truth were known, and having a great fight up there with Dickens". He bought this issue, and flung it down in *Punch's* office, exclaiming that there was no writing against such powerful writing as this. Lord Jeffrey wrote to Dickens: "What a no. 5 you have given us! I have so cried and sobbed over it last night, and again this morning, and felt my heart purified by those tears ..." (Letter dated January 31st. 1847.) But it was felt that Dickens had now shot his bolt, and public interest fell off - Florence and the Carker-Edith story were considered no substitute for the central interest in the story of young Paul.

In his letter to Forster detailing his plans for *Dombey* (July 1856) he had said that the death of Paul would be "a death blow" and it was nearly so as far as the popularity of the novel was concerned. His problem was to throw the weight and interest of the story onto Florence and public interest in this was understandably a bit slow.

6. February 1847.

In this issue, which contained chapters seventeen to nineteen, the novelist throws all the emphasis onto Florence Dombey. Her fortunes seem to be declining, although she is the heir to the business, Paul is dead, Walter is gone, and her father continues to ignore her. Toots arrives from Blimber's and brings the dog, Diogenes, who was a friend of Paul's.

7. March 1847.

This episode contains chapters twenty to twenty two, and prepares us for Mr. Dombey's second marriage, to Edith Granger, whom he meets through Major Bagstock's old flame, Mrs. Skewton.

8. April 1847.

Here we have chapters twenty three to twenty five. Florence is now firmly established in the centre of the interest, and there is the bad news that Walter Gay has been lost at sea when the "Son and Heir" went down on the way to the West Indies.

9. May 1847.

The purpose of this episode, which brings us to chapter twenty eight, was to "bring on the marriage gradually" and to connect Carker with Edith before the wedding with Mr. Dombey, and to get in the relationship between Edith and Florence.

10. June 1847.

Dombey and Edith are married. He spends a fortune on the house to make it suitable for his new bride. Mrs. Skewton moves in too and the materialistic aspects of life are stressed.

11. July 1847.

In this number Dickens explores the analogy between prostitution and arranged social marriages - Carker has seduced, ruined and abandoned Alice, who is Edith's cousin. Dombey's relationship with Edith is seen as social prostitution. Mrs. Skewton and Goodmother Brown are seen in parallel.

Edith Granger

12. August 1847.

This episode shows how Dombey's relationship with his wife goes into sharp decline. Socially she is a great disappointment to him and he has to fall back on using Carker as a go-between. Dickens contrasts this with the warmth and heartiness of life at Polly Toodle's household.

Mr. Toodle, the centre of his domestic universe.

13. September 1847.

Dickens confessed to Forster that this number was a great strain to write: "It requires to be so carefully done" he wrote to him. The main part of this issue was the chapter "Domestic Relations" which is the showdown between Dombey and Edith. The flight with Carker is already designed by the author, though it was later to be severely qualified after protest from readers. This was the halfway point of the novel's construction, and Dickens looks back as well as forward: Mrs. Skewton is taken in her final illness to Brighton, and Dr. Blimber's academy is visited once more. Dombey drives Edith away by failing to communicate with her - fatally employing Carker in the role of go-between.

14. October 1847.

Mr. Dombey has a riding accident and this immobilises him downstairs. This gives Carker unhampered access to Edith. Dickens is preparing us for what he called the "Thunderbolt".

15. November 1847.

He had laid the ground well for this episode - chapters forty six to forty eight. He had planned originally that the "Thunderbolt" was to fall at the end of this issue, but that would have left readers in the most terrible suspense over the Christmas period. This chapter was, in fact, written first, so he pushed it into middle space and the month's issue then ended with Florence safely under Captain Cuttle's protection.

16. December 1847.

This issue contains the idyll of Walter and Florence. He returns safely and they are together. This is ideal "Christmas" material, and it shows the peculiar problems of the serial writer. Dickens went over the previous chapters now before writing this, to establish Florence's age - she would now be about seventeen. The marriage would have to be brought on, so that Florence's child (a son of course!) would be of age to represent the third generation of the Dombeys in time for the great reconciliation number which was to end the novel.

The return of Walter Gay - a happy shadow on the wall.

17. January 1848.

Another important alteration - Dickens heard from Lord Jeffrey (letter dated 21st. December 1847) who would not believe that Edith would actually commit adultery with Carker. Dickens wrote to Forster asking him what he thought of the idea of making it seem as if she hated both Dombey and Carker and only used Carker to "escape" from Dombey. He decided to write a tremendous scene "of her undeceiving Carker, and giving him to know that she never meant that..." Forster thought this was a good idea, and Dickens recorded in his notes: "Edith **not** his mistress ..." And so it was - and we are given one of the most genuinely melodramatic scenes in all of Dickens, as Edith rounds on Carker at Dijon. It creaks, more than a bit.

Mr. Carker in his hour of triumph.

18. February 1848.

This issue contained chapters fifty five to fifty seven. Carker is now pursued by Dombey and is killed in a railway accident. The illustration of Dombey's pursuit is one of the famous "dark" plates in the book - where the illustrator works his effect by adding light to dark on the engraving.

Sol Gills returns from his travels. He is now a richer man, of course. Florence and Walter Gay are married. Susan Nipper marries Mr. Toots. The threads of the story are gradually coming together, Dickens is preparing the readers for the final, double number, which will round off the whole performance.

19 and 20 - Double Number. March 1848.

This special number contains the last five chapters and was issued with a set of additional portrait engravings of Mr. Dombey, Miss Tox, Mrs. Skewton, Mrs. Pipchin, Old Sol and Captain Cuttle, Joe Bagstock, Miss Nipper, Polly, Paul, Florence, Edith and Alice. It was widely advertised and sold well. The problems in a serial novelist's rounding off a novel which has appeared over a period of some eighteen months are considerable. In *Dombey* Dickens had to show Florence and her father reconciled. He prepares the way carefully. Dombey's illness softens him from within, and the collapse of his business empire influences from without. Dickens' notes read "The birth of Florence's child and her relenting towards her father" and "The scene in his own room". This will introduce the theme of the three generations of Dombey - and Walter Gay continues to operate the old firm.

Mr. Dombey's heart is taken by storm. Captain Cuttle is married off. Mrs. Skewton has died. Alice has repented and died. He had planned a deathbed repentance for Edith, with Florence present, but this was scrapped in the final version. (Few Dickensians would lament its loss, I think.) In the final proof version the author was forced by lack of space to cut seven lines, and consequently the novel was published without the following: "The voices in the waves speak low to him of Florence, day and night, plainest when he, his blooming daughter, and her husband, walk beside them in the evening, or sit at an open window, listening to their roar. They speak to him of Florence and his altered heart; of Florence and their ceaseless murmuring to her of love, eternal and illimitable, extending still, beyond the sea, beyond the sky, to the invisible country far away. Never from the mighty sea may voices rise too late, to come between us and the unseen region on the other shore! Better, far better, that they whispered of that region in our childish ears, and the swift river hurried us away!" This passage was based on his careful notes for this final number which read: "End with the sea - carrying through, what the waves were always saying, and the invisible country far away." Everything is

tied up - even Diogenes, the dog was remembered a week before publication and Dickens wrote to Forster and asked that an additional line be
inserted at proof stage - "and an old dog is generally in their company."
The Skettles and Miss Tox were also only inserted at proof stage.

In summarizing the main effects of this kind of publishing of a major
work of fiction, I would say this - serial publication was made possible by
technological and market factors by the eighteen thirties, and the very
considerable developments in printing and in illustrating made possible
the publishing and wide distribution of very attractive issues. Serial
publication made careful planning of a novel of vital importance, and we
know from all the evidence that Dickens did plan and work from plans -
he did not (contrary to literary mythology) write with the printer's boy at
his elbow. We know that he carried in his mind a very detailed and
elaborated view of the whole novel before he began composition and
during the whole period of a novel's construction. This is a very important
claim, and I would cite some significant evidence. Frederick Chapman,
one of Dickens publishers, said that Dickens had told him when he wanted
to begin a book he would start by "getting hold of a central idea" which he
then "revolved in his mind until he had thought the matter thoroughly
out" and then he would make "a programme of his story with the
characters" and finally "upon this skeleton story he set to work and gave
it literary sinew, blood and life." This was in a published interview with
Chapman in *The Daily Chronicle* for June 25th. 1892. Dickens told
Forster that when he reached this stage **he saw everything** and only
had to write it all down. *Dombey and Son* is a fascinating example of how
this original conception becomes altered as a result of the very processes
of serialization. Advertising revenue is fundamental in serial publication,
therefore the readership has to be pleased, otherwise they won't buy. If
they won't buy, then the advertisers cannot be guaranteed that their
goods will be seen by numerous readers. The public, therefore, has to get
what they expect. Walter Gay, for example, was altered by Dickens to
conform to the Dick Whittington stereotype expected by the audience.
Edith did not become Carker's mistress. Edith did not die (she went to
Italy instead). Then there is the important matter of the shaping of the
actual plot line. A serial must always be issued in parts which (a) explain
the last episode's cliff-hanger (b) carry the narrative forward one whole
and entire stage, and (c) leave off at a point where the readers will want
to know more, so that they go out and buy next week's or next month's
issue. If you look at the number plans and the published numbers of

Dombey and Son you will see how Dickens does, in fact, follow this pattern. Then there is the matter of the space available - and the evidence of Dickens' actually cutting sections so that they fit the space that has been rehearsed. This may be why the section which should have shown Dombey as an MP (foreshadowed in the frontispiece) was scrapped although in embryo it exists in the otherwise quite unnecessary character of Sir Barnet Skettles MP Another important consideration in the serial form used by Dickens is the essentially aural nature of Dickens' art - we know that his works were read aloud in families and in factories and workshops, and they were written so that this was possible. Dickens made a fortune reading them in public himself and they still read aloud very well - the comparison with Scott or Henry James or Joseph Conrad is vital here, they were written for a vastly different market. We should note that Dickens was a reporter and used shorthand, he was the most brilliant parliamentary shorthand reporter of the day, he was used to regarding the English language in terms of **sound**. He was not a "literary" author at all - in fact the modern Oxbridge view (e.g. Cockshut et al.) regard him as an ignorant "maker" uttering his "wood notes wild". There is something very importantly idiosyncratic in the very texture of Dickens' fiction, and it is to do with the way Dickens uses the English language - and this is essentially a quality - I do not say made inevitable by serialization - but very largely fostered by the circumstances of serialization which I have attempted to discuss.

Finally, I would stress the fact that Dickens' celebrated symbolism, poetry, dream, myth, archetype - call it what you will - is also the result of serialization. Dickens, as a creative artist, was faced with the fact that he could express his imaginings to his public in long term serial form: to give each work a symbolic cohesion, a recognisable quality of imagination, he used images and symbols to aid readers' imaginations in a long imaginative flight. Each Dickens novel is like no other - the world of *Dombey*, for example, is quite unlike *Bleak House* or *Great Expectations*. *Dombey and Son* is poetically held together - by myth and archetype (Dick Whittington in Walter Gay and Cinderella in Florence Dombey) which the audience subliminally respond to - and by groups of images and symbols which are totally appropriate to the world of Dickens is portraying in *Dombey and Son* - the sea is one such image: this is appropriate to the world of *Dombey* as Dombey is a merchant whose trade is wholly dominated by the sea - Paul is early associated with the sea (what the waves were saying) and his mother when she dies drifts out "upon the dark and unknown sea that rolls round all the world" - Walter goes to sea on The Son and Heir - Cuttle and Sol Gills are associated with the sea - the sea is used as an emblem of time and immortality which binds the performance together and this is very elaborately featured by Dicken's art. Then there are time pieces, clocks and watches - both the sea and chronometers of various kinds feature in the design of the superb frontispiece, which would indicate that they were an essential part of the fabric of this novel right from the start: there are the doctors' watches, the ticking clock at Dr. Blimber's, the ticking watch of the doctor who looks after Paul, Mr. Dombey's loud ticking watch, the watch Cuttle winds up and gives to Walter when he leaves and so on - these are all symbolic of time, mortality and the mechanization of life. Then there is the contrast between the warmth and golden sunny qualities of Gills' household contrasted to the dark tenebrous home of the Dombeys and so on and so on. Many hundreds of books have been written on Dickens' symbolism but few have noted that it was almost certainly the result of the serialization of Dickens' fiction.

The fact that Dickens is our first "poetic" novelist might well be the result not only of his staggeringly creative imagination but also of the circumstances of the publications of his work. What I am suggesting in fact is that literary form (or forms) is not a matter of being organic at all, but that the form taken by creative literature is very closely related to the mode of literary production. I am also urging that these considerations should be exploited so that they provide useful insight into the evaluation of literature. Take another case - Henry James. The modish litterateurs who are the opinion leaders of the academic teaching profession, those who stand in apostolic succession to the late F. R. Leavis, all agree in praising (? lauding) the "organic" - compressed - subtle - rich - poetic symbolism of the later Henry James. They neglect to consider the mode of production which may be cited to help us really understand these qualities: by the time this fiction was written there had been changes in the material mode of literary production and this meant there was a shift away from the densely populated 'three decker' novel - with its diffuse and complex plot structure, numerous characters and situations - to the more organic single volume novel.[7] Writing in 1674 Nicolas Boileau said in his *L'Art Poetique* that no man who could not limit himself has ever been able to write: the real test is to see how the powerfully creative imagination thrives within the complex of limitations posed by the very means of production - and here Dickens' triumph is unqualified, and we should love him for it. Balzac's novels were serialized in newspapers, *mais ça c'est une toute autre histoire!*

NOTES

1. Print and Public.

1   Angus Wilson: *The World of Charles Dickens* (Harmondsworth, Penguin 1972) p. 62.

2   Sylvere Monod: *Dickens the Novelist* (Norman, Oklahoma, University of Oklahoma Press 1968) pp. 30-31; Edgar Johnson: *Charles Dickens: His Tragedy and Triumph* (Boston, Massachusetts, Little, Brown and Company 1952) pp. 294-5 and Peter Ackroyd: *Dickens* (London, Sinclair Stevenson Ltd., 1990) p. 288.

3   Raymond Williams: *Communications* (Harmondsworth, Penguin 1976) pp. 14-15.

4   Wordsworth: *Preface* to *The Lyrical Ballads* in *English Critical Texts* edited by D. J. Enright (Oxford, Oxford University Press 1964) p. 166.

5   Quoted in *Coleridge: Selected Poetry, Prose and Letters* edited by Stephen Potter (London, The Nonesuch Press 1971) p. 459.

6   For material for this section I am considerably indebted to E. P. Thompson: *The Making of the English Working Class* (Harmondsworth, Penguin 1972); Louis James: *Fiction for the Working Man* (Harmondsworth, Penguin 1976); Dennis Richards and J. W. Hunt: *Modern Britain* (London, Longman 1974) and Raymond Williams: *The Long Revolution* (Harmondsworth 1973).

7   Dennis Richards and J. W. Hunt op.cit. p. 381.

8   *Autobiography of William Lovett* edited by R. H. Tawney 1920.

9   Angus Read: 'The Coffee Houses of London' in *New Parley Library* Volume I (1843) pp. 293 ff.

10   Although R. M. Miles: *Serial Publication in England* dates it as early as 1677. Smollett's *Sir Launcelot Greaves* was serialised in *The British Magazine* in 1760 — see Robert Giddings: *The Tradition of Smollett* (London, Methuen 1966) pp. 14 ff.

11   Victor E. Neuburg: *Popular Literature* (Harmondsworth, Penguin 1976) pp. 171-2.

12   Raymond Williams: *Communications* op.cit. p. 15.

13   Ibid.

14   J. William Palmer: *Meliora* 2nd. series 1853.

2. Serial Parts and Advertising Revenue.

1   Charles Dickens: *Nicholas Nickleby* (London, Macmillan 1930) p. 111. There is an interesting study of the advertisements in the various monthly serial parts of Dickens's novels, Bernard Darwin: *The Dickens Advertiser* 1930.

2   Charles Dickens: *The Old Curiosity Shop* Chapter 27.

3   Ibid.

4   Ibid Chapter 28.

5   Ibid Chapter 29.

6   Philip Collins: *Charles Dickens — The Critical Heritage* (London, Routledge 1971) pp. 27 ff.

7   Preface to the 1847 edition of the *Pickwick Papers.*

8   W. Dexter (editor) *The Letters of Charles Dickens* (London, The Nonesuch Press 1938) volume I p. 165.

9   Preface to the 1847 edition of *The Pickwick Papers.*

3. The Meat between the Sandwich.

1   A major influence in this movement was Edmund Wilson's essay 'Dickens—The Two Scrooges', published in *The Wound and the Bow* 1941. His arguments were followed up by Angus Wilson, Edgar Johnson, A. E. Dyson, Christopher Hibbert, Sylvere Monod and the Leavises. See Robert Giddings 'A Cockney in the Court of Uncle Sam' in *Dickens Studies Newsletter* June 1975, and the review of John Carey's *The Violent Effigy: A Study of Dickens's Imagination* in *Dickens Studies Newsletter* June 1976.

2   Edgar Johnson op.cit. p. 149.

3   Ibid p. 151.

4   Ibid pp. 304 ff.

5   *The Dickensian* Volume XV p. 96.

6   Edgar Johnson op.cit. p. 453. The discussion of the construction of *Dombey and Son* which follows was considerably inspired by John Butt and Kathleen Tillotson's *Dickens at Work* (London, Methuen 1957).

7   Terry Eagleton: *Criticism and Ideology* (London, New Left Books 1976) p. 104.

VI
Mark Twain
and the
King of the Belgians

Twain personified and embodied the American Dream. Born in a log cabin in Missouri he became one of the most famous men in the world, honoured wherever he went. In his life he bodied forth the history of his nation — he moved from the frontierland to life in the modern city; he lived through the great changes from transport by river steam boat to railroad; he served in the Civil war, in whose blood the modern America was born; he went West; he was among the earliest great print journalists and became a best-selling author. Yet, from time to time, when some of his various commercial enterprises went wrong, he returned to the ancient traditional role of story-teller, the public orator, the touring lecturer — all forms of the original art on which all authorship is ultimately based. In one of his immortal scripted one-man shows he presents the representative figure of the modern international capitalist imperialist. The bard is here no longer the spokesman of the race. He has now returned as a one-man global warning.

"There are many humorous things in the world; among them the white man's notion that he is less savage than other savages." (Mark Twain, FOLLOWING THE EQUATOR, 1897)

1.

One evening in Monte Carlo Frank Harris and Lord Randolph Churchill had a really heart-to-heart talk about politics. It was after a good dinner at the Hotel de Paris, and the garrulous Harris found that they were poles apart: 'I pointed out that just as village communities were superseded by nations', he recorded, 'so nations now were in process of being superseded by world empires; already two were being formed, Russia and the United States, which must soon dwarf all nations ...'[1] The anecdote is not dated by Frank Harris, but Lord Randolph Churchill died in 1895. Mark Twain lived and worked during the opening stages of America's rise to global imperialism and was certainly fascinated by it.[2]

The foundations of the United States' early imperialism were laid in the immediate post-Civil War period, in the systematic denial to the Red Indians of the territories they had inhabited and of the very means by which they had survived. As Gareth Stedman Jones has so convincingly argued, there are several significant misconceptions about the historical development of American imperialism which successfully mask its basic continuity. The fact that in its initial stages it was not territorial or colonial, but was a westward movement across its own continent, involving the destruction of the indigenous population and the conquest of aboriginal territory, has made it seem essentially unlike the British colonization of the West Indies, India, the Antipodes, or the French, Belgian, German or Dutch colonial ventures in Africa and the Far East. U.S. imperialism was initially non-territorial. This has allowed the Land of the Free to pose as a champion of national liberation, whereas the opposite was essentially the case. The national stance is buttressed and supported by the most powerful ideological superstructure:

"... the construction of a mythological, non-communist, non-socialist and even non-nationalist road to political independence for the countries of the Third World. To woo aspiring politicians of these new states, the United States has offered the model of the 'American Revolution' of 1776. It was on this basis that Franklin Roosevelt considered that the United States was uniquely equipped to advise India on the road to independence, and it was again on the basis of this claim that Eisenhower felt entitled to ditch his Anglo-French imperialist allies at the time of the Suez crisis in 1956 ... "[43]

The opening up of the West, which occurred after Twain returned from Europe and Palestine (*Innocents Abroad,* 1869) and his marriage and setting up household in Hartford, Connecticut, was the first stage of a rapacious progress which has never felt retiring ebb, but kept due on to the Pacific and beyond. Yet Twain hardly deals with the American Indian in his fiction, except insofar as he features in 'character' roles from time to time.[4] The great land grab and the massacres which featured as a staple diet in the American press while he experimented with humorous inventions, wrote essays, short stories and published *The Gilded Age* (1873), *A Tramp Abroad* (1880) and *Following the Equator* (1897) seemed hardly to interest him. He told the American press in 1900, after his return from another set of travels: ' I am anti-imperialist. I am opposed to having the eagle put its talons on any other land.' His failures in printing and publishing enterprises had brought him to bankruptcy, and he launched into a world-wide lecture tour to get himself in funds. What he saw of European imperialism in the South Pacific, Asia and Africa made his blood run cold. These European nations, he argued, did not deserve the term 'civilized'. Of the colonization of Australia, for example, he said:

"We are obliged to believe that a nation that could look on, unmoved, and see starving or freezing women hanged for stealing twenty-six cents' worth of bacon or rags, and boys snatched from their mothers, and men from their families, and sent to the other side of the world for long terms of years for similar trifling offences, was a nation to whom the term 'civilized' could not in any large way be applied. And we must also believe that a nation that knew, during more than forty years, what was happening to those exiles and was still content with it, was not advancing in any slow way toward a higher grade of civilization." [5]

He wrote ironically of the need to annex the Sandwich Islands in order to bring to them the unspeakable benefits of civilization:

"We must annex these people. We can afflict them with our wise and beneficent government. We can introduce the novelty of thieves, and all the way up from street-car pickpockets to municipal robbers and government defaulters, and show them how amusing it is to arrest them and try them and then turn them loose - some for cash and some for 'political influence'. We can make them ashamed of their simple and primitive justice ... We can give them juries composed entirely of the most simple and charming leatherheads. We can give them railway corporations who will buy their Legislatures like old clothes, and run over their best citizens and complain of the corpses for smearing their unpleasant juices on the track.... We can give them Tweed ... we can furnish them some Jay Goulds who will do away with their old-time notion that stealing is not respectable .... And George Francis Train. [6] We can give them lecturers! I will go myself. We can make that little bunch of sleepy islands the hottest corner on earth, and array it in the moral splendour of our high and holy civilization. Annexation is what the poor islanders need. 'Shall we to men benighted, the lamp of life deny?' " [7]

At the time when Mark Twain's creative energies were blooming in a series of works which obviously still retain the power to dazzle the imagination, the Americans were gradually depriving the Red Indians of their land by deceit, slaughter, military might and starvation. The land, once possessed, was soon so abused that the wildlife which had supported generations of numerous Indian tribes[8] was destroyed without hope of regeneration. This is still to a considerable extent a buried part of the nation's consciousness. As John Upton Terrell writes:

"It is incomprehensible to me how a people can benefit by deliberately suppressing and ignoring opprobrious episodes of their past. By what means can they measure their social, economic and cultural progress without taking into account the mistakes, faults and crimes of their ancestors? Persons whose minds are open only to pleasant legends of bygone years are, in effect, condoning the half-truths customarily disseminated by chambers of commerce and advertising agencies and abetting the immoral practices of pseudopatriots and political demagogues."[9]

The curious thing is that Mark Twain seems, on the surface at least, to have done his best to have forgotten it as well. There are moments of outburst, of course, and it would dishonour Twain's memory to deny them. They are so fiery that we should relish them. But they are scattered. For a man who professed and proclaimed his vehement hatred of imperialism, and American imperialism no less than any other proprietary brand, the random nature of his outbursts on behalf of the redskin is very interesting.

2.

Mark Twain wrote in his notebook in 1882 that the U.S. government had spent a lot of money killing indians: 'We have killed 200 Indians. What did it cost? $2,000,000. You could have given them a college education for that.' Three years later he urged Grover Cleveland, President of the U.S.A. to protect the Indians in the West from the terrible treatment they were getting both from the private citizenry (settlers and prospectors) and from U.S. government officials: 'You not only have the power to destroy the scoundrelism of many kinds in this country, but you have amply proved that you also have the unwavering disposition and purpose to do it.' Enclosed with this letter he sent the President a cutting from the *Southwest Sentinel*, published in Silver City, New Mexico:

$250 REWARD

The above reward will be paid by the Board of County Commissioners of Grant County to any citizens of said county for each and every hostile renegade Apache killed by such citizen, on presentation to said Board of the scalp of such Indian.

By Order of the Board, E. Stine, Clerk [10]

The great humorist was here attempting to swim against a very strong ideological tide.

Social Darwinism was a powerful current in American thinking. [11] The doctrine of the Anglo-Saxon superiority was spread at colleges and universities, where the ideas of such scholars as Edward Augustus Freeman (1823-92) - enshrined in his *Comparative Politics* (1874) - were deeply influential. Freeman asserted that history was a science comparable to the biological sciences, and that

" For the purposes of Comparative Politics, a political constitution is a specimen to be studied, classified, and labeled, as a building or an animal is studied, classified, and labeled by thosed to whom buildings or animals are objects of study. "[12]

What is arresting here is the fact that romantic notions of 'nationhood' and the 'manifest destiny' which predate Darwinism (cf. John Mitchell Kemble, *The Saxons in England* (1849) and Charles Kingsley, *The Roman and the Teuton* (1864)) lean on a perverted understanding of biology for their ultimate justification.

As the nineteenth century advanced and manifested European and American nationalism and imperialism - which are among the later stages of the imperatives of capitalism and thus have essentially economic causes[13] - history was distorted to present the justification for favouring certain races over others, by means of a brand of scientific determinism which demonstrated the inevitability of the triumph of certain political and economic systems over others. In other words, the colonial conquest of the West Indies, India, Africa, Asia and the New

World by Caucasians was part of God's plan for the world. This was certainly how such matters were in fact taught to those whose happy duty it was to serve the British Empire. J. Fitzgerald Lee, author of a work first published in 1902, but regularly reprinted until the 1930s - recommended to military students and dedicated (with permission) to His Excellency Lord Kitchener - comes right out and says in so many words that the whole thing was God's idea right from the start:

"It is not without some reason, beyond our ken, that the greatest empire in the world, the greatest of the White Race, happens to hold these lands on the other side of the globe, as well as the temperate regions in North America and South Africa. The wonderful growth of the British Empire, from Pole to Pole, has been attributed to various causes: by our friends, to British enterprise and statesmanship; by our enemies, to our alleged qualities of greed and cunning; although recent world-events have proved that these latter characteristics are the monopoly of no one people under the sun. And they cannot be reasonably held to account for such geographical phenomena as the Gulf Stream bearing warm breezes to the British Islands, or the monsoons coming at the right time to water the parching plains of British India. The same inscrutable causes which placed England's geographical position in the centre of the land hemisphere arranged that the great mass of the habitable lands on earth should be in the temperate zone, where men can best live; into these things it is not the business of the geographer to enquire, but only to deal with them as he finds them. [14]

This is the thrust of much influential 'history' produced at this period - cf. John Richard Green, *Short History of the English People* (1874), *The Making of England* (1881) and *The Conquest of England* (1883), and James K. Hosmer, *Short History of Anglo-Saxon Freedom* (1890). These volumes may be seen as more or less respectable history, quite different in kind from the more bizarre products of the racism and imperialism of the time, produced by such persuasive cranks as Comte Arthur de Gobineau, whose seminal *Essai sur l'Inégalité des Races Humaines* was published in 1853-55, and Houston Stewart Chamberlain, whose *Die Grundlagen des neunzehnten Jahrhunderts* (1899) was published in English in 1910. Gobineau's dangerous thesis was that it was only the white races who alone were capable of creating culture and true civilization. Unfortunately, he claimed, they had become enervated as the result of no longer being 'pure'; he put into circulation the idea of the superman and in several respects was the intellectual parent of Nietzsche. Chamberlain, son of an English admiral and public school educated, was a lifelong Germanophile and anti-semite. He published a biography of Wagner and married his daughter. During the First World War he became a naturalized German subject and published much anti-British propaganda. For him it was the Germans alone who could produce culture and political organization and stability. [15]

In the mid-nineteenth century when free trade was at its height, even a colonial power such as Britain was actually opposed to territorial expansion. It was almost universally believed that the colonies were an albatross round the national neck and that their ultimate separation and independence from Britain was both desirable and inevitable. That great British imperialist Benjamin Disraeli actually declared in 1852: 'The colonies are a millstone round our necks.' [16] Colonies had been accumulated as the result of various wars, with little thoughts of their development or exploitation as overseas empire. [17] It was not until the second part of the century that the British began in practice to realize the potential of empire - as John George Lambton, Earl of Durham wrote:

"The experiment of keeping colonies and governing them well, ought at least to have a trial, ere we abandon forever the vast dominion [Canada] which might supply the wants of our surplus population, and raise up millions of fresh consumers of our manufactures."

He had been appointed Governor-General of Canada, and his recommendations for reforming the administration of the colony, embodied in the *Durham Report* (1839) are an important staging-post in Britain's development as an imperial nation. [18] The vast accumulation of capital made colonial expansion inescapable. [19] Between 1884 and 1900 Great Britain acquired 3,700,000 square miles of territory and 57,000,000 inhabitants; France got 3,600,000 square miles, with 36,500,000 inhabitants; Germany 1,000,000 square miles and 14,700,000 inhabitants; Belgium 900,000 square miles and 30,000,000 people and Portugal obtained 800,000 square miles and 9,000,000 people. [20] As the Rev. C.S. Dawe so sweetly put in a little book often given to children as a school prize:

" The British Empire consists not only of the United Kingdom and such large countries as Canada, Australia and India, but it comprises also a host of small settlements dotted about the world, and valuable either for purposes of war or commerce. In consequence of our Empire being world-wide, there is scarcely a month when peace reigns in every part of it. We have generally some little war on hand ..." [21]

There are few things as strong as ideas at the right time. These ideas gained generous circulation in the U.S.A. at the close of the nineteenth century as the result of their dissemination in educational institutions which turned out so many of the policy-makers of the nation. To take just one example: at Columbia University Theodore Roosevelt was a student of John William Burgess, who had been educated at Amherst, and at Gottingen, Leipzig and Berlin. In 1873 he had been appointed Professor of History and Political Science at Amherst and later became Professor of Political Science and Constitutional Law at Columbia. In his *Political Science and Comparative Consitutional Law* (1890) Burgess argued that he had a new approach to the subject. It was a comparative study which applied the method successful in the natural sciences to political science and jurisprudence. His findings included the demonstration that political capacity was not a gift which was to be found equally distributed among the peoples of the earth. Only a few races had it at all, and of these the Aryan races stood supreme:

"The Teuton really dominates the world by his superior political genius ... It is therefore not to be assumed that every nation must become a state. The political subjection or attachment of unpolitical nations to those possessing political endowment appears, if we may judge from history, to be as truly a part of the world's civilization as is the national organization of states. I do not think that Asia and Africa can ever receive political organization in any other way... The national state is ... the most modern and complete solution of the whole problem of political organization which the world has yet produced; and the fact that it is the creation of Teutonic political genius stamps the Teutonic nations as the political nations *par excellence*, and authorizes them, in the economy of the world, to assume the leadership in the establishment and administration of states..."[22]

The lesson was not wasted on Theodore Roosevelt, whose *The Winning of the West*, published in four volumes (1889-96), portrayed the struggles of the frontiersmen with the Indians as a final working-out of a racial war which was inevitable and in the nature of things. As Richard

Hofstadter writes, in Roosevelt's eyes the great expansion of American influence, over the Indians in the West and in extra-territorial American imperialism, was simply the final stages of an expansion to be traced back

" many centuries to the days when German tribes went forth to conquest from their marshy forests. American development represents the culminating achievement of this mighty history of racial growth." [23]

In the words of Horace ('Go West, young man, and grow up with the country') Greeley, writing in *An Overland Journey, from New York to San Francisco* (1860):

"It needs but little familiarity with the actual, palpable aborigines to convince anyone that the poetic Indian - the Indian of Cooper and Longfellow - is only visible to the poet's eye. To the prosaic observer, the average Indian of the woods and prairies is a being who does little credit to human nature - a slave of appetite and sloth, never emancipated from the tyranny of one animal passion save by the more ravenous demands of another. As I passed over those magnificent bottoms of the Kansas which form the reservations of the Delawares, Potawatamies, etc., constituting the very best corn-lands on earth, and saw their owners sitting around the doors of their lodgings at the height of the planting season and in as good, bright planting weather as sun and soil ever made, I could not help saying: 'These people must die out - there is no help for them. God has given this earth to those who will subdue and cultivate it, and it is vain to struggle against his righteous decree'... "[24]

But the appalling and horrific scandal of the destruction of the indigenous Indian population of the South West seems to a large extent to be submerged in Twain's writing. He is determined to play down with all his considerable energies the 'noble savage' stereotyping of the Redskin, whom he refused to view - in his own words - 'through the mellow moonshine of romance'. Does this mean that so unquestionably a great American writer, who lived through what was, in effect, the colonization of the American West, ignored such human suffering, and that all he had to say about Indians will be found in his portraits of the less attractive side of Indian behaviour?

3.

There is ample evidence that Twain found ideas of racial superiority repugnant, and that he had a deep loathing for contemporary European rapaciousness. It is found scattered through his writings, but finds exemplary expression in the extraordinary work, *King Leopold's Soliloquy*, published in Boston in 1905, and in London a year later. It seems to me that he projects his loathing of the criminal treatment of savage people by white colonists and their willing military and government agents in this satiric attack on King Leopold's production of personal wealth from the resources of the Free State of the Congo by a policy of terror, repression, rape and genocide in the guise of a civilizing and christianizing mission to the dark continent.

In the Autumn of 1904 Mark Twain was approached by the English radical and reformer E.D. Morel, head of the Congo Reform Association, [25] who asked him to give his support as a writer to 'the cause of the Congo natives'. The east coast expedition of Verney Lovett Cameron to relieve Livingstone in 1873, which started from Bagamoyo and reached Benguela in November 1875, led to the formation of the Association International Africaine under the auspices of Leopold, King of the Belgians. The proclaimed ambition of the Association was to suppress slavery and civilize Africa. The movement was given considerable impetus by the discoveries of Henry Morton Stanley, who had traced the Congo to the sea. Supported by Leopold he founded the Congo Free State in 1879. This led to the Congo Congress in Berlin in 1884-85, which gave the Free State international status. Before the slave trade could be abolished, war broke out between the Belgians and the Arab slavers under Tippoo Tib. It was this crisis which caused Leopold to adopt the concessional system to exploit the natural resources of the area to recoup the cost of the war. This was the system of obtaining rubber and other materials by exerting terror on the population who were thus compelled to labour in order to produce the supplies for which the country was ransacked.

Leopold had never exhibited the slightest doubt that he knew what colonies were for. He was one of the earliest European statesmen to realize the vast economic advantages to be had from a systematic exploitation of overseas possessions in the tropics. His ideas on this matter predate his acquisition of the Congo Free State in 1885 by over twenty years: witness his famous Letter on the Advantages of Colonization, dated 26 July 1863. Discounting the usefulness of slave colonies, such as Cuba, and bearing in mind the problem which would exist in getting the best out of colonies in cases where the working class in the home European country will not emigrate and the home middle class lack opportunities, he concentrates on the value of 'Colonies inhabited by a numerous native race, which have been made a dependency of some European state'. The native population, he is willing to grant, will have to be 'subordinated to a European people', but the economic advantages to the European country are considerable: 'Such countries are not real colonies but external possessions which are very productive if well chosen ...' He admits that 'forced labour' is usually the only way of 'civilizing and imposing moral standards on these lazy and corrupt peoples ...' Those who assist the cultivation of the colony properly will one day be able to 'buy back their liberty from the state and become landowners. Taxes will replace labour obligations ...' The advantages for the investment of domestic capital are considerable. It is a perfect solution to the vexing problem of capital accumulation, as the colony, if properly selected, will provide investment potential, careers and work, while adding nothing to the budget of the mother country - on the contrary - the colony will support the mother country with an annual bonus of millions, more than paying the costs of government administration and the army and navy needed to run and to police such a scheme. [26] What did it mean for the Congo when these theories were put into practice?

On 10 December 1865 Leopold succeeded his father and became Leopold II, King of the Belgians. Ten years later he organized and assumed the presidency of the International Association for the Exploration and Civilization of Central Africa. Henry Morton Stanley had hoped to interest British capital or the British goverment in developing the lower Congo, but he failed to do so. He was supported by Leopold, who sent him back to Africa to stake claims for the Association. The United States officially recognized the Association as an 'independent state' in 1884, and in 1885 Leopold became King of the Independent State of the Congo.

The Berlin Conference admitted Leopold's claim but supported the idea of free trade, the suppression of the slave trade and the moral well-being of the native population. But, in effect, Leopold was the owner of a million miles of land, with a population of twenty million natives. He sent agents to exploit the resources of the land - mainly rubber and ivory at this stage, before the discovery of the land's vast mineral wealth. The realization of the Congo's economic properties required the people to be dispossessed of their land and put into camps. Their job was to collect rubber, and they were punished if they failed to deliver the required quota. The incentives were the amputation of hands and feet and other barbarities. Within twenty years it was estimated between five and eight million men, women and children died, others surviving as cripples. But the system was efficient. Output increased from $30,000 in 1886 to $8,000,000 in 1900.[27]

From the early 1890s stories of atrocities committed in the Congo began to filter back to Europe and across the Atlantic from missionaries, explorers and reformers. Initially these stories were simply not believed. In 1903 Roger Casement, then British Consul at Boma, in the Belgian Congo, released an official report on the administration of the Congo Free State. The document was a terrible catalogue of fiendish acts and told the story of forced labour and coercion - the latter included amputation of limbs and genitals, village-burning and the murder and mutilation of children. Those in charge of the labour gangs carried baskets full of hands (smoked to preserve them in the tropical climate) to demonstrate their authority. Women were raped and sent to brothels for Leopold's military or official personnel. The tax system levied on the native workers ensured they returned whatever miserable wages they actually earned. The entire process was making Leopold into one of the richest men in the world.

E.D. Morel learned of these atrocities very largely from Casement's disclosures and was prompted to form the Congo Reform Association and to contact Mark Twain. But Twain had the Congo on his mind before this. His correspondence shows his awareness of Leopold's record in the Congo, [28] and there is an unpublished *Thanksgiving Sentiment*, which dates from 1904:

"We have much to be thankful for. Our free Republic being the official godfather of the Congo Graveyard, first of the Powers to recognise its pirate flag & become responsible through silence for the prodigious depredations & multitudinous murders committed under it upon the helpless natives by King Leopold of Belgium in the past twenty years: now therefore let us be humbly thankful that this last twelvemonth has seen the King's usual annual myriad of murders reduced by nearly one & one half per cent; let us be humbly grateful that the good King, our pet &

protégé, due in hell these sixty-five years, is still spared to us to continue his work & ours among the friendless & the foresaken; finally let us live in the blessed hope that when in the Last Great Day he is confronted with his unoffending millions upon millions of robbed, mutilated & massacred men, women & children & required to explain, he will be as politely silent about us as we have been about him." [29]

In some ways *King Leopold's Soliloquy* is, in effect, like a vicious parody of a Robert Browning monologue. Twain seems to have taken Browning's basic ironic method of having a character, speaking in monologue, attempt to explain or apologise for his life or career, and in the process actually condemn himself out of his own mouth, realizing those lines in *Hamlet*: 'So full of artless jealousy is guilt,/ It spills itself in fearing to be spilt.' [30] But Twain pushed the *genre* to the extremes of grotesque self-revelation. It is written as a script for an actor, complete with stage directions. Twain masterfully works in material additional to Leopold's musings - extracts from official reports of such activities in the Congo, eye-witness accounts of atrocities and authorial footnotes to add detail. The effect is devastating. The work is beautifully constructed, developing from rather crude knock-about comedy at the opening, through a whole range of brilliant and often moving effects - pathos, bathos, melodrama, comedy and savage irony.

Leopold is placed before us deeply disturbed and anxious at the fact that the truth about the Congo is cominout. He curses and prays by turns:

"In these twenty years I have spent millions to keep the press of the two hemispheres quiet, and still these leaks keep occurring. I have spent other millions on religion and art, and what do I get for it? Nothing. Not a compliment. These generosities are studiously ignored, in print. In print I get nothing but slanders - and slanders again - and still slanders, and slanders on top of slanders! Grant them true, what of it? They are slanders all the same, when uttered against a king. Miscreants - they are telling **everything**!" [31]

'Everything' turns out to have consisted of Leopold's cunning mixture of hypocrisy, guile and mendacity for his civilizing/christianizing mission which gave him supremacy in the Congo. He is proud of the way he duped European states and tricked the U.S.A.

"Oh, well, let them blackguard me if they like; it is a deepsatisfaction to me to remember that I was a shade too smart for that nation that thinks itself so smart. Yes, I certainly did bunco a Yankee ... Pirate flag? Let them call it so ... All the same, **they were the first to salute it.**" [32]

He goes on to call the American missionaries, British consuls and Belgian officials who have published the truth about the Congo 'pests' who have 'kept back nothing!' Shame should have kept them silent since these exposures place a king in an insufferable light: '... they were exposures of a king, a sacred personage and immune from reproach, by right of his selection and appointment to his great office by God himself ...' [33] Twain has now raised our curiosity. What have these pests been saying Leopold tells us:

"... how I levy incredibly burdensome taxes upon the natives - taxes which are a pure theft; taxes which they must satisfy by gathering rubber under hard and constantly harder conditions, and by raising and furnishing food supplies gratis - and it all comes out that, when they fall short of their tasks through hunger, sickness, despair, and ceaseless and exhaustive labour without rest, and forsake their homes and flee to the woods to escape punishment, my black soldiers, drawn from unfriendly tribes, and instigated and directed by my Belgians, hunt them down and butcher them and burn their villages - reserving some of the girls ... But they never say ... that I have laboured in the cause of religion at the same time ... and have sent missionaries there ... to teach them the error of their ways and bring them to Him who is all mercy and love ..." [34]

He goes on to read some of the evidence of these missionaries and meddlers, who work statistics up into offensive kindergarten object lessons, 'whose purpose is to make sentimental people shudder, and prejudice them against me ...' He reads out some of these object lessons:

"if the innocent blood shed in the Congo by King Leopold were put in buckets and placed side by side, it would stretch 2,000 miles; if the skeletons of his ten millions of starved and butchered dead could rise up and march in single file, it would take them seven months and four days to pass a given point; if compacted together in a body, they would occupy more ground than St. Louis covers, World's Fair and all ... " [35]

In order to refute and to minimize the evidence, the King has to read it. This enables us to hear it. He then turns to a pamphlet by the Rev. A.E. Scrivener, a British missionary, which describes a journey made in July, August and September 1903. It is a sickening catalogue of barbarities. The Rev. Scrivener's account ends with his seeing the bones of numerous victims of Leopold's system, and watching the file of rubber collectors coming in:

"with their little baskets under their arms [I] saw them paid their milk tin full of salt... saw their trembling timidity, and in fact a great deal that all went to prove the state of terrorism that exists and the virtual slavery in which the people are held." [36]

Leopold is offended at the depths to which his enemies will sink to discredit him - why, Mr. Casement even reprints private diaries and journals not intended for general circulation, which distastefully reveals the mutilation of adults and the killing of children with the butts of rifles. Leopold attempts to excuse 'severing hands, unsexing men etc.' by saying that these were already native customs in which we Europeans simply followed local traditions. And these reformers have the nerve to retort:

"If a Christian King can perceive a saving moral difference between inventing bloody barbarities, and **imitating them from savages,** for charity's sake let him get what comfort he can out of his confession!" [37]

A report by the Rev. W.H. Sheppard included an interview with a black raider in Leopold's service who describes how he took part in the massacre of between eighty and ninety natives and mutilated their bodies. One victim's skull was made into a tobacco bowl. He saw eighty-one hands (which he counted) being smoked over a fire to preserve them. Leopold turns to the evidence gathered by E.D. Morel and exclaims: 'This Morel is a king's subject, and reverence for monarchy should have restrained him from reflecting upon me with that exposure.'

The climax of Leopold's monologue is his denunciation of the camera - this is the most damaging weapon used against him. It is interesting to note that Twain submitted the *Soliloquy* to American magazines, but none dared to print it. He gave it to the American Congo Reform Association and it was published by the Warren Company of Boston. On Twain's personal advice this edition carried photographs and drawings of mutilated negroes - men, women and children.[38] Leopold now almost begins to despair:

"The kodak has been a sore calamity to us. The most powerful enemy indeed. In the early years we had no trouble in getting the press to 'expose' the tales of mutilations as slanders, lies, inventions ... and by the press's help we got the Christian nations everywhere to turn an irritated and unbelieving ear to these tales .... Yes, all things went harmoniously and pleasantly in those good days, and I was looked up to as the benefactor of a down-trodden and frienless people. Then all of a sudden came the crash! That is to say, the incorruptible kodak and all the harmony went to hell! The only witness I have encountered in my long experience that I couldn't bribe."[39]

How is he going to escape universal condemnation? He reads one last dreadful pamphlet which further summarizes the appalling inhumanities for which he is responsible:

"He is sole master there; he is absolute. He could have prevented the crimes by his mere command; he could stop them today with a word. He withholds the word. For his pocket's sake." [40]

The end of the *Soliloquy* is a striking example of that cynicism and pessimism which is typical of the mature Twain. Having driven Leopold to the point where there seems no escape, Twain reveals that in human nature itself lies his refuge. The pamphlet the King reads ends with the words:

"'We see this awful King, this pitiless and blood-drenched King, this money-crazy King ... but **we do not wish to look**; for he is a King, and it hurts us, by ancient and inherited instinct it shames us to see a King degraded to this aspect; and we shrink from hearing the particulars of how it happened. **We shudder and turn away** when we come upon them in print."

As Leopold says, this is his salvation: 'Why, certainly, THAT IS MY PROTECTION. And you will continue to do it. I know the human race.'
[41]

This work is vintage Twain, the distillation of a lifetime's experience in using words to amuse, persuade, cajole, moralize, satirize, inform, educate and disturb. In it he combines the skills learned in his long apprenticeship to authorship in the widest sense - *King Leopold's Soliloquy* is a *tour de force* which displays Twain in several aspects of his trade - journalist, lecturer, playwright, preacher, story-teller, and - above all - satirist.

4.

The *Soliloquy* did a lot of good. It was a shot in the arm for the American Congo Reform Association. Henry I. Kowalsky, an agent employed by the Belgian government, notified King Leopold in December 1904:

" Mark Twain, or Samuel Clemens (which is his proper name) must certainly have a retainer from the English people. The fight here (in the U.S.A.) is organized as it has never been before. Monster petitions have been circulated and signed; the industry of the opposition is very manifest, and I can assure you that you cannot afford to turn a deaf ear to what I am saying." [42]

The *Soliloquy* had a good press in England and was publicized in the pages of *The Athenaeum, Punch*, the *Bookman* and its author congratulated by E.D. Morel. Twain gave all his income from this work to the American Congo Reform Association. At this time several leading American capitalists - John Pierpont Morgan, John D. Rockefeller, Thomas Fortune Ryan and Daniel Guggenheim - were negotiating investment in the Congo. The publicity of Twain's work had given the Congo was understandably embarrassing, and they spent out large sums to counteract its effects, hiring academics and churchmen to disclaim the atrocity stories. The stakes were very high, for, in the same year which saw the composition of *King Leopold's Soliloquy* , it became clear that the wealth to be made out of the Congo was immense; deposits of copper, zinc, cobalt, cadmium, tungsten and diamonds were discovered. International tension over the Congo mounted in the light of the condemnation of Leopold. For example, Sir Edward Grey, British Foreign Secretary, declared: 'The Congo state has morally forfeited every right to international recognition.' In February 1908 a British parliamentary paper, *Africa No. 1*, which contained reports from the British Consul at Boma,

W.G. Thesiger, further fanned international opinion. In March 1908 Leopold attempted to make the best terms he could, but in August the same year the Belgian government adopted a treaty of cession and the Congo was annexed as a Belgian colony. On 14 November 1908 the Congo Free State ceased to exist. [43] Leopold died the following year.

The Congo horrors remain as fresh now as the time when Mark Twain produced his vehement and effective satire. That this continues to be so underlines the fact that although these personalities and events are historically specific, they nevertheless conform to the depressing and recurring configuration of human experience which consitutes an inescapable ingredient in the paradigm of capitalism - Cuba, the Phillippines, Latin America, Burma, Indo-China, India, the scramble for Africa .... The ultimate Twainian irony may be found in the fact that the New World was itself discovered by Christopher Columbus in an earlier version of the same old sordid story. He hoped to capitalize discovery by means of slaves and gold. Slavery proved unprofitable, hundreds of Indians died *en route* to Europe. So it had to be gold. At Hispaniola every man, woman and child was to collect gold for the Spaniards. Every three months they had to bring in a hawk's bell filled with gold dust. Chiefs had to bring in ten times that amount. If they failed, they had their hands chopped off. There were no goldfields. The task was clearly impossible. The wretched natives tried panning for gold, which was fruitless. If they attempted to flee, they were hunted by Spaniards with dogs. Resistance was impossible. Many of them committed mass suicide with cassava poison. By 1496 there was clearly no gold left, and the remaining members of the population were used as slave labour on *encomiendas*. By 1540 the entire nation of Arawack Indians had vanished from the face of the earth - totally exterminated. [44] Mark Twain's identification with anti-imperialism was total. He opened his speech at the annual dinner of the New England Society in 1881: 'My first American ancestor, gentlemen, was an Indian, an early Indian. Your ancestors skinned him alive, and I am an orphan.

NOTES

1.   Frank Harris, *My Life and Loves*, edited by John F. Gallagher (New Jersey: Castle Books, 1963), p. 485.

2.   See Gareth Stedman Jones, 'The History of U.S. Imperialism' in Robin

Blackburn (ed.), *Ideology in Social Science* (Collins, 1973), pp. 207-37.

   3.   Gareth Stedman Jones, ibid., pp. 207 and following.

   4.   See Leslie Fiedler, *The Return of the Vanishing American* (Paladin, 1972), pp. 17, 26, 123-28 and 177-78.

   5.   Mark Twain, *Following the Equator*, quoted in Philip S. Foner, *Mark Twain - Social Critic* (New York: International Publishers, 1975), p. 314.

   6.   Jay Gould (1836-92): U.S. financier, celebrated for his attempt to corner the gold market. Began life in the leather trade. Entered Wall Street and was a millionaire before he was 21. Lost his fortune in the panic of 1857. Involved in various speculations, investments and deals after the Civil War, made additional fortunes in railway investments and by 1890 was alleged to own half the mileage in the Southwest. Always suspected of chicanery, bribery and sharp practice. Left over $100,000,000. William Marcy Tweed (1823-78): 'Boss Tweed', was a New York politician who became the prototype corrupt city boss. When he ran City Hall the aldermen were known as the 'Forty Thieves'; contracts were only accepted after payment of between 10% and 85% to Tweed and his ring. It was estimated that the Thieves took some $30,000,000 to $200,000,000 from the city of New York. Exposed by the *New York Times* and a committee of investigation, Tweed died in jail. George Francis Train (1829-1904): transport magnate, traveller, millionaire and eccentric, orphaned as a boy in New Orleans, then successively farmworker, grocer's boy, shipping clerk, manager and partner in Train and Company, famous for his clippers and railway construction and tramway systems. Organized French Commune, Marseilles 1870. Train went round the world in 80 days and was the original of Jules Verne's character Phileas Fogg. He ran for the presidency against Grant and Greeley, 1871-72. He styled himself 'Champion Crank'; he was in his day a celebrated lecturer, merchant, promoter, author and character. Went round the world four times in all; the final time (1892) he made it in sixty days.

   7.   Mark Twain, 'The Sandwich Islands' (1873), in *The Complete Essays of Mark Twain*, edited Charles Neider (New York: Doubleday and Company, 1963), pp. 27-8.

   8.   Robert Silverberg, *Home of the Red Man* (New York: Washington Square Press, 1973), pp. 101-19; Dee Brown, *Bury My Heart at Wounded Knee: An Indian History of the American West* (Barrie and Jenkins, 1970), pp. 1-12; Thomas R. Detwyler, *Man's Impact on Environment* (New York: McGraw-Hill Book Company, 1971), pp. 515 and 615 - see also M.S. Garretson, *The American Bison* (New York Zoological Society, 1938).

   9.   John Upton Terrell, *Land Grab; The Truth About 'The Winning of the West'* (New York; The Dial Press, 1972), p. vii.

   10.   Quoted in Foner, op. cit., p. 308.

   11.   See Richard Hofstadter, *Social Darwinism in American Thought* (Boston;Beacon Press. 1955), pp. 172-200.

   12.   Edward Augustus Freeman, *Comparative Politics* (New York, 1874), p. 23. Freeman made considerable claims for the Teutonic origins of British institutions-see W.R. Stephens, *The Life and Letters of Edward Augustus Freeman* (1895). Freeman's *The History of the Norman Conquest of England, its Causes and its Results* (1867-76) provides useful insights to late nineteenth-century Anglo-Saxon racial ideology. Freeman was a Fellow of Trinity College, Oxford, where he was later Regius Professor of Modern History from 1884 until his death in 1892.

   13.   Lenin, *Imperialism, The Highest Stage of Capitalism* (Moscow; Progress

Publishers, 1970), pp. 117 and following. See also C. Morris, *The History of Coloni- zation* (New York, 1900), Vol. 2, pp. 88 and following.

14.   J. Fitzgerald Lee, *Imperial Military Geography* (William Clowes and Sons Ltd., 1923), p. 16.

15.   Emil Ludwig, *The Germans* (Hamish Hamilton, 1942), pp. 306 and follow- ing. See also Michael Banton (ed) *Darwinism and the Study of Society* (1961); Jacques Barzun, *Darwin, Marx and Wagner* (Boston: Little, Brown & Co., 1941) and Carlton J.H. Hayes, *A Generation of Materialism 1871-1900* (New York: Harper and Bros., 1941), pp. 12-13. 246 and 255 and following; cf.General Friedrich von Bernhardi, *Germany and the Next War,* translated by Allen H. Powles (Edward Arnold, 1914), pp. 56 and following.

16.   See M. beer, 'Modern British Imperialism' in *Die Neue Zeit,* Vol. XVI, No.1 (1898), p. 302.

17.   See Edward Grierson, *The Imperial Dream: British Commomwealth and Empire 1775-1969* (Collins, 1972), pp.55-64.

18.   See Gerald S. Graham, *A Concise History of the British Empire* (Thames and Hudson, 1972), pp. 173 and following.

19.   E.J. Hobsbawm, *Industry and Empire* (Penguin, 1969), pp. 192 and following; Michael Barratt Brown, *The Economics of Imperialism* (Penguin, 1974), pp. 133-45; Anthony Nutting, *The Scramble for Africa* (Constable, 1970), pp. 15-31; cf. Richard Shannon, *The Crisis of Imperialism 1865-1915* (Paladin, 1974), pp. 105 and following. See also Joseph Schumpeter, 'The Sociology of Imperialism' in *Imperialism and Social Class,* translated by Heinz Norden (New York: Meridian Books, 1971), pp. 3 and following.

20.   The figures are from John Atkinson Hobson, *Imperialism* (1902).

21.   C.S. Dawe, *Queen Victoria and Her People* (The Educational Supply Association Ltd., 1897), p. 162.

22.   John William Burgess, *Political Science and Comparative Constitutional Law* (Boston: Ginn and Company, 1890), Vol. W. pp. 39 and 44-5.

23.   Richard Hofstadter, *Social Darwinism in American Thought* (Boston: Bea- con Press, 1955), p. 175.

24.   Horace Greeley, *An Overland Journey, From New York to San Francisco* (1860), quoted in *Westward the Way: The Character and Development of the Louisiana Territory as Seen by Artists and Writers of the Nineteenth Century,* edited by Perry T. Rathbone (City Art Museum of St. Louis in Collaboration with the Walker Art Center, Minneapolis 1954), p. 111. The catalogue of this systematic working out of God's will may be perused in the photographic record taken by W.S. Prettyman - see *Indian Territory: A Frontier Record* by W.S. Prettyman, selected and edited by Robert E. Cunningham (University of Oklahoma Press, 1958). William S. Prettyman of Arkansas City, Kansas, took his photographic equipment by wagon and oxen through the Indian territory of Oklahoma in 1880-1909 and made some ten thousand plates which record the historic moment of the opening up of Indian territory to white settlement.

25.   E.D. Morel was a well known English radical and reformer, who once described himself as 'one of the best abused men in the British Isles'. The son of a French father and an English mother, he was a life-long campaigner against imperialism and militarism. Before he contacted Twain he had already written extensively about European colonization of Africa - *Affairs of West Africa* (1902), *The British Case in French Congo* (1903) and *King Leopold's Rule in Africa* (1904). In 1906 he published *Red Rubber: The Story of the Rubber Slave Trade in the Congo* which went through five editions between 1906 and 1908.

26.   Leopold, Duke of Brabant (1835-1909), 'Letter on the Advantages of Colonization', 26 July 1863, in *Documents d'histoire précoloniale belge 1861-65*, edited by L. le Febvre de Vivy (Brussels: Academie royale des Sciences coloniales, 1955), translated by D.K. Fieldhouse (ed.) *The Theory of Capitalist Imperialism* (Longman, 1967), pp. 46-9.

27.   P.T. Moon, *Imperialism and World Politics* (New York: MacMillan and Co., 1926), p. 28.

28.   See Foner, op. cit., pp. 384 and following.

29.   Quoted in the *Introduction* to Mark Twain, *King Leopold's Soliloquy* (New York: International Publishers, 1971), pp. 16-17.

30.   Shakespeare, *Hamlet*, Act IV, scene 5, 19-20. Semantic changes have slightly distorted the meaning of these lines for us - **jealousy** meant for Shakespeare suspicion, or apprehension of evil or mistrust - so the Queen's comment means that the guilt is itself to full of suspicion that unskilfully it betrays itself in fearing to be betrayed. See C.T. Onions, *A Shakespeare Glossary* (Oxford: Clarendon Press, 1972), p. 120. The comment suits Twain's portrait of Leopold admirably.

31.   Mark Twain, *King Leopold's Soliloquy* (New York: International Publishers, 1971), p. 29.

32.   Ibid., p. 31.

33.   Ibid., p. 32.

34.   Ibid., pp. 33-4.

35.   Ibid., p.36 This is a telling stroke. The Louisiana Purchase Exposition, held in 1904, was still fresh in the public memory. Up to this time it was the greatest world exhibition ever held and covered more ground and offered more exhibits, from more parts of the world, than any other fair. Every state of the U.S.A. was represented, and most major world powers. It incorporated the 1904 Olympic Games. In the seven months of its duration it was visited by 20,000,000 spectators. There was a Belgian exhibition hall but the Congo was not featured. Colonization and imperialism were among the great unmentioned in the exhibition, though the collision of advanced and savage cultures, which is the essence of imperialism, did surface from time to time. The Official catalogue describes a group of statuary entitled 'The Destiny of the Red Man' in these words: 'This group by Adolph Weinmann, is one of the most impressive works of sculpture at the Exposition, expressing forcibly the fate of the aboriginal inhabitants of America. The Indian, with all his trappings and superstitions is departing, along with the bison of the plains. The group expresses the departure of barbarism, driven out by civilizing institutionss and influences that are making the Indian self-supporting and fitting him for citizenship.' *The Greatest of Expositions: Official Catalogue of the St. Louis World's Fair 1904* (St. Louis, Missouri: Riverside Press, 1975), p. 144. See Robert Iddings, St. Louis: Doughnut City, in *New Society*, 9 September 1976, p. 541.

36.   Mark Twain, *King Leopold's Soliloquy*, op. cit., p. 43.

37.   Ibid., p. 45.

38.   Foner, op. cit., p. 388.

39.   Twain, op. cit., p. 68.

40.   Ibid., p. 70.

41.   Ibid., pp. 70-1.

42.   Foner, op. cit., p. 389.

43.   See M. Cattier, *Etude sur la situation de l'état indépendant du Congo* (Brussels, 1906) and Neal Ascherson, *The King Incorporated* (1963). The accounts by Roger Casement may be read in *Correspondence and Reports Respecting the Adminstration of the Free State of the Congo* (H.M.S.O., 1904).

44.   See Hans Koning, *Columbus: His Enterprise* (New York: Monthly Review Press, 1976), pp. 85-9. Koning bases his account on the record of a Dominican priest, Batholomé de la Casas, whose eye-witness account, *Devastation of the Indies* (New York: Seabury Press, 1974), in a new English translation, makes a salutary comparison with the account of Columbus's contribution to the history of America in the much acclaimed B.B.C./Time-Life Alistair Cooke version. See Alistair Cooke, *America* (New York: Alfred A. Knopf, 1974), pp. 26-36; cf. Robert Giddings, 'Cooking the Books', in *New Society*, 14 June 1979, pp.652-53.

VII
Tolkien:
Climbing Mount Olympus
by Escalator

An obscure Oxford Anglo-Saxon don, J.R.R. Tolkien, wrote a children's best-seller, *The Hobbit*. He was plagued by his enterprising publisher to write a sequel. He found this very difficult. Eventually, drawing on his love of the trappings of medieval myths and legends, boys adventure stories beloved by him and his circle at Oxford he produced *The Lord of the Rings* which realized his publisher's dream and continues to fulfil particular appetites in its readers. It has become a modern classic and has created a cult following. Its impact is hypnotic. It seems like "great literature" and yet mercifully it is easy to read. It recycles and propagates reactionary social and political attitudes. It divides the complexities of the world into black and white, good and evil. The production of such an essentially modern work as *The Lord of the Rings* with all the appearances of a medieval saga is a triumph of modern means of literary production.

It is strange, but true, that *The Lord of the Rings* has been very seriously neglected by literary criticism in Britain. Although it has a tremendous cult following here and has been subject to critical exegesis in America, Middle-earth is almost an undiscover'd country through whose bourn few British academics or critics have travelled. The snobbism is curious. On the one hand we have a text read by thousands and thousands of readers, and an author with a cult following; a book perceived as a 'good' book-that is to say, one held to be emphatically the opposite of corrupting, willingly handed over by librarians to young and old and bought by doting aunts for younger relatives; a work broadcast on Radio Four twice recently more or less in its entirety, and turned into a popular animated cartoon film. On the other hand we have the fact that serious literary evaluation of *The Lord of the Rings* has hardly begun here. It has not even been taken up in the school curriculum-it has not been prescribed as a G.C.E. text. Yet the book must mean something to millions of people. But what does it mean? As Claud Cockburn wrote in *Bestseller: The Books that Everyone Read 1900-72*:

"...you cannot deny that if book X was what a huge majority of book-buyers and book-borrowers wanted to buy or borrow in a given year, or over a period of years, then Book X satisfied a need, and expressed and realized emotions and attitudes to life which the buyers and borrowers did not find expressed or realized elsewhere...of all indices to moods, and, above all, aspirations, the best-seller list is one of the most reliable."

There is no way of fudging it. What must be asked is what are these needs, emotions and attitudes which *The Lord of the Rings* satisfied, and what is the nature of the moods and the aspirations which this reveals?

An understanding of the need *The Lord of the Rings* was seen to supply may help us to an awareness of the book's real qualities. One thing which it seems clearly to satisfy is the need for a complete, whole and entire world - an environment, which although complex and vast, does make whole, complete and entire sense. The world which Tolkien offers readers is one which they can comprehend within the context of its own laws. Problems are proposed, and difficulties are encountered, but there are, ultimately answers. Tolkien's world offers the same kind of security as that offered by institutions, say, public schools, colleges, the armed forces, hospitals - self-contained worlds which may exact the cost of certain losses of freedom and individuality, but in which it is possible to negotiate the establishment of identity, gradations, obedience, authority, power. Deeply buried in the structure of *The Lord of the Rings*, it might be argued, is the image of the British traditional school - Gandalf as headmaster, Aragorn as head-boy, with the obviously identifiable prefects, Upper and Lower Shell, fags, and all the ceremony and ritual which holds such a performance together. There are heroes, and there are bounders and cads. *The Lord of the Rings* may be viewed as a discourse through which fundamental categories and relations which constitute the contextual culture we all recognize are denoted and demonstrably manipulated. [1] This is particularly true in Tolkien's portrayal of the power structure, of class relations and the construction of maleness and femaleness. [2] It is here that the verbal texture of the book is so significant.

Although it offers itself to the reader as something which approximates to high literature (it has the length and the trappings of an epic), its syntax and its vocabulary bespeak an antique quality. Several of its characters strain towards assertion of the archetypal - yet it is not actually difficult to read, provided the reader has the staying power required of its many pages. Reading *The Lord of the Rings* can give the illusion of handling 'great literature' - yet it is easy, compared, say, with effort required to accomplish a reading of Henry James, George Eliot, Joseph Conrad or even D.H. Lawrence. *The Lord of the Rings* is like climbing Mount Olympus by escalator. It is a vast province, a colony, an empire, which is easily claimed, explored and conquered. You can **possess** it easily. This is an important element in the Fashion for Tolkien. The fraternity are very possessive. Anyone who has ever written or broadcast anything about the master's work will know that the slightest slip of name, incident or geographical nomenclature will result in massive and often strenuously corrective mail. You have trespassed on the domain. It is very much to the point that the B.B.C.'s *Mastermind* final was won in 1981 by a competitor who had all the information on Middle-earth in his mental retrieval system.

Here lies one of the importances of the style of *The Lord of the Rings*. Its differences from the work of Michael Moorcock, Douglas Hill, David Lindsay, or other masters of fantasy writing, are deeply significant. The fact that it tells its story in that compulsively archaic mode literally makes it more telling. Because the tone of voice is partly scriptural and partly that of a chronicler, the world view gradually assembled in *The Lord of the Rings* seems God-willed, long matured by human experience and the lessons of history. There is a useful analogy to be made here between the way texts operate on the imagination, and the use of images in advertising and publicity. John Berger in *Ways of Seeing* (1972) talks about the effective use publicity images make of classical images which they echo. Does the language of publicity, he asks, have anything in common with that of oil painting, which, until the advent of photography, dominated the European way of seeing for so many centuries? There is a direct continuity, he claims:

" Only interests of cultural prestige have obscured it. At the same time, despite of continuity, there is a profound difference.... There are many direct references in publicity to works of art from the past.

Sometimes a whole image is a frank pastiche of a well-known painting. Publicity images often use sculptures or paintings to lend allure or authority to their own messages ... A work of art 'quoted' by publicity serves two purposes. Art is a sign of affluence; it belongs to the good life; it is part of the furnishing which the world gives to the rich and the beautiful. But a work of art also suggests a cultural authority, a form of dignity, even of wisdom ... The continuity, however, between oil painting and publicity goes far deeper than the 'quoting' of specific paintings. Publicity relies to a very large extent on the language of oil painting. It speaks in the same voice about the same things ..."

The parallels with the art of Tolkien are fascinating and assist in qualifying the real nature of Tolkien's achievement. [3]

This frequently undervalued aspect of Tolkien's art manifested in *The Lord of the Rings* is his immensely professional ability to provoke very deep echoes in the reader's consciousness which lie immediately beneath the glittering surface structure of his narrative. At its lowest level this is rightly perceived as cheap (if slick) legerdemain, a kind of quality-by-association technique, analogous to the skill used in composing film and T.V. scores which subconsciously remind one of various moments in music by the classical masters and work on the imagination by exploiting these associations. Much of the success of Annigoni portrait-painting was the result of a masterful ability to draw on a massive collection of half-forgotten visual memories of the work of other painters and visually to orchestrate these memories, so as to create a patina or surface quality of Old Masterliness through which to perceive modern portraits of the world's leading figures. It strikes me that much of Tolkien's success in moving and pleasing and satisfying so many readers is the result of his capacity to manipulate our memories of the classics. This is especially true of those moments in *The Lord of the Rings* where something of an epic kind is required. The battle scenes draw upon memories of Shakespeare and medieval romances. [4] The Edwardian-nostalgic-Georgian qualities of the idyllic landscape of the Shire are to a considerable extent conjured up by association with memories of *The Wind in the Willows* and Matthew Arnold's *The Scholar Gypsy*, vaguely recalled from school English lessons. Rural nostalgia is a powerful magnetic pull in the British suburbanite ideology and links up with yearnings for unspoiled romantic innocence with an almost universal appeal. [5] In Tolkien's case the feelings were personal and very deep, as the Thames and the county landscape he loved so much became by a curious accident of industrial development one of the centres of British motor manufacturing. It is usually the case in advanced capitalism that the life enjoyed by the privileged élite and the means of production needed to produce the wealth to support it are kept separate and discrete. In Tolkien's experience the two collided. Oxford meant not only the Thames valley, dreaming spires, college life, but also Cowley, Morris motors and all that mass production industry involves. In Tolkien the situation was at once personal, but with a huge general appeal. The conclusion of Frodo's epic endeavours certainly affects readers, because Tolkien is able to remind you at all sorts of levels of translations of Greek heroic myths read in childhood and of the more rhapsodic sections of Tennyson's version of the passing of Arthur. In his cosy insularity and undying enthusiasm for the cult of the past - not the immediate past, but a past well beyond the Renaissance - Tolkien tuned in to a very powerful frequency in British ideology. It is claimed that urban dislocation has created a passion for local history and archaeology which may be evidenced by enrolment at evening classes all over the country. Figures show that more people want to study archaeology and local history in adult education courses than want to study English literature, politics, economics and sociology. Professor W.G. Hoskin's two television series on the history of the English landscape were followed by an average audience for each programme of 1,000,000 viewers in 1976 and 1978. For those who do not share much of an affinity with the Middle-earth cult it is all too easy to dismiss the wearing of the home-made armour and the Queen Guinevere outfits, the half-jokey half-sincere adoption of Middle-earth names, the various 'moots', etc. as so much silly display behaviour, but these are all significant pieces of evidence of very deeply held beliefs about the nation and its history which have surfaced at a period of great uncertainty and anxiety.

The Lord of the Rings persistently strikes chords in its readers, which set up very powerful sympathetic resonances which Tolkien harmonizes and develops, often using themes from very well-known sources, familiar to us all. This is basic professionalism in the skill of mass communication. The obvious parallel is the successful politician, who is able to detect what the public is thinking, what it fears, what it aspires to, and is able to articulate views and opinions already widely in circulation. The politician then proceeds to tell the public what it wants to hear.

This is one important aspect of Tolkien's art, which is amply demonstrated in *The Lord of the Rings*. It is the art of the demagogue transferred to authorship and developed to the height of genius. It is impressive that Tolkien's imagination functions simultaneously at several levels, operating on the readers' deep need for consolation and assurance that the world need not change, exploiting nationalist paranoia and in a world of complex and baffling materialistic problems, political and economic, supplying spiritual and 'other worldly' answers to intractable mundane questions. It is characteristic of *The Lord of the Rings* that the surface quality of its medievalism, its consciously harking back to the chivalrous past, its 'Northerness' and all the accoutrements of its cult, should be little more than skin deep, and its real subject matter should be modern.

It is essentially a modern phenomenon. As a commodity it is a product of the age of mass publication. *The Lord of the Rings* became a massive best-seller in an age of the mass production of books. Two thirds of all the books ever published were published after 1950.[6] It was written at the direct request of its publisher, rather than at the promptings of the relentless pressures of its author's own inspiration.[7] It was hyped by all the methods of advertising and public relations possible at the time. A very large proportion of its success is obviously the result of its author's ability to reach into deeper recesses of the collective minds of its readership. For all its talk of the 'ominous and disquieting' Evil Powers released upon the world, being driven out by the White Council, all the references to Mordor and the Dark Tower 'from where the power was spreading far and wide', in the face of all the dwarfs, knights, hidden kings, turrets, battles, banners, funeral pyres, wizards and orcs - the anxieties and tensions are modern ones and beneath the top dressing of its self-conscious medievalism its world is our world, or, rather, it is the world as perceived by Tolkien's readers. In *The Lord of the Rings* the evil striven against seems to have been disembodied and then to have gone on and infected other people and other creatures. Some creatures are damned beyond recall, nothing whatever could be done to save them. The orcs, for example, are totally irredeemable. The evil in the world as portrayed by Tolkien has nothing whatever to do with social or economic causes. It is evil, pure and simple. Consequently there is no need for change of socio-economic conditions, the environmental conditions of life, relations between different classes, etc., etc. - all these things which make up the very fabric of society, of **any** society, are perceived by Tolkien as totally beyond any need or possibility of change. As Bob Dixon comments:

" The effect of this kind of literature, as with tract literature, is to divert people from the here and now and persuade them that it's not possible to do anything about the problems of the world. Of course, some people find this a very comforting thought ... *The Lord of the Rings* isn't an allegory but of course it does have a meaning. It says something. It says a lot of things about power and hierarchy. "[8]

Class relationships are vividly portrayed in *The Lord of the Rings*. Tolkien's lower orders are fairly efficient in being deferential to their betters. The strong implication is always present that this is all part of an immutable plan for the world. Another deep chord which *The Lord of the Rings* struck in its readers which set up long sounding sympathetic resonances was the conspiracy theory. It is interesting that the great success of Tolkien's epic has been coincidental with the cult of James Bond,[9] the fashion for Len Deighton and John le Carré, which collectively form such a revealing aspect of Cold War ideology. The author of *The Lord of the Rings* believed that its success was without explanation. It was just a mater of personal taste. W.H. Auden claimed that 'Nobody seems to have a moderate opinion, either people find it a masterpiece of its genre, or they cannot abide it.' The word **genre** is a useful clue. Tolkien created a work which locates itself in a long tradition which has always had a great pull for English readers - the conspiracy story. A foreign power is plotting to invade/overthrow/destroy this green and pleasant land ... As Roland Barthes put forward, a book may often mean something to its readers which was not deliberately intended by its author, and there is a close analogy between fashion and literature which may both be seen as homeostatic systems:

" ... that is to say, systems whose function is not to communicate an objective, external meaning which exists prior to the system but only to create a functioning equilibrium, a movement of signification." [10]

Stories which detail the intentions of a wicked power to take over the world, or to invade the island homeland of the British, or to work for the overthrow of democracy as we know it, etc. have continually exerted a deep fascination for English readers since industrial and colonial rivalries created the tensions in international relations which found expression in Bismarck's foreign policy and the whole network of secret diplomacy which laid the foundations of the First World War and the apparently never ending international unease which is the legacy enjoyed by succeeding generations.

Robert Erskine Childers published *The Riddle of the Sands* in 1903 after a yachting expedition to the German coast. It purported to portray the fiendish cunning of the Germans in secretly planning for war. German ambitions he wrote, were perverted by two principles,

"perfect organization: perfect secrecy.... Germany is pre-eminently fitted to undertake an invasion of Great Britain. She has a great army ... in a state of high efficiency, but a useless weapon, as against   us, unless transported over seas. She has a peculiar genius for organization .... She has a small navy, but very effective for its purpose ... She has little to lose and much to gain ..." [11] The hero of *The Riddle of the Sands* actually sees with his own eyes an experimental rehearsal of a great scene:

" to be enacted, perhaps, in the near future - a scene when multitudes of sea-going lighters, carrying full loads of soldiers ... should issue simultaneously, in seven ordered fleets, from seven shallow outlets, and, under escort of the Imperial Navy, traverse the North sea and throw themselves bodily upon English shores ... recent as are the events I am describing, it is only since they happened that the possibility of an invasion by Germany has become a topic of public discussion." [12]

In 1909 the play *An Englishman's Castle* was performed at Wyndham's Theatre. It was written by Guy du Maurier, brother of the actor, Sir Gerald du Maurier. In substance it is a piece of national paranoia which portrays the homeland a victim to foreign invaders. Joseph Conrad's *The Secret Agent* had only recently bodied forth the idea that the enemy was already amongst us and had projected the vision of 'an anarchist haunted London', in Terry Eagleton's phrase. [13] 'Criminal aliens' - 'anarchists'. etc. - provided ideal news-copy for the sensational press during the Tottenham Affair of 1910 and the panic caused by the Siege of Sidney Street in 1911. Some desperadoes, described by the police as 'anarchists', shot their way out of a house in Houndsditch. Three policemen were killed. A police raid at another house revealed the body of an armed man as well as guns and ammunition, some oil paints and a painting signed 'Peter'. Such were the origins of the saga of 'Peter the Painter' - which ended in Sidney Street, Stepney, in January 1911 and involved 750 police, a detachment of Scots Guards, two field guns, machine guns and the personal appearance of Mr. Winston Churchill, the then Home Secretary. A bill was put before Parliament in favour of new expatriation orders aimed at foreigners.

H.H. Munro's pro-war fantasy *When William Came* was published in the year the First World War started, and portrayed Britain conquered and occupied by the armies of Kaiser Wilhelm II.[14]

The second year of the war saw the U-boat blockade of Britain, the attack on the Dardanelles, the first use of Chlorine gas by the Germans at the Battle of Ypres, the sinking of the *Lusitania*, the execution of Edith Cavell, the collapse of the Russian war effort and the publication of John Buchan's *The Thirty-Nine Steps*. Buchan captured exactly the mood of the readers of the day. In his autobiography Claud Cockburn describes how middle-class families of the time actually expected the German conspiracy to come to fruition any day and that they would see German troops in the street: 'Guests came to lunch and talked about the coming German invasion', he says.

On Sundays, when my sister and I lunched in the dining room instead of the nursery, we heard about it. It spoiled afternoon walks on the hills with Nanny ... I thought Uhlans with lances and flat-topped helmets might come charging over the hill any afternoon ... It was frightening, and a harassing responsibility, since Nanny and my sister had no notion of the danger." [15]

The essential delusion of this invasion paranoia is supported by the fact that if there were plans for war and invasion, it might well seem that Germany was the beleaguered nation. In 1910 British defence estimates reached £68,000,000, France's reached £52,000,000 and Russia's £7,000,000. Germany's was £64,000,000 and Austria's £17,000,000. Great Britain had fifty-six battleships in commission and under construction, Germany had thirty-three. By 1914 defence estimates in Britain had reached £76,800,000 and France's topped £57,400,000. Germany's reached £110,800,000. Britain had nineteen Dreadnoughts and thirty-nine pre-Dreadnoughts. Germany had thirteen Dreadnoughts and twenty-two pre-Dreadnoughts. The naval expenditure of Germany's potential foes exceeded her own expenditure and that of Austria in the decade prior to the outbreak of war by £461,986,392. Taking military and naval expenditure together, Russia and France had between them spent £229,868,853 more than Germany and her ally on armaments in the period 1905-14.

John Buchan wrote in the dedication to his classic novel of German espionage in these days: 'The wildest fictions are so much less improbable than the facts.' The facts would seem to suggest that it was Germany who was threatened. At the end of the Second World War, when German Foreign Office and military archives were captured and sorted and analysed it was revealed that as late as 1914 there were no plans for an invasion of Britain. In 1914 Bertrand Russell wrote of the 'universal reign of fear' which had caused the system of alliances, 'believed to be a guarantee of peace', which was proving to be a cause of world wide disaster, [16] despite the undisputed fact that with the single exception of a guerilla war against a Hottentot tribe in South West Africa, Germany had been at peace since the Franco-Prussian War.

Nevertheless, the strength and the fascination of the conspiracy myth continued. From the early days of the 1914 War, right up to 1939, spy stories proved successful mass entertainment provided by the film industry - *I Was a Spy, The Man Who Knew Too Much, The Thirty-Nine Steps, Lancer Spy, The Spy in Black, Dark Journey, British Agent, Secret Agent, The Lady Vanishes, Espionage Agent, Confessions of a Nazi Spy* - all seemed to play to a powerful public demand. Hitchcock's version of Buchan's yarn (1935) is a fine example of the genre. It seems he had not even read the original [17] and played to the fears of the time by having baddies talk with upper-class Mosleyite accents. He even wished to insert a whole new sequence showing the underground hangars in the High-lands of Scotland built by the cunning Huns for our destruction. [18]

During the Second World War espionage drama boomed and in-cluded *Foreign Correspondent, Night Train to Munich, Casablanca, The Conspirators, They Came to Blow Up America, Berlin Correspondent, Across the Pacific, Escape to Danger, Ministry of Fear, Continental Agent, Sherlock Holmes and the Secret Weapon, Hotel Reserve.* To reveal that the villains were really enemy agents was an oft repeated trick in films of this kind, especially in comedy thrillers. [19]

In the immediate post-war years two new fashions in spy films became noticeable. [20] With the introduction of the new leading figure, downbeat, neurotic, guilt-torn, often seedy heroes made their appearances for the first time - *Orders to Kill, Hotel Berlin* - while there also appeared the now-it-can-be-told story - *The Man Who Never Was, Diplomatic Courier.* In the opening decade of the Cold War Nazis and Japs were dethroned in favour of 'Reds' - *I Married a Communist, I Was A Communist for the F.B.I.* The mania for spy films spilled over into comedies and gave the world *Gasbags* (with the Crazy Gang), *To Be or Not to Be* (with Jack Benny), *Top Secret* (with George Cole), and, ultimately, *Carry on Spying*. The romantic spy figure re-emerges in the late '50s and reaches his box-office apotheosis in James Bond films, beginning with *Dr. No* in 1963. The film version of Richard Condon's assassination-conspiracy thriller, *The Manchurian Candidate*, was released the previous year, but Fleming's novels fully exploited the world conspiracy theory. Bond clearly owed a great deal to Bulldog Drummond and the Fu Manchu stories, but their avid consumerism, sexism and technological obsession mark them unmistakably a product of their moment.[21] Imitations of Bond were legion and all the leading male stars attempted the genre - Cary Grant in *Charade*, Paul Newman in *Torn Curtain*, Frank Sinatra in *The Naked Runner*, Yul Brynner in *The Double Man* and Robert Vaughn starred in a James Bond-derived American television series, *The Man From U.N.C.L.E.* which lasted from 1964 to 1967. British television series such as *The Avengers* and *The Professionals* further testify to the tenacity of the genre.

Star Wars (1977) was a science fantasy revamp of the same old yarn. Invariably the leading ingredients of these narratives feature a plot by a sinister gang who work for a 'power' - another nation/galaxy/aliens, etc. - an informer on the good side tells the hero, whose integrity is tested and whose task is therefore defined. Post-war fears of Soviet Russia gave *The Lord of the Rings* an amazingly powerful resonance as Tolkien's epic cued itself so smoothly into a long loved archetypal pattern.

The world-view constructed in Reaganite American foreign policy involved a re-awakening to the Soviet 'threat' and the spread of the belief in the Soviet world conspiracy. In Ronald Reagan's own words about the Vietnam War:

"I think we were right to be involved. The problems in South Vietnam weren't just internal affairs, and we weren't there because we were imperialistic, as the communists claimed, or altruistic, as we tried to appear. The plain truth of the matter is that we were there to counter the master plan of the communists for world conquest, and it's a lot easier and safer to counter it 8,000 miles away than to wait until they land in Long Beach."[22]

The view through this transatlantic refraction recently prompted E.P. Thompson to say that it was based on infantile perceptions of political realities:

"derived, I suppose from too much early reading of The Lord of the Rings. The evil kingdom of Mordor lies there ... while on our side lies the nice republic of Eriador, inhabited by confused liberal hobbits who are rescued from time to time by the genial white wizardry of Gandalf figures such as Henry Kissinger, Zbigniew Brzezinski, or, maybe, Richard Allen."

Now although a devout Tolkien fanatic would attempt to pick holes in Thompson's comment by indicating his poor Middle-earth scholarship - Eriador is hardly a republic, it was at one time ruled by the Kings of Arnor; the Hobbits' Shire is but one small region of Eriador and is to some extent a self-governing democratic republic of sorts; Mordor is not a kingdom, etc., etc.-the fact remains that he does seem to be describing a world view in which one kind of manichaeism invokes another. This is the essential nature of the struggles which convulse Middle-earth. [23]

All texts signify, but not all texts are significant. It seems to me that insofar as The Lord of the Rings shapes, textures and conditions the nature of our perceptions of the world we live in, insofar as it is used in negotiating the construction of our realities, then it is extremely significant. It is frankly an impossibility to regard it simply and purely as a fine piece of writing, devoid of political, economic or ideological significance. It cannot be regarded simply as an arrangement of sounds, in spite of some of its advocates who seem anxious so to describe it. [24] It is in the nature of Tolkien's genius that he took an old war-horse like the conspiracy yarn and threw over it a certain medieval charm, decorated lavishly with the trappings of chivalric romance, decked it out with his unique wit and sent it charging out armed with an unmistakable theological force which seemed to identify itself with quite respectable blazonry. This again demonstrates Tolkien's skill in drawing on deep reservoirs of experience which we seldom recognize while reading the words on the page. Yet it is those unconscious hardly identified textual echoes which reinforce the seeming inevitability and God-willed plan for the world which is at the heart of The Lord of the Rings, and renders the 'common sense' world of Tolkien (in Gramsci's phrase) in terms of scriptural authority. [25] Tolkien seems to share a world-view with Evelyn Waugh, a writer he is not usually linked with, but, as David Lodge has pointed out, Waugh accepts the doctrine of original sin and with it the sense of mankind as exiled from a lost Paradise. The Faith is perceived as a haven, an institution under providential guidance in a world where civilization has fallen into decline. These ideas constantly recur in Waugh,[26] even if satirically: *A Handful of Dust* takes its title from Eliot's *The Waste Land* and accepts Eliot's view of modern times, but the basis of the narrative is sexual betrayal, which is basic in the raw kind of Christian mythology Waugh adopted. The New Jerusalem appears to Tony Last during the hallucinations of his fever. Sexual betrayal, the decadence of modern times, and the operation of divine grace are likewise the basis of *Brideshead Revisited*. In a review of Graham Greene's *The Lawless Roads* in the *Spectator* of 10 March 1939 Evelyn Waugh wrote:

"Mr. Greene is, I think, an Augustinian Christian, a believer of the dark age of Mediterranean decadence when the barbarians were passing along the frontiers and the City of God seemed yearly more remote and unattainable."

In the Sunday Times of 16 July 1961 he wrote that for P.G. Wodehouse 'there has been no fall of man....the gardens of Blandings Castle are that original garden from which we are all exiled.' The description of Tony Last's deranged vision in the Brazilian jungle is worth careful regard:

" Looking up from the card table, Tony saw beyond the trees the ramparts and battlements of the City; it was quite near him. From the turret of the gatehouse a heraldic banner floated in the tropic breeze...the sound of music rose from the glittering walls; some procession or pageant was passing along them....The gates were before him and trumpets were sounding along the walls, saluting his arrival; from bastion to bastion the message ran to the four points of the compass; petals of almond and apple blossom were in the air; they carpeted the way, as, after a summer storm, they lay in the orchards at Hetton. Gilded cupolas and spires of alabaster shone in the sunlight. [27]

Of course Waugh writes as a satiric ironist, and the imitation of Bunyan and *Revelations* are almost carried to the level of parody.[28]

In *The Lord of the Rings* it is all played straight, played for all it is worth, and is spread over several pages of highly wrought prose.[29] *The Return of the King* moves slowly to its climax:

" And so they stood on the walls of the City of Gondor, and a great wind rose and blew, and their hair, raven and golden, streamed out mingling in the air. And the Shadow departed, and the Sun was unveiled, and light leaped forth; and the waters of Anduin shone like silver, and in all the houses of the City men sang for the joy that welled up in their hearts from what source they could not tell...."

After the appearance of the great Eagle bearing tidings from the Lords of the West which cause the people to sing in all the ways of the City, it begins to grow and build up in the manner of a Rossini crescendo:

"The days that followed were golden, and Spring and Summer joined and made revel together in the fields of Gondor. And tidings now came by swift riders from Cair Andros of all that was done, and the City made ready for the coming of the King...."

The prose now takes on a rather self-conscious antique glint and moves with stilted syntax reminiscent of the King James Bible:

" All things were now made ready in the City; and there was great concourse of people, for the tidings had gone out into all parts of Gondor, from Min-Rimmon even to Pinnath Gelin and the far coasts of the sea; and all that could come to the City made haste to come. And the City was filled again with women and fair children that returned to their homes laden with flowers; and from Dol Amroth came the harpers that harped most skilfully in all the land; and there were players upon viols and upon flutes and upon horns of silver, and clear-voiced singers from the vales of Lebennin. At last an evening came when from the walls the pavilion could be seen upon the field, and all night lights were burning as men watched for the dawn. And when the sun rose in the clear morning above the mountains in the East, upon which shadows lay no more, then all the bells rang, and all the banners broke and flowed in the wind.... "

The great moment arrives and Aragorn shows himself:

"But when Aragorn arose all that beheld him gazed in silence, for it seemed to them that he was revealed to them now for the first time. Tall as the sea-kings of old, he stood above all that were near; ancient of days he seemed and yet in the flower of manhood; and wisdom sat upon his brow, and strength and healing were in his hands, and a light was about him."

As Faramir cries 'Behold the King', at that moment

" all the trumpets were blown, and the King Elessar went forth and came to the barrier...and amid the music of harp and of viol and of flute and the singing of clear voices the King passed through the flower-laden streets, and came to the Citadel, and entered in; and the banner of the Tree and the Stars was unfurled upon the topmost tower...."

What is important here is the effect of applying the imprimatur of almost divine revelation upon a set of values and social assumptions implicit if not explicit throughout *The Lord of the Rings* which are well worth exploring and deserve properly to be questioned.

NOTES

1.   Cf. Paul Bouissac, 'The Meaning of Nonsense,' in Ino Rossi (ed.), *The Logic of Culture: Advances in Structural Theory and Methods* (London: Tavistock, 1982), pp. 202-3, for an hypothesis similar to the meta-cultural phenomena I am trying to identify in *The Lord of the Rings*. See also Janet Wolff, *Aesthetics and the Sociology of Art* (London: Allen & Unwin, 1983), pp. 49 and following.

2.   See Lucy Bland, Trisha McCabe and Frank Mort, 'Sexuality and Reproduction: Three "Official" Instances', in Michele Barrett, Philip Corrigan, Annette Kuhn and Janet Wolff (eds.), *Ideology and Cultural Production* (London: Croom Helm, 1979), pp. 78 and following; and cf. Naomi Weisstein, ' Psychology Constructs the Female', in *The Norton Reader: An Anthology of Expository Prose*, edited by Arthur M. Eastman (New York: Norton & Co., 1973), pp. 1010 and following. See Kenneth Plummer, *Sexual Stigma: An Interactionist Account* (London, 1975), pp. 5-8 and 23 and following, and P.L. Berger, *Invitation to Sociology: A Humanist Perspective* (London: Penguin, 1966), pp. 180 and following: 'Sexual roles are constructed within the same general precariousness that marks the entire social fabric. Cross cultural comparisons of sexual conduct bring home to us powerfully the near flexibility that men (sic) are capable of in organizing their lives in this area ...'

3.   John Berger, *Ways of Seeing* (London: Penguin/B.B.C., 1972), pp. 134-37.

4.   Robert Giddings and Elizabeth Holland, *J.R.R. Tolkien: The Shores of Middle-earth* (London: Junction Books, 1981), pp. 58, 62, 63, 94-8, 138-39, 230-31.

5.   See Christopher Caudwell, *Illusion and Reality* (New York: International Publishers, 1973), pp. 125-27; Raymond Williams, *The Country and the City* (London: Paladin, 1975), pp. 18 and following; and cf. Robert Giddings, 'A Myth Riding By', in *New Society*, 7 December 1978, and Richard Norton Taylor, *Whose Land Is It Anyway? - Agriculture, Planning and Land Use in the British Countryside* (Northamptonshire: Turnstone Press, 1983), pp. 269 and following. The destruction of the unique character of the British countryside is the subject of Marion Shoard's

provoking book, *The Theft of the Countryside* (London: Temple Smith, 1980). The contemporary fascination with the past is discussed on pp. 178 and following.

6.   George H. Ford (ed.) *Victorian Fiction: A Second Guide to Research* (New York: Modern Language Association of America, 1978), p. 34.

7.   See Robert Giddings and Elizabeth Holland, op. cit., pp. 7-9.

8.   Bob Dixon, *Catching Them Young: Political Ideas in Children's Fiction* (London: Pluto Press, 1978), p. 149.

9.   See Umberto Eco, 'The Narrative Structure in Fleming', in Tony Bennett and Graham Martin (eds.), *Popular Culture: Past and Present* (London: Croom Helm, 1982), pp. 242-62.

10.   Roland Barthes, *Essais Critiques* (Paris, 1964), p.. 156, in *Critical Essays* (Northwestern University Press, 1972); see also Diana Laurenson and Alan Swingewood, *The Sociology of Literature* (London: Paladin, 1972), pp. 11-12; and Pierre Macherey, *A Theory of Literary Production*, translated by Geoffrey Wall (London: Routledge and Kegan Paul, 1978), pp. 32-40.

11.   Erskine Childers, *The Riddle of the Sands* (London: Penguin, 1978), pp. 320-21.

12.   Childers, op. cit., pp. 304-5.

13.   Terry Eagleton, 'Form, Ideology and "The Secret Agent"', in Diana Laurenson (ed.), *The Sociology of Literature: Applied Studies* (University of Keele: Sociological Review Monograph, 1978), p. 55.

14.   J.B. Priestley, *The Edwardians* (London: Heinemann, 1970), p. 88.

15.   Claud Cockburn, *Cockburn Sums Up* (London: Quarto, 1981), pp. 1-2.

16.   E.D. Morel, *Truth and the War* (London: National Labour Press, 1916), pp. 161 and following.

17.   *Grierson on the Movies*, edited by Forsyth Hardy (London: Faber, 1981), p. 165.

18.   John Russell Taylor, *Hitch: The Life and Work of Alfred Hitchcock* (London: Faber, 1978), p. 129; see also K.R.M. Short (ed.), *Feature Films as History* (London: Croom and Helm, 1981), p. 103.

19.   *Halliwell's Filmgoer's Companion*, 7th edition (London: Granada, 1980), p. 616.

20.   Ibid.

21.   Robert Blair Kaiser, 'The Case is Still Open', in Peter Dale Scott, Paul L. Hoch and Russell Stetler (eds.), *The Assassinations: Dallas and Beyond: A Guide to Cover-Ups and Investigations* (New York: Vintage, 1976), pp. 330-31.

22.   *Ronald Reagan's Call to Action* (New York: Warner, 1976), p. 40.

23.   'America's Europe: A Hobbit Among Gandalfs', in *Nation*, 24 January 1981. I am indebted to Jessica Yates of the Tolkien Society for bringing this to my attention.

24.   This was the claim made in a radio broadcast by Humphrey Carpenter. In conversation with Michael Oliver he said: 'You must remember that Tolkien's professional work was concerned really, technically at least, with language rather than with literature and really all his literary academic work, his edition of *Sir Gawain and the Green Knight*, his lectures on *Beowulf* and on the *Ancrine Wisse*, and things like that, these are almost thrown off by a detailed study of the language so the academic work gets spun from the language, now so did the imaginative writings. He often said that he found it hard to convince people that *The Lord of the Rings*

had really grown from a wish to express certain aesthetic linguistic preferences, by which he meant that he wanted to create a world in which it was possible for certain sounds to exist. Now those sounds exist in fact, manifest themselves in his books as the various elvish language is spoken by elves in the stories and they are the centre of it, he begun to make up these languages when he was in his teens and the language has developed so much and so fast they required a history and a habitation so again it was the imaginative writing that sprang from the language' (*Kaleidoscope*, B.B.C. Radio Four, 2 January 1981).

25.   *Selections from the Prison Notebooks of Antonio Gramsci*, edited and translated by Quintin Hoare and Geoffrey Nowell Smith (London: Lawrence and Wishart, 1971), pp. 326 and following.

26.   David Lodge, *Working With Structuralism* (London: Routledge and Kegan Paul, 1981), pp. 136 and following.

27.   Evelyn Waugh, *A Handful of Dust* (London: Penguin, 1983), p. 203.

28.   Cf. John Bunyan, *The Pilgrim's Progress* (London: Penguin, 1976), pp. 202 and following, and the *Bible Designed to be Read as Literature*, edited and arranged by Ernest Sutherland Bates (London: Heinemann, 1963), pp. 1224 and following.

29.   J.R.R. Tolkien, *The Lord of the Rings, 3. The Return of the King* (London: Unwin Paperbacks, 1974), pp. 212 and following.

VIII

Scott Fitzgerald in Hollywood: The Writer as Projectionist

Several modern writers have successfully turned themselves into screen writers — R.C. Sherriff, who achieved fame with his stage play *Journey's End* in 1929, went on to write brilliant screenplays for Alexander Korda. Aldous Huxley, famous as a novelist, went to Hollywood and wrote the screen version of *Pride and Prejudice*. Frederic Raphael earned his name as a novelist before writing such worthy screenplays as *Far From the Madding Crowd* and *The Glittering Prizes*. Scott Fitzgerald worked in Hollywood as a scriptwriter and was not a resounding success, yet his unfinished novel *The Last Tycoon* has enormous importance in the story of literary production, as it examines cinema as industry and film as a means of telling stories.

"Please do not turn on the clouds until the show starts. Be sure the stars are turned off when leaving." - Notice on the backstage switchboard of the Paradise Theatre, Farubault, Minnesota. Quoted in Ben M. Hall, THE GOLDEN AGE OF THE MOVIE PALACE: THE BEST REMAINING SEATS (1961)

"Irving Thalberg carried with him the accoutrements of an artist; hence he was unique in the Hollywood of he period. I don't know of anyone else who has occupied the position. He was like a young pope." - Budd Schulberg

It has become widely accepted that Fitzgerald was at his best when writing about experiences known and observed first-hand. In no respect has this been more alleged than in the matter of the Jazz Age, Fitzgerald as its celebrant and victim and in whose 'Jazz Age' fiction and essays (especially as collected in *The Crack-Up*) the very essence of American history, the decades of the 1920s and 1930s at least, apparently, had been caught on the wing. This may have started out as a way of praising Fitzgerald, but it has produced its problems. Was Fitzgerald the master or the servant of his materials? Other than in *The Great Gatsby* (1925), by common agreement his one sure masterpiece, did he in truth write as more than the chronicler, the historical painter of his period? And more to immediate purposes, when the issue is *The Last Tycoon* - admittedly unfinished at his death in 1940 - which so conspicuously takes for its central figure of Monroe Starr a model literally as large (if not more so) as life, the studio mogul Irving Thalberg (1899-1936), can it be said that Fitzgerald not only kept but mastered his imaginative distance?

Arthur Mizener usefully set out Fitzgerald's own exhilaration at the prospect of writing *The Last Tycoon:*

"Less than a year before his death, when he began the actual writing of *The Last Tycoon*, he was filled once more with the old, irrepressible excitement; you can hear it in the letter he wrote his daughter; 'Scottina: ... Look! I have begun to write something that is maybe **great** ... It may not **make** us a cent but it will pay expenses and it is the first labor of love I've undertaken since the first part of 'Infidelity!' " [1]

Mizener goes on to speak of *The Last Tycoon* as indeed fulfilling Fitzgerald's hopes, and essentially because, as always with Fitzgerald at his best, it offers not 'social history or even nostalgically evocative social history' but 'the history of a consciousness'. Fitzgerald, in other words, whatever the temptation to see this last novel as overwhelmingly tied only to its time and place and Hollywood materials, manages infinitely more. A torso only *The Last Tycoon* may be, but on my estimate at least, it truly ranks among Fitzgerald's most glittering prizes, and precisely in how it takes the 'life' figure of Thalberg, whose mogulship Fitzgerald had every occasion to observe in his Hollywood script-writing days, and transforms aspects of him into Monroe Stahr. So that one immediately says yes, Monroe Stahr **is** Irving Thalberg, but yes, also, and mercifully, he is so much more, a portrait - a fiction - indeed as 'maybe great' as Fitzgerald so fervently hoped he had it within him to create. And one also says that *The Last Tycoon* goes beyond even that, beyond any one figure or phase of American history, into a vision of how Art, as Fitzgerald conceived it, might 'project' History itself.

But to return first to Thalberg: his life has not wanted for documentation. Witness, for example, Samuel Marx, *Mayer and Thalberg: The Make-Believe Saints* (1975), Bosley Crowther, *Hollywood Rajah: The Life and Times of Louis B. Mayer* (1960) and Bob Thomas, *Thalberg: Life and*

Legend (1969). It all makes for fabulous reading. It is openly acknowl-edged that although Thalberg's name was technically not part of the company's title, he was the real driving force and elemental genius which made Metro-Goldwyn-Mayer the prosperous empire which it had become by the opening years of the 1930s.

And what an empire it was! It was the largest of the 124 subsidiaries owned by the huge conglomerate founded by Marcus Loew, the Austral-ian-American tycoon, Loew's Incorporated. Its plant in Culver City, California, covered fifty-three acres and was valued at $2,000,000. Its stars were paid $6,000 a week. It boasted the highest paid writing staff in the business with a payroll of $40,000 a week. Its parkland could be turned into anything required from battlefields to palace gardens. It had twenty-two sound stages and twenty-two projection rooms. Its films made the most money in the trade, each movie costing on average about $500,000. A billion people annually paid some $100,000,000 worldwide to go and see the products turned out by Metro-Goldwyn-Mayer. It could boast it had more stars than there were in Heaven - including Greta Garbo, Clark Gable, John Gilbert, Spencer Tracy, Lewis Stone, Laurel and Hardy, the Barrymores, Lon Chaney, Wallace Beery, Joan Crawford, William Powell, the Marx Brothers, Franchot Tone and Norma Shearer - and among its first productions were *The Big Parade, Anna Christie, Grand Hotel, Ben Hur, The Thin Man* and *Mutiny on the Bounty.* These were not all produced during Irving Thalberg's period with Metro-Goldwyn-Mayer. He died in 1936, before the making of such money-spinning commodities as *Goodbye Mr. Chips* and *The Wizard of Oz,* which are such typical products of Culver City's active imperialism.

The company originated from Loew's which was initially an exhibiting company which bought into Metro Pictures in 1920. Immediately afterwards it produced two extremely successful films - *The Four Horse-men of the Apocalypse* in 1921, directed by Rex Ingram, which introduced Rudolph Valentino as a star, and *The Prisoner of Zenda* in the following year, again directed by Rex Ingram, with Lewis Stone and Ramon Navarro. By 1925 it had merged with the Goldwyn production company and been joined by Louis B. Mayer Pictures. Mayer epitomized the American dream. He was a Jewish refugee from Russian persecution who had crawled from the very bottom of the pile to the very top of executive power. Early in his career he had sold junk and this was a reputation he was to carry with him forever, whether he deserved it or not. He said himself, 'Look out for yourself or they'll pee on your grave', but he probably would accept Bob Hope's famous comment as his most fitting epitaph: 'Louis B. Mayer came west in the early days with twenty-eight dollars, a box camera, and an old lion. He built a monument to himself - the Bank of America.' Herman Mankiewicz, the scriptwriter immortally associated with *Citizen Kane,* was less generous: 'There but for the grace of God, goes God.' Nevertheless with Mayer as its production head the company thrived, though stories of his tyranny are infamous, including his physical violence upon the persons of Charlie Chaplin, Robert Taylor and John Gilbert, and his emotional violence upon the likes of Myrna Loy, for whom he faked a heart attack in order to blackmail her into playing a particular role. He lay on the floor murmuring: 'No ... No ... Don't play the part, Myrna ... I understand. Please don't play the part ... I understand ... People will only say you played it so as to please a sick man.' She went on her knees to him and begged to be allowed the role she had originally refused. He reluctantly gave in as a doctor was called to his side. When she had left his office, Mayer leaped up from the floor and yelled 'Well, who's next?' and continued to keep his business appointments. Mayer dominated Metro-Goldwyn-Mayer for a quarter of a century. But this was the strange business world into which the frail but determined Irving Thalberg, original of Scott Fitzgerald's Monroe Stahr, entered as a young man. He was to provide the artistic flair, the cultivated and sophisticated tone, to counterbalance Mayer's shrewd understanding of mass public appetites.

During the early years of the decade following the Wall Street crash it has been estimated that Irving Thalberg was paid $500,000 a year, partly the result of a generous bonus system on Metro-Goldwyn-Mayer's productions. He worked very hard for it. His business methods and habits were strange, but they earned huge dividends. The Metro-Goldwyn-Mayer executive offices were a white wooden building, and Thalberg's office was on the second floor. He had a private projection room which had three desks, a couple of pianos and about thirty armchairs. He was seldom there before 10 a.m. But once there he devoted all his energies into ensuring that the company produced the best films in the world. His life story is another version of the American myth of the ordinary guy who makes it to the top of the tree. After leaving high school in Brooklyn, he worked as an office boy in Universal Pictures, where he had been 'discovered' by Carl Laemle, Snr., who was an executive producer, associated particularly with the success of *All Quiet on the Western Front* in 1930.

Thalberg's major business activity seemed to be talk and he used words quietly, sacredly and preciously, almost like a poet. He was fragile in appearance and less than 5' 2" in height. He used his hands to great effect when he spoke and was given to pacing up and down his office with his hands clasped behind his back when deep in thought. His voice was always calm and contained, as if he was determined to be sparing in its use. The items noticeable on his desk were his dictaphone, a large box of cigarettes which he never opened, plates of apples and dates which he frequently dipped into and many bottles of medicine. He did not give out the impression of massively good and robust health.

All those who have written about the professional qualities possessed and employed by Irving Thalberg agree that two particular qualities were outstanding: his ability to deal thoroughly with all aspects of motion picture production, and his ability to come up with ideas. To an outsider the activities of a typical day in Thalberg's working life might seem to lack cohesion and purpose. But he knew what he was doing, and the industry knew that he knew. Mae D. Huettig gives a reasonable account of what he actually seemed to do for a living:

" There is naturally no chance that Mr. Thalberg's activities will fall into routine. His efforts follow no pattern whatsoever, except that theyconsist almost exclusively of talk. He deals with actors, whose simple wants of avarice or vanity he finds it easy to appease. He deals with writers, with whom he seldom commits the unpardonable blunder of saying: 'I don't like it, but I don't know why.' He is ceaselessly aware of Delores Del Rio's gifted husband, Cedric Gibbons, who designs MGM scenery, and of the tall, twittering hunchback of Adrain, who drapes MGM's loveliest bodies. He deals with M.E. Greenwood, the gaunt studio manager, who used to be an Arizona faro dealer and now tells MGM's New York office how much the company has spent every week and how much to place on deposit for MGM's account at the Culver City branch of Bank of America. Through Mr. Greenwood. and sometimes more directly, Irving Thalberg observes the two thousand of the skilled but unsung: 'grips', assistant cameramen, 'mixers', cutters, projectionists, carpenters, unit managers, artisans, seamstresses, scene painters. Often he calls a group of these underlings into the projection room to consider pictures with him."[2]

But none of this Thalberg-supervised activity would have existed had it not been for the ideas which were the genesis of all movies. Here Thalberg's genius was even more apparent, his mind a seeming fount of good basic scripting ideas as well as brilliant ideas about points of detail.

Thalberg could sense the basic need at the very core and centre of a movie; it was his idea to borrow Tallulah Bankhead from Paramount to give much needed zest to *Tinfoil*. *Rasputin and the Empress* (1932) gave Lionel Barrymore one of his biggest and best roles, but it was Thalberg's idea to have the movie directed by Richard Boleslavsky, the Polish stage director who came to Hollywood in 1930 from the Moscow Arts Theatre (he went on to direct *The Painted Veil, Clive of India* and *Les Miserables*). It was Thalberg who recognized and exploited the particular gifts of Howard Hawks, who had been in the industry since 1918 and who had become a household name certainly from *Scarface* 1932 on; Hawks had a penchant for grainy realism and action-packed drama as well as very polished and professional comedies. (He made *The Criminal Code* for Thalberg in 1931.) He encouraged the very cosmopolitan talents of Sidney Franklin, who directed *Beverly of Graustark* (1926), *The Last of Mrs Cheyney* (1929), *Private Lives* (1931), *Smiling Through* (1932), *The Guardsman* (1932) and *The Barretts of Wimpole Street* (1933) and went on to produce the immortal *Mrs. Miniver* in 1942. The many-sided W.S. Van Dyke was another director in Thalberg's stable, whose films included *White Shadows in the South Seas* (1928), *Trader Horn* (1931), shot on safari in Africa, *Tarzan the Ape Man* (1932), which introduced the greatest of all ape-men, the former Olympic athlete Johnny Weissmuller, *Manhattan Melodrama* (1934) and the still very impressive disaster movie prototype, *San Francisco* (1936). Sam Wood, director of *A Night at the Opera* and *A Day at the Races*, who had a gift for football and college pictures and left his mark on *Goodbye Mr. Chips* (1939) and directed the future president of the United States in *Kings Row* in 1942, was another of Thalberg's favourites. Edgar Selwyn, master of soggy melodrama, who directed such films as *Night Life of New York, The Girl in the Show, War Nurse, The Sin of Madelon Claudet, Turn Back the Clock* and *The Mystery of Mr. X*, is additional evidence of Thalberg's range of interests, as was Tod Browning, who made his name directing early masterpieces of the cinema's gothic horrors: *The Unholy Three, London After Midnight, Dracula* and *Freaks*.[3] A director whose talents and inclinations might have seemed the most suited to Thalberg's taste was Clarence Brown, who specialized in rather fussy period subjects - *The Last of the Mohicans, Anna Christie, Anna Karenina* - but who showed a very sure touch in such dramas as *Goosewoman* (1925), which is still considered a picture of immense stature and authority and contains a brilliant performance by Marie Dressler as a retired opera singer who unwittingly implicates her own son in a murder case. Irving Thalberg seemed able to work harmoniously with these versatile creative talents. But as well as exercising his diplomacy in dealing with these lofty persons, he could also deal with minute details of finance, committee work, casting, preparing and supervising scripts, conferring with his team of writers and resolving the numerous minor and not so minor industrial disputes between personnel during day-to-day production activities. All this was done with little external sign of anxiety or neurosis. He briefly developed one irritating habit which was soon cured. His therapeutic rolling of a twenty-dollar gold coin on his desk top during discussions was immediately cured by ridiculous satirical imitation by his colleagues.

Notoriously, Thalberg's day did not end at 5 p.m. The day's toiling over, the bargains all struck (J.B. Priestley wanted $50,000 for *The Good Companions* - Thalberg got it off him for half the price), Irving Thalberg drove back to his mansion at Santa Monica overlooking the Pacific Ocean where he pored over scripts and watched Metro-Goldwyn-Mayer movies in his sitting room. He lived and died for the movies and nothing else seemed to interest him very much. He was married to Norma Shearer, star of *The Barretts of Wimpole Street* and *Romeo and Juliet*. His dying words seem humdrum enough: 'Don't let the children forget me.' But we shall not look on his like again. As Gene Fowler remarked: 'On the way down, I saw Thalberg's shoes in the hall, and no one has filled them.'

The remarkable thing about his treatment at the hands of Scott Fitzgerald in *The Last Tycoon* is the fact that very little of this is captured at all in the character of Monroe Stahr. What Fitzgerald preferred to do was to focus exclusively on just one or two aspects of Thalberg's character as far as it was revealed in his professional life and to work these facets up into very high definition. His identification of these particular aspects of Thalberg's personality, considering that he knew the Hollywood tycoon personally and professionally, tells us a great deal about Fitzgerald, even though the book may in fact do less than justice to Irving Thalberg.

The Last Tycoon is not a thinly disguised biography of Irving Thalberg. Although it deals with a leading figure in the motion picture industry, it is not even really about films. To read *The Last Tycoon* properly we must be careful not to mistake the evidence, impressive and convincing though much of it is, for the case Fitzgerald wanted to present. This fragment may only partially be described as 'his unfinished novel of Hollywood'.[4] For this mistaken emphasis, among several other things, we have Edmund Wilson to thank. [5] It is certainly the case that we are led into the novel's major themes by means of constant references to an omnipresent Hollywood right from the start:

" Though I haven't ever been on the screen I was brought up in pictures. Rudolph Valentino came to my fifth birthday party - or so I was told. I put this down only to indicate that even before the age of reason I was in a position to watch the wheels go round.

I was going to write my memoirs once, *The Producer's Daughter*, but at eighteen you never quite get round to anything like that. It's just as well - it would have been as flat as an old column of Lolly Parsons. My father was in the picture business as another man might be in cotton or steel ... I accepted Hollywood with the resignation of a ghost assigned to a haunted house. I knew what you were supposed to think about it but I was obstinately unhorrified."[6]

Thus (and more) Cecilia Brady, college educated daughter of Monroe Stahr's partner in Hollywood. At the opening of the book we are given the traditional stereotypical view of the Hollywood producer. It is significantly embedded in an anecdote of Wylie White's:

"Listen, Cecilia: I once had an affair with the wife of a producer. A very short affair. When it was over she said to me in no uncertain terms, she said: 'Don't you ever tell about this or I'll have you thrown out of Hollywood. My husband's a much more important man than you!' "[7]

We cannot help but contrast this with the first impression of Monroe Stahr we are given only a few pages on. He is not presentedd as a money-mad mogul, crazy with his own power, but as a man with an almost magnetically spiritual quality about him. Cecilia falls over him accidentally, but there is a symbolic dimension here. She would easily fall for him.

He was a man, she says, that any girl would go for with no encouragement at all. They would not be able to help it. They would be drawn to him. As his dark eyes look at her she wonders what they would look like if he was to fall in love:

"They were kind, aloof and, though they often reasoned with you gently, somewhat superior. It was no fault of theirs if they saw so much. He darted in and out of the role of 'one of the boys' with dexterity - but on the whole I should say he wasn't one of them. But he knew how to shut up, how to draw into the background, how to listen. From where he stood (and though he was not a tall man, it always seemed high up) he watched the multitudinous practicalities of his world like a proud young shepherd to whom night and day had never mattered ...."[8]

Stahr is a mysterious figure. Initially he hides himself behind the mundane name 'Smith', but this only temporarily masks his star quality. Fitzgerald is at pains when introducing him to stress his superior attributes: he seems tall, even though he may not be; he has dark, mysterious eyes; qualities of gentle superiority are emphasized; he is in the world, yet not really part of it, as he watches the multitudinous practicalities proudly like a shepherd. He has a god-like indifference to night and day as he seems removed from the passing of time which affects other mortals. As he twists the ring on his finger it seems to have a magical effect on Cecilia, who comes to believe that she has been rendered invisible. She can barely summon the power to address so charged a being: 'I never dared look quite away from him or quite at him ... and I knew he affected many other people in the same manner.'[9]

His figure is a strange combination of the ethereal and the pugnacious. She reflects how the bulky ring on his finger contrasts with his delicate fingers and slender body. He has a slender face and arched eyebrows. His hair is dark and curly:

"He looked spiritual at times, but he was a fighter - somebody out of his past knew him when he was one of a gang of kids in the Bronx, and gave me a description of how he walked always at the head of his gang, this rather frail boy, occasionally throwing a command backward out of the corner of his mouth."[10]

Monroe Stahr is a Prince, an aristocrat among robber barons and warlords. He seems to stand for a particular set of values which include personal courage, skills and expertise, professionalism and ambition combined, but buffed and polished with sophistication, delicacy and refinement. He has all the American virtues, but they are refined to an almost aristocratic essence. But there is a very important element in this aristocratic personality as presented in Scott Fitzgerald's hero: he is not a patron of the arts, he is a creative person. This seems to interest Fitzgerald very much in his portrait of the last tycoon. Yes, it is undeniable that Stahr works for the motion picture industry, whose job it is to provide entertainment for the masses, but he is emphatically not presented to us merely as an executive of the industry. He is a man who expresses the essence of himself in what he does: he is an artist. Much of the essential Monroe Stahr is revealed in his relationship with the writer, George Boxley. This is particularly true of the scene where Stahr explains to Boxley how films tell stories and indicates that film is not a narrative medium which apes printed literature; it is a language of its own, with its own vocabulary, grammar and syntax, **its own way of telling you things.** Significantly, Boxley is British, with all the associations of history, tradition and an old-fashioned way of doing things which far too many Americans mistake automatically for 'class' and 'quality'. Typically, Boxley the novelist tends to despise the modern means of cultural production which feeds him and pays his mortgage and his other living expenses. Boxley feels that he is the victim of a conspiracy, that the 'hacks' who work with him on film scripting have a vocabulary of a mere few hundred words. Stahr tells him that the trouble with what he writes is that it is not appropriate to the medium he is writing for: 'it was just talk, back and forth ... Interesting talk but nothing more.'

Boxley finds this insulting. How dare this American film executive, this example of senior management whose concern is the proper control of finance and budgeting, tell him, the established British novelist, how to write?

" I don't think you people read things. The men are duelling when the conversation takes place. At the end one of them falls into a well and has to be hauled up in a bucket." [11]

Monroe Stahr rightly perceives that Boxley would consider writing for the movies cheap and vulgar, something beneath his real dignity as a **writer.** Part of the trouble is that Boxley himself does not even go to the movies. Why does he feel that way about the movies? Because people are always duelling and falling down wells 'and wearing strange facial expressions and talking incredible and unnatural dialogue'. But Stahr has brought Boxley to Hollywood because he wants his films to be properly written. He is employing him as a professional writer, but he must not be so proud as to feel superior to the very matter he is expected to write:

"Slip the dialogue for a minute ... Granted your dialogue is more graceful than what these hacks can write - that's why we brought you out here. But let's imagine something that isn't either bad dialogue or jumping down a well. Has your office got a stove in it that lights with a match? "

Boxley seems to think that it has, but he never uses it. Never mind, says Stahr, imagine that you are in your office:

"You've been fighting duels or writing all day and you're too tired to fight or write any more. You're sitting there staring - dull, like we all get sometimes. A pretty stenographer that you've seen before comes into the room and you watch her - idly. She doesn't see you, though you're very close to her. She takes off her gloves, opens her purse and dumps it out on a table -." [12]

Stahr stands up and tosses his key-ring on the desk. Boxley listens as he goes on:

"She has two dimes and a nickel - and a cardboard matchbox. She leaves the nickel on the desk, puts the two dimes back into her purse and takes her black gloves to the stove, opens it and puts them inside. There is one match in the matchbox and she starts to light it kneeling by the stove. You notice that there's a stiff wind blowing in the window - but just then your telephone rings. The girl picks it up, says hello - listens - and says deliberately into the phone, 'I've never owned a pair of black gloves in my life.' She hangs up, kneels by the stove again, and just as she lights the match, you glance around very suddenly and see that there's another man in the office, watching every move the girl makes -" [13]

Here Monroe Stahr pauses again, and picks up his keys and puts them in his pocket. Boxley is really interested now and asks what happens next? Stahr replies: 'I don't know ... I was just making pictures.' Boxley then attempts to indicate that he was not really interested, merely curious. It was just a 'melodrama' he says. Stahr replies:

"Not necessarily ... In any case, nobody has moved violently or talked cheap dialogue or had any facial expression at all. There was only one bad line, and a writer like you could improve it. But you were interested.[14]

This is a key moment in Fitzgerald's portrait of Stahr. It gives Stahr the artist, the creator, the man who makes things. It is of overriding importance to grasp this point as it is vital in the character construction of the leading figure in *The Last Tycoon*, and the novelist's investigation of the value system he has undertaken depends wholly on the use he makes of particular qualities selected from his observations of 'the boy wonder' - Irving Thalberg. Monroe Stahr is a man who is clearly aware that in his daily work as a man who wants to make motion pictures of quality for the mass market which depends on the Hollywood studio system, he must negotiate the best relationship he can between the creative and the productive elements of the industry. Fitzgerald establishes this as a central problem for Monroe Stahr, as it was to him and as it was to Shakespeare, and Dickens and Trollope and D.H. Lawrence and the entire host of imaginative and sensitive and insightful storytellers before Scott Fitzgerald's time.

The writer - like the film maker - is immediately faced in modern times with a complex of relationships between himself and what he wants to tell the world (the stuff of literature) and the means of literary production - economic, technical, cultural and social - which have to be resolved as harmoniously as possible. No modern writer is able directly to address his audience. Monroe Stahr, the great film tycoon, stands emblematically for the figure of the storyteller in his relationship with the means of production and distribution on which the survival of literature depends. The strength and fascination of Fitzgerald's Monroe Stahr is the result not of his having based him on Irving Thalberg whom he knew in Hollywood, etc., etc. but in what Stahr stands for. This conversation with George Boxley brilliantly demonstrates Stahr's understanding of how man-made art works on the imagination. But he also understands, as a later discussion with Boxley shows, how important is the relationship between the artist and the means of production. These matters cannot be left to chance. The artist must understand them if he is fully to realize himself as an artist. It is no good feeling superior to them. **The economics and the technology of artistic production are as important as the creative and imaginative aspects of art.**

In the greatest art, they become one and the same thing, and the greatest writers understand this - to the positive advantage of their development as artists in realizing the potential of the means to communicate what they have to say. [15]

Monroe Stahr puts this case to Boxley in the hope that the novelist will understand what motion pictures can do: suppose you were in a chemist's shop, buying medicine for a relative who was very ill, then whatever caught your attention through the window and distracted you would be material for pictures. Such as a murder outside the window, asks Boxley. Stahr implies that in motion pictures there is not always the necessity to pile into melodrama at the first possible opportunity. It might be a spider, working on the pane:

" 'Of course - I see.' 'I'm afraid you don't, Mr. Boxley. You see it for **your** medium, but not for ours. You keep the spiders for yourself and you try to pin the murders on us.' "
'I might as well leave,' says Boxley. 'I'm no good to you. I've been here three weeks and I've accomplished nothing. I make suggestions, but no one writes them down.'
'I want you to stay. Something in you doesn't like pictures, doesn't like telling a story this way - '
'It's such a damn bother,' exploded Boxley. 'You can't let yourself go - ' " [16]
As he speaks, Boxley realizes that Stahr was a helmsman with many matters to take into account in steering a true course. He senses the stiff wind that must be sensibly battled against and the creaking of the rigging of a ship sailing in great awkward tacks along an open sea. Another analogy Fitzgerald uses is the feeling Boxley has that they are in a huge quarry where even the newly cut marble bears the tracery of old pediments and half-obliterated inscriptions from the past:

" 'I keep wishing you could start over,' Boxley said. 'It's this mass production.'

'That's the condition,' said Stahr. 'There's always some lousy condition. We're making a life of Rubens - suppose I asked you to do portraits of rich dopes like Billy Brady and me and Gary Cooper ... when you wanted to paint Jesus Christ! Wouldn't you feel you had a condition? Our condition is that we have to take people's own favourite folklore and dress it up and give it back to them. Anything beyond that is sugar. So won't you give us some   sugar, Mr. Boxley?'" [17]

This seems to me a very good summing up of the assumptions Irving Thalberg had about the motion picture industry. He once said: 'The medium will eventually take its place as art because there is no other medium of interest to so many people.' [18] These are qualities of an ideal nature which Fitzgerald strongly indicates in his portrait of Monroe Stahr, and make him at once a powerful and vigorous figure, yet one prone to destruction. It is important to note the symbolic use Fitzgerald makes of leading figures taken from American history in this novel as well as in others - *Tender is the Night*, for example, with its echoes of Ulysses Grant. [19]

Fitzgerald was considerably influenced by his reading of the historical works of Henry Adams (1838-1918) whom the novelist knew personally. Adams was educated at Harvard and studied law in Germany. He taught history at Harvard for a time and published *The History of the United States During The Administration of Thomas Jefferson and James Madison* (1889-91). In much the same way as another major American writer - T.S. Eliot - Adams found modern times disturbing and believed civilization was about to disintegrate. Like Eliot, he, too, looked to the Middle Ages for that harmony and permanence he found lacking in the twentieth century. This is the essential theme of Adams's *Mont-Saint-Michel and Chartres* (1904). General Grant was Adams's hope for maintaining liberalism, virtue and humanism in modern America. Grant was elected president, Adams believed, because he stood for moral order against the rising tide of greed, mammonism and anarchy. Adams came to see in Grant's two terms of office - 1868-72 and 1872-76 - a surrender of moral and political virtue to those very forces of materialism and corruption that he so feared would destroy the American nation. It is of considerable significance that Fitzgerald compares Dick Diver to Grant, and shows that he, like Adams's failed hero, succumbed to temptation when he found himself surrounded with the wealthy and socially distinguished. Like Grant, Diver is a dreamer destroyed by realities which he is too frail to combat. [20] In the character of Monroe Stahr Fitzgerald again draws on American history to provide symbolic texture to his themes.

Two other outstanding figures from the nation's history in this respect add conspicuous gravity to the thematic structure of *The Last Tycoon*:

Andrew Jackson and Abraham Lincoln. Jackson is introduced quite early in the book as the group of ill-assorted characters stranded by transport problems go to visit the home of Old Hickory. In the zappy words of Wylie White:

" Just in time ... The tour is just starting. Home of Old Hickory - America's tenth president. The victor of New Orleans, opponent of the National Bank, and inventor of the Spoils System."

Making allowances for the Hollywood scriptwriter's shorthand this does summarize the values and associations of Andrew Jackson (1767-1845). Jackson was, in fact, the seventh president, but in essence the career given here does embody the major features of his folkloric reputation. Andrew Jackson fought in the War of Independence and was captured by the British. He helped to frame the constitution of Tennessee and represented the state in Congress in 1796 and in the Senate in 1797. He was a judge of the supreme court of Tennessee.

He became a national hero during the 1812 war with the British after a series of brilliant victories against the Indians and defeating Sir Edward Michael Pakenham's army of 16,000 veterans at New Orleans. Jackson was governor of Florida and ran for the presidency in 1825 as a Democrat against John Quincy Adams, W.H. Crawford and Henry Clay. Jackson had the highest number of popular votes but not a majority. In 1828 he was elected with a majority of electoral votes. The strength of Jackson's image in popular history is to be located in the values he stood for: he was a genuine self-made man, a product of the socio-economic and political philosophy on which the United States was founded, he was courageous and he was a man of principle.

He was re-elected in 1832. To get things done he swept great numbers of officials from office and replaced them with his own partisans, coining the phrase, 'To the victor belong the spoils', to cover these actions. But it meant that he got things done. In spite of the censure of the Senate he broke the power of the Bank of the United States, asserting that it had too much power and was a corrupting element in American political life. During his second administration the national debt was fully paid and the surplus was distributed to the several states of the union. He retired at the end of his second term and died at his house, the Hermitage, Nashville, Tennessee. In *The Last Tycoon* the stranded party look at Jackson's house:

"It was still not quite dawn. The Hermitage looked like a nice big white box, but quite a little lonely and vacated after a hundred years. We walked back to the car ... "[21]

One member of the party considers that even if people do not know much about Jackson or why he is important in American history, there must be something significant about him, if they have preserved his house all these years, and that Jackson must have been 'some one who was large and merciful, able to understand'. At both ends of life man needed nourishment: 'a breast - a shrine'. Significantly the visiting party are unable to gain access to the Hermitage, the house is locked. It is as if the values Jackson stood for are nor longer available to these representatives of a more rapacious America in the twentieth century.

Monroe Stahr is directly associated with Abraham Lincoln. It is George Boxley who recognizes:

"that Stahr like Lincoln was a leader carrying on a long war on many fronts; almost single-handed he had moved pictures sharply forward through a decade, to a point where the content of the 'A productions' was wider and richer than that of the stage. Stahr was an artist only, as Mr. Lincoln was a general, perforce and as a layman." [22]

There is another important reference to Lincoln, seen through the eyes of a distinguished visitor to the studios, the Danish Prince Agge, who is described in Scott Fitzgerald's list of characters as an 'early Fascist'. [23] Agge obviously believes in the superiority of some races to others:

" He was hostile to Jews in a vague general way that he tried to cure himself of. As a turbulent man, serving his time in the Foreign Legion, he thought that Jews were too fond of their own skins. But he was willing to concede that they might be different in America under different circumstances ..." [24]

But the panoramic view he gets of the crowded film studios is like the Melting Pot of Nations itself:

" Coming out of the private dining room, they passed through a corner of the commissary proper. Prince Agge drank it in - eagerly. It was gay with gipsies and with citizens and soldiers, with sideburns and braided coats of the First Empire. From a little distance they were men who lived and walked a hundred years ago, and Agge wondered how he and the men of his time would look as extras in some future costume picture.

Then he saw Abraham Lincoln, and his whole feeling suddenly changed. He had been brought up in the dawn of Scandinavian socialism when Nicolay's biography was much read. He had been told that Lincoln was a great man whom he should admire, and he hated him instead, because he was forced upon him ..." [25]

But now that he sees Lincoln before him he cannot help staring at him. The actor sits there, with his legs crossed, his kindly face fixed on his forty-cent dinner, 'including dessert', with a shawl wrapped round his shoulders to protect himself from the erratic air-conditioning: 'This then, was Lincoln ...' Agge realizes that this is what they all meant to be. Much to his surprise this glimpse into the inner meaning of things in this new society, this man-made nation, is shattered as the living presence from the past of American history, the great and good Abraham Lincoln, father of the new nation state, unexpectedly raises his hand and stuffs a triangle of pie into his mouth. In the United States the extraordinary and the ordinary are all mixed up together, and the best and the brightest can be seen rising from humble origins and at the same time reasserting absolute ordinariness; the historic and the humdrum are one and the same. It is the dynamic of this society which has created Monroe Stahr, and as Fitzgerald's plans for *The Last Tycoon* survive to indicate, it was these same forces which would threaten and destroy him. [26] As Charles E. Shain opines, *The Last Tycoon* has the mark of the '30s on it as surely as the early fictions had taken the American boom as their theme: 'The subject was Hollywood as an industry and as a society, but also as an American microcosm.'[27] But there is mercifully more to it than that. *The Last Tycoon* is an impressive and moving fragment, not just because it is a faithful portrait of the motion picture industry at a particular period of its development - to say that is to mistake the Hollywood for the trees - but because Fitzgerald convincingly uses this material to explore some of his driving interest in the creative processes and their relationship with industry and mass society. As a creative artist himself he could not fail to be interested in the compromise and negotiation which must take place between the various stages of the processes between ideas and conception, on the one hand, and production and consumption on the other. Had he lived to finish it, our impression of *The Last Tycoon* might well be gloomier. As it stands it remains a brilliant and dazzling achievement.

The novel was filmed in 1976 with Robert de Niro as Monroe Stahr. It was not a very good movie, but its weaknesses are significant. It saw itself as part of a particularly strong tradition in film-making - the movie about movie-making, sardonically lifting the lid on the whole business. This line stretches back from *Sunset Boulevard* in 1950, through *The Star, The Barefoot Contessa, Hollywood Boulevard*, the various versions of *A Star is Born, The Day of the Locust* and *The Carpetbaggers*. Its period detail was excellent, and the recreation of the industry's technology and management was impressive. But its focus was awry. It was like a bad cake made with the best ingredients. *The Last Tycoon* is not about films. It is about art. Scott Fitzgerald wrote in his notebook: 'There never was a good biography of a good novelist. There couldn't be. He's too many people if he's any good.' [28] But *The Last Tycoon* is very nearly a great novel about a maker, unfinished as indeed it is.

NOTES

1. Arthur Mizener, *Introduction, F. Scott Fitzgerald: A Collection of Critical Essays* (New Jersey: Prentice-Hall, 1963). pp. 3-4.

2. Mai D. Hueling, 'Fortune-Metro-Goldwyn-Mayer', in Tino Balio (ed.), *The American Film Industry* (Madison, Wisconsin: University of Wisconsin Press, 1976), p. 259.

3. *Freaks* was completed in 1932 but was withheld from public showing by censorship for thirty years. It is a circus melodrama featuring genuine freaks. An odd movie to have been sponsored by the fastidious Irving Thalberg.

4. Marcus Cunliffe, *The Literature of the United States* (Harmondsworth: Penguin, 1968), p. 292.

5. For a discussion of *The Last Tycoon* as 'Hollywood novel' see Arthur Mizener, 'The Maturity of Scott Fitzgerald', in the *Sewanee Review*, LXVII (Autumn 1959), 658 ff.

6. F. Scott Fitzgerald, *The Last Tycoon*, in *The Bodley Head Scott Fitzgerald* (London: Bodley Head, 1966), Vol. 1, 167.

7. *The Last Tycoon*, ibid., p. 175.

8. Ibid., p. 180.

9. Ibid., p. 180.

10. Ibid., p. 181.

11. Ibid., pp. 197-98.

12. Ibid., p. 198.

13. Ibid., p. 198-99.

14. Ibid., p. 199. This is, in fact, an excellent account of how stories are told in pictures, and suggests that F. Scott Fitzgerald learned much from his days in Hollywood - cf. James Monaco: *How to Read a Film: The Art, Technology, History*

and Theory of Film and Media (New York: Oxford University Press, 1981), pp. 125 ff.;
J. Dudley Andrew, *The Major Film Theories* (New York: Oxford University Press, 1976),
pp. 220 ff.; Robert Scholes's essay 'Narration and Narrativity in Film' in Gerald Mast
and Marshall Cohen (eds.), *Film Theory and Criticism: Introductory Readings* (New
York: Oxford University Press, 1979), pp. 417-33, and Robert Richardson, *Literature
and Film* (Bloomington, Indiana: University of Indiana Press, 1969), pp. 65 ff.

15.   An obvious example would be Dickens, who seized the opportunities of
reaching a growing readership by means of serial publication. *Bleak House, Great
Expectations* and *Our Mutual Friend* are not masterpieces in spite of the mass
production of literature in mid-Victorian Britian; they are masterpieces because of
the means of production available to Dickens at that time.

16.   F. Scott Fitzgerald, *The Last Tycoon*, op. cit., pp. 277-78.

17.   Ibid., p. 278.

18.   Quoted in John Robert Columbo (ed.), *Wit and Wisdom of the
Moviemakers* (London: Hamlyn, 1979), p. 116.

19.   C.W.E. Bigsby, 'The Two Identities of F. Scott Fitzgerald' in Malcolm
Bradbury and David Palmer (eds.), *The American Novel and the Nineteen Twenties*
(London: Edward Arnold, 1971), pp. 142 ff.

20.   The case is persuasively argued by C.W.E. Bigsby, see 'The Two Identities
of F. Scott Fitzgerald', ibid., pp. 14 ff.

21.   *The Last Tycoon*, op. cit., p. 178.

22.   *The Last Tycoon*, ibid., pp. 278-79.

23.   Ibid., p. 211.

24.   Ibid., p. 213.

25.   Ibid., pp. 216-17.

26.   Ibid., pp. 303-8.

27.   Charles E. Shain, 'F. Scott Fitzgerald' in *Seven Modern American Novelists:
An Introduction*, edited by William Van O'Connor (Minneapolis: University of
Minnesota Press, 1964), p. 116.

28.   Quoted in *The Bodley Head Scott Fitzgerald*, op. cit., p.7.

IX

John Le Carré
and the Writing
on the Igloo Walls

At last fiction learns a few lessons from film. Writers tried to sponge a living from the film industry for generations, but literature was always a bit snobby about the cinema. Yet the profession of authorship has always learned something from new modes of production. Novelists learned a great deal about the creation of character and about dialogue from what they saw and heard on the stage — Dickens is your best expert witness for that — but "serious" writers have tried for years to keep literature and entertainment separate, as Grahame Greene will tell you. But at last in John Le Carré we have a novelist, accepted by the literary establishment, who has undoubtedly learned some basic lessons from watching films. And none the worse for that.

"Nothing amuses the Eskimo more than for the white man to crane his neck to see the magazine pictures stuck on the igloo walls. For the Eskimo no more needs to look at a picture right side up than does a child before he has learned his letters on a line ... The extreme bias and distortion of our sense-lives by our technology would seem to be a fact that we prefer to ignore in our daily lives." - Marshall McLuhan, UNDERSTANDING MEDIA (1964). [1]

One major result of the impact of French structuralism on English and American literary criticism has been the energy expended in deconstructing the role of the 'author'. This has been a long time in coming. Susan Sontag claims the movement has been going for a century.[2] Be that as it may, the movement is in full cry now:

"Inevitably, disestablishing the 'author' brings about a redefinition of 'writing'. Once writing no longer **defines** itself as responsible, the seemingly common- sense distinction between the work and the person who produces it, between public and private utterance, becomes void. All pre-modern literature evolves from the classical conception of writing as an impersonal, self-sufficient, free-standing achievement. Modern literature projects a quite different idea: the romantic conception of writing as a medium in which a singular personality heroically exposes itself. This ultimately private reference of public, literary discourse does not require that the reader actually know a great deal about the author ..." [3]

Thus (and more) Susan Sontag. Many issues come into play in the discussion of authorship and the role of the reader, and, as Susan Sontag is generously the very first to admit, consciousness as given can never wholly constitute itself in art but must always strain to transform its own boundaries and to condition the boundaries of art. Within these boundaries the reader needs to know why, and how, so many of John le Carré's effects can be rendered cinematically with such apparent ease. Le Carré's pictorial imagination can be **placed**.

Between the 'author' and the 'reader' - the creator and the consumer, as it were - the shape, texture and condition of form, which is the result of the technology of production and distribution, intrudes itself. The means of production will have an immense, immediate and obvious impact on the nature of the art produced in any culture. Artists work within the technical limitations of their day. Geniuses transcend them. Whether Homer existed as the identifiable unique individual is not the issue here; the important fact is that 'Homer' produced the unique and overwhelming masterpieces the world now knows as the *Iliad* and the *Odyssey* in the way that he did because the existing mode of literary production of the day favoured the telling of long stories rhapsodically. [4] Oral culture reached the mind through the ear; its culture had to be memorable.

The advent of printing seriously eroded the necessity of patterned language, as literary works no longer required memory and recitation for their production and consumption. As prose narrative began to replace epic a noticeable exactitude of geography and chronology became a feature of what we now recognize as 'the novel' - although its beginnings are clearly to be seen in much Elizabethan prose. John Lyly goes to some trouble to create a believable sense of time, smattering the narrative with

times and days and months, in *Euphues: The Anatomy of Wit* (1578) and
Euphues and his England (1580):

" Euphues, having gotten all things necessary for his voyage into
England ... tooke shipping the first of December, by our English Compu-
tation ..." [5]

In sixteenth- and early seventeenth-century drama, location is not
always important. If the audience need to know where the action is taking
place, they will be told ('Ay, now am I in Arden: the more fool I ...'), but
otherwise the action could be located generally in a forest, in a street, a
palace, a hovel, a coastline or a battlefield. But at the same time we begin
to notice that the writers of narrative prose fiction are starting to
particularize time and place. Miguel de Cervantes went to considerable
trouble to get time and place correctly ascribed in his *Exemplary Novels*,
which were published in 1613. Samuel Putnam comments on the exact
topography of *Rinconete and Cortadillo*:

"The Molinillo inn at which the two lads meet was situated on the road
from Toledo to Cordova; it was two leagues from Tartanedo and four
leagues from Almodovar del Campo; and the Alcade inn, as stated, was
half a league distant ... The allusions to sites in and about Seville are
similarly accurate ..."[6]

Similar comments could be directed at the realistic elements in le
Carré's beloved *Simplicissimus* (think of Smiley, in *Tinker Tailor,* con-
templating the sale of an early edition of Grimmelshausen).

Hearing, rather than sight, had dominated the more ancient poetic
world which preceded writing, and even those societies which experienced
the revolution of writing and became manuscript cultures were still oral-
aural. Texts could be written down and preserved, but a large part of what
we would recognize as 'literature' was still committed to memory. The
reasons are obvious - manuscripts were expensive and not in very wide
circulation, they were often not easy to read and a high proportion of the
population were not literate. The coming of print revolutionized the way
we wrote about the world and the way we perceived the world. In the
words of Walter Ong:

" ... print replaced the lingering hearing-dominance in the world of thought and expression with the sight- dominance which had its beginnings with writing but could not flourish with the support of writing alone. Print situates words in space more relentlessly than writing ever did ...   Most readers are of course not consciously aware of all this locomotion that has produced the printed text confronting them. Nevertheless, from the appearance of the printed text they pick up a sense of the word-in-space quite different from that conveyed by writing. Printed texts look machine-made, as they are. Chirographic control of space tends to be ornamental, ornate, as in calligraphy. Typographic control typically impresses more by its tidiness and   inevitability: the lines perfectly regular, all justified on the right side, everything coming out even visually ... This is an insistent world of cold, non-human, facts ..."[7]

As the means of literary production seemed to emphasize this sense of reality as a result of the very shape and texture of their product, so the creative imaginations of writers inclined, during the centuries which succeeded the invention and development of printing and paper manufacture, to concentrate on an output which attempted credible reality. Sometimes the technology gave rise to an almost immediate reaction in literature. Clearly the modern novel is the child of the printing revolution. Samuel Richardson's creation of a new literary genre, the epistolary novel - which plays so significant a part in the course of Leavis's Great Tradition and led directly to the rich psychological novels of George Eliot and Henry James - was the direct result of technical developments in the industry which employed him.

Richardson was born the sone of a London joiner but was apprenticed to the printer John Wilde at Aldersgate when he was 17 years old. He became compositor, proof-reader and later printer on his own account. He published newspapers and books, printed the Journals of the House of Commons and as Master of the Stationers' Company and Law-Printer to the King was a solid citizen. His contribution to literature had been minor. He compiled a few indexes and wrote a few dedications, but that was that. But he was approached by two successful booksellers, Charles Rivington of St. Paul's Churchyard and Thomas Osborne of Paternoster Row, who asked him to write a model letter-writer for such 'country readers' as 'were unable to indite for themselves'. Richardson compiled a book which they published, *Letters written to and for Particular Friends, on the most Important Occasions*. But Richardson also realized that a story could be told as a series of letters and that telling a story in this way would have several significant advantages. Letters are human documents. They are personal to those who write them and to those for whom they are intended. In reading letters the consumer of a novel so constructed would believe they were overhearing an unfolding series of real events involving real people. Point of view could be exploited. Motives could be explored. All this could be done in ways which were new to the novel and which would in turn be absorbed into the way succeeding novelists created novels. The publication of Richardson's *Pamela; or Virtue Rewarded* in November 1740 ensured that the novel would never be the same again. The following February a second edition had appeared; a third appeared in March and a fourth in May. Ladies held up copies of the book at public gardens to show that they had got it, and Dr. Benjamin Slocock of Southwark commended it from his pulpit.

Impressive though its immediate vogue obviously was, the importance of Richardson's *Pamela* is deeper than that, and for all the mockery of Henry Fielding and the author of *An Apology for the Life of Mrs. Shamela Andrews* (1741) - they may have been one and the same person - the novel had made a leap forward and there would be no retreating, although masked for a while by the triumph of *Tom Jones* and the earlier novels of Smollett whose great strength was in narrative synthesis, Richardson had definitively pointed the way forward to the novel of analysis.

The application of steam power to printing and the development of the railway complex throughout Britain were changes which brought great opportunities not only to periodic journalism but to novel 'authorship' in the widest sense. William Nicholson took out a patent for a cylinder press in 1790, but it was Frederick Koenig in Germany who constructed the first power-driven press in 1811. His pioneering work was built on by Andrew Bauer who made a flat-bed printing machine with a continually revolving cylinder. The issue of *The Times* for 29 November 1814 proclaimed that it 'was printed by steam power'. This machine could produce 1,100 impressions an hour, and by 1827 these machines could print on both sides of the sheet. Applegarth and Cowper produced a machine for *The Times* before 1830 which could print 4,000 impressions an hour. The age of popular publishing, much of it financed by serial publication, had dawned.[8] An essential aspect of Dickens's genius lay in its ability to adapt itself to the new developments in literary production and distribution. Serial publication was a good way for a story-teller to earn a living, but a narrative extended over eighteen months - and most of Dickens's novels were serialized in monthly parts over a year and a half - required the ability to handle a vast canvas with complex plots and numerous characters, [9] but he was influenced significantly by other technological developments in the arts in the early nineteenth century, notably melodrama. [10] There are numerous passages in Dickens's novels which are obviously influenced by the craze for melodrama, where we can see the novelist deliberately and often painstakingly seeking to reproduce on the printed page some of the gaslit and - to modern tastes - garish and crude excitement of the stage:

" 'I have learnt it!' cried the old man. 'From the creature dearest to my heart! O, save her, save her!' He could wind his fingers in her dress; could hold it! As the words escaped his lips, he felt his sense of touch return, and knew that he detained her. The figures looked down steadfastly upon him. 'I have learnt it!' cried the old man. 'O, have mercy on me in this hour, if, in my love for her, so young and good, I slandered Nature in the breasts of mothers rendered desperate! Pity my presumption, wickedness, and ignorance, and save her.' "

This is Dickens writing under the power of a good head of steam in the *Fourth Quarter* of *The Chimes*, published by Chapman and Hall in December 1844, and even allowing for the fact that it is the narrative of a series of dreams experienced by Toby Veck who falls asleep on New Year's Eve while reading a newspaper, it must be admitted that the language is hardly what we would expect from a London ticket-porter in reduced circumstances. But the language of melodrama becomes absorbed into the general apparatus of the novelist's craft, as Edith Granger's rejection of the advances of Mr. Carker in *Dombey and Son* (1846-48) will testify. The requirements of the lending library also had an impact on the novelist's art. As an undergraduate I remember being constantly reminded by my mentors of the brilliant compression of Henry James's imagination and the deep, rich, vast, bottomless hugeness of his mind as it expressed itself in slender volume form. Many years later I was to learn that by the time Henry James came upon the scene considerable changes in the material mode of literary production had meant a shift from what Terry Eagleton has described as 'the densely populated "three-decker" novel, with its diffuse, multiple plots', to the 'more "organic" single volume'.[11]

In the early cinema we see film working on the basic assumptions of narrative prose fiction and drama and basing its grammar and syntax initially on the existing literary traditions. This early literary allegiance is well demonstrated in examples which enshrine a profound contradiction in terms - silent versions of Shakespeare, such as Emil Janning's *Othello* (1922), Johnston Forbes Robertson's *Hamlet* (1913) and Herbert Beerbohm Tree's *Macbeth* (1916, directed by D.W. Griffith). Moving film was able to exploit the innate authority of photography, which - as Marshall McLuhan has argued - extends and multiplies the human image to the proportions of mass-produced merchandise, yet, by drawing on the western European experience of print and painting, creates a false world which we fully believe in; characteristically he coined a pun for it - the reel world.

The cinema was originally called 'The Bioscope' because it was claimed that it could present the actual forms of life, in the form of a public spectacle. Moving film, McLuhan claims, is a spectacular wedding of the old mechanical technology and the new electric world. In a brilliant minor masterpiece, only a few pages in length, McLuhan likened the cinema spectator to Don Quixote.

Like Cervantes' hero the viewer of film is wholly and completely transferred from one world - his own - to another, that world created by typography and film:

"That is so obvious, and happens so completely, that those undergoing the experience accept it subliminally and without critical awareness. Cervantes lived in a world in which print was as new as movies are in the West, and it seemed obvious to him that print, like the images now on the screen, had usurped the real world. The reader or spectator had become a dreamer under their spell ..." [12]

McLuhan goes on to elaborate his argument that moving film as a non-verbal experience may be compared with photography, as a form of statement without syntax. Like print and photography, moving film assumes a very high-level literacy in those who use film. Film is baffling to the non-literate. Although film is an imitation of life, it has to be read, and we have to learn to read it. Film does have some kind of powerful impact on those who have not seen it before. McLuhan quotes the celebrated examples of the African natives who wanted to know where characters went when they went off screen as evidence of the case that the linear logic and grammar of film has to be learned; nevertheless the surface quality of film itself, even in its black and white form and with no sound track, does show a world of movement which looks like life. It is an historically attested fact, and a fact of considerable significance, that on 10 March 1895 when the first celluloid film was projected to an audience by Louis Lumière, the viewers left their seats in fright when they saw film of a train arriving in a station. [13] The point appears to need some emphasis; film is its own language, with its own way of telling things. The full cultural apprehension of film may not come until we have learned the grammar and syntax of the new language - let us go that far with McLuhan as the argument seems on the whole to be a sound one - but the initial, immediate impact of film seems charged with innate information. After all, the Lumière film of the train was totally silent, [14] and yet it carried enough information to convince its audience that what they were seeing was 'real'. It is a strong part of McLuhan's argument that a literate audience, used to following printed imagery line by line without questioning the logicality of lineality, will be more ready to accept film sequence. It seems, then, that when film appears in our culture at the turn of the nineteenth and twentieth centuries, it is able to build on the very sturdy foundations laid in western European culture by our long experience of writing and printing and reading. In other words, cinematography was an extension of literacy.

As McLuhan points out, it was René Clair - whose early professional experience was literary (he was a journalist) but who went into films from beginning as an actor, and wrote and directed many films, including *A Nous la Liberté, Quatorze Juillet, Le Dernier Milliardaire, Les Belles de Nuit, Les Grandes Manoeuvres* - who observed that if three characters were on stage, the dramatist ceaselessly has to strive to explain or motivate their being there, whereas a film audience will simply accept mere sequence as rational. Whatever the moving camera shows us, we accept as part of what the film-maker wants to tell us. We are transported into another world:

" The close relation, then, between the reel world of film and the private fantasy experience of the printed word is indispensable to our Western acceptance of the film form. Even the film industry regards all of its greatest achievements as derived from novels, nor is this unreasonable. Film, both in its reel form and in its scenario or script form, is completely involved with book culture." [15]

The emphasis on associating literature and film owes a great deal for its surviving success in film theory to the imprimatur of almost classical authority granted it by Sergei Eisenstein. It was Eisenstein who locate the primal springs of Griffith's genius as a film-maker in the novels of Dickens. [16] A theorist who comes to the matter from the other direction is Siegfried Kracauer. Kracauer has a great deal to say about the surface quality of film, about matters of style and the flexibility of film as a language which, he believes, are the result of its ultimate derivation from photography:

" Like the embryo in the womb, photographic film developed from distinctly separate components. Its birth came about from a combination of instantaneous photography ... with the older devices of the magic lantern and the phenakistoscope. Added to this later were contributions of other nonphotographic elements, such as editing and sound. Nevertheless, photography, especially instantaneous photography, has a legitimate claim to top priority among these elements, for it undeniably is and remains the decisive factor in establishing film content. The nature of photography survives in that of film." [17]

The craze for structuralist analysis of texts has tended to emphasize the importance of deep structural meanings, hidden agendas, and mythic structures of narrative meaning based on the relationship between characters. This has often been extremely valuable, but the work of Propp and Eco has tended, in the main, to divert attention from the surface structure of works which attempt something in the narrative mode. [18] Kracauer's words bring us back to focus our attention on those qualities we immediately perceive, that we perceive with such immediacy that we do not notice them: the photographic quality of moving film, its ability to be stuck together as a raw material by a film-maker of genius and turned into an artwork; the latent charge in film which can be so edited in montage that new meanings can be constructed in a process which cinematographically parallels dialectic materialism - thesis/antithesis/ synthesis [19]; the manner in which film enables us to concentrate on reaction as much as on action; and on all the tricks of the trade in terms of sound and vision. Kracauer is correct to assert that it is the very nature of photography which survives in film and which establishes film con-

tent. The argument that film is a degenerate art and that to adapt classic novels for films is to corrupt sacred texts is a familiar one in British culture. (Its leading exponent is Dr. Jonathan Miller.) It is impossible literally to translate a novel into film terms. Certain things possible in literature (which are among the things which make literature the great high cultural commodity which it is assumed to be) are not possible in film. For example, in *Great Expectations* Dickens likens Wemmick to a post-box. He does more than this, of course, being the great poet that he is: he says that Wemmick does not so much eat his food as post it. Now, how can we show that in film? We can show Wemmick eating and then cut in (or even fade up) a post-box. But what will that do? It will make viewers think that Wemmick is thinking about posting a letter as he is eating. Or it may suggest that Wemmick works for the Post Office. But it cannot convey what Dickens wants to convey.

Much as we may respect the argument that the way we read film owes much to our experience of reading written or printed words, there are numerous ways in which the language of film must be seen as unique to itself and not just an extension of literature.

Moving film can show a whole scene, a room full of people, a landscape, a street - all in one moving shot - so that a great deal of information can be delivered in one go. This is beyond literature. It has enormous powers, then, of exposition - and it is significant that exposition is one of the most difficult things convincingly to bring off in literature. The fact that film can be shot in pieces then stuck together at will in the editing process gives film a whole battery of effects not available in literature: fading, dissolving, cutting. An effect such as the scream of the landlady suddenly cutting to the shriek of express train bound for Scotland in Hitchcock's *The Thirty-Nine Steps* (1935) would not be possible in literature. [20] The multiplicity of angles and points of view which can be brought together all in the same moment - such as the murder of Marion in *Psycho* (1960) - can only be constructed in film. It is a tribute to film, and of course to the genius of Hitchcock, that many people who have seen *Psycho* believe the murder-in-the-shower scene to be in colour and that they have seen the knife enter Marion Crane's bare body. This amazing sequence is a superb example of the film-maker's art. It is a combination of photography (it needed a week of filming, and seventy-eight set-ups), editing (it lasts only a minute on screen) and sound(the music by Bernard Herrmann adds to visual effects rather than simply supporting them). [21]

In film it is possible much more easily than in drama or narrative prose to concentrate on reaction. For example, we can see the face and changing reactions of a person as we hear the voice and sounds providing the information which prompts those reactions. Our response to what we see can be conditioned by the angle and distance of camera shots selected by the director and editor of film. This is not possible in drama. This quality in film is repeatedly exploited by Eisenstein. Flashback is extremely effective in film but very difficult indeed in drama or narrative prose, as film is very strong at creating the idea of 'present' time - the time that you are actually watching the action - and then reverting easily into a sequence clearly signalled as the 'past'. Orson Welles constantly exploits this in Citizen Kane (1940). [22] The endless tricks possible with the camera - deep focus, multiple image, mixing, fading, filtering, point-of-view, zooming and tracking - add a whole new vocabulary to narrative which does not exist elsewhere. [23] To dismiss film as degenerate and of lower intrinsic aesthetic merit than drama or the novel is to be a cultural Luddite. But the mythology is very strong.

Film and television are media with their own languages - languages no less worthy of respect than the printed text. But it is in the nature of the production and consumption of 'high culture' in our society that there is an in-built snobbery about print. Bernard Levin commented, in a book review in the *Sunday Times* in September 1983, that a particular author's technique 'of undercutting ... has a cinematic gloss but also a cinematic superficiality.' So there you have it, stated for all its worth - literature is *ipso facto* a higher art than film.

Cultural snobbery has always demonstrated itself by its allegiance to the immediately preceding mode of production. This is an essential part of the grammar of culture. It is the argument of fashion and anti-fashion. The trick is to resist change, which is always perceived as a sign of degeneracy. The classics are relics from previous modes of production. The ability to adapt to change, Charles Darwin believed, was one of the things which enabled life to survive. But we still resist new forms of cultural production and distribution. The classics are good for you. It is as simple as that. They are to the soul what a high-fibre diet is to the body. It is vastly more upmarket to consume the wholemeal of 'literature' and 'the theatre' (e.g. the West End theatre) than to consume the junk food of the mass media.

Very recent cultural history will show how this grammar actually works. Hollywood musicals of the '30s and '40s were originally regarded as shallow, cheap, ephemeral entertainment. The next stage was the development of a camp interest in the genre. Today, the 'best' of them are regarded as classics, worthy of being shown on B.B.C. 2, the channel of opera, Jane Austen and documentaries about Evelyn Waugh. The consequences of this are considerable. It means that the more what is seen on television, for example, is 'like' literature, the 'better' it is. That is to say *Barchester Chronicles, Brideshead Revisited, Kilvert's Diary, Mansfield Park, The Jewel in the Crown, Tender is the Night, Hotel du Lac* - O.K. But *Minder, Rumpole, The Likely Lads, Auf Wiedersehen Pet* and other popular favourites are hardly acceptable. It means that a lacklustre, overdressed movie such as *A Room with a View,* in which a team of well-intentioned British thespians seem to be enunciating their lines as if fearful that the actual words might come to some harm as they leave their lips, was hailed as a great film in 1986.

But there have now been several generations of writers who lost their innocence by being exposed to the cinema. It could be argued that the cinema has influenced developments in modern narrative prose fiction. It is well-documented fact that Evelyn Waugh loved going to the pictures. No one would claim that Waugh was, by any stretch of critical generosity, a 'novelist's novelist'. His novels are markedly free from literary associations. Poor Tony Last is condemned to reading the novels of Dickens to the end of his life. The narrative sequence of *Brideshead Revisited* is constructed as one vast flashback. Len Deighton is another interesting example. He was educated at art school and has always admitted his admiration for the movies, especially espionage movies. The narrative infrastructure of his novels owes much to his experiences at the cinema and indeed, unlike the heavyweights of the British literary establishment (that is to say, those who are more likely to win the Booker Prize than Len Deighton is), he was never exposed to an Eng. Lit. education. In his creation of his working-class hero - Harry Palmer - and the series of adventures in which he is usually placed (*The Ipcress File* (1962), *Horse Under Water* (1963), and *Funeral in Berlin* (1964)) he seems to have created a kind of novel whose genre really belongs, root and branch, to the cinema. Alistair MacLean is another novelist whose espionage/adventure novels seem naturally made for the cinema - in particular *Puppet on a Chain, Where Eagles Dare* and *Bear Island.* Interestingly enough, when the considerable literary abilities of Graham Greene (novel) and Tom

Stoppard (screenplay) were combined in *The Human Factor* (1979) the results were emphatically not good cinema. John le Carré has achieved a considerable feat in combining some very characteristic elements of the cinema with the requirements of prose narrative. He has created a *genre* unmistakably his own: the espionage story in the form of a novel with 'class'. He has his entry in Margaret Drabble's edition of *The Oxford Companion to English Literature* (1985) [24] and his novels have been serialized on B.B.C.2 as starring vehicles for Sir Alec Guinness. The similarity with Graham Greene is worth recalling for several reasons. Like Greene, le Carré had a public school and Oxford education, and worked for the British Foreign Office. Both authors share an interest in the seedy and the ambiguous as qualities of life in the modern world, both in terms of private and public life.

Graham Greene spent four-and-a-half years immediately before the outbreak of war in 1939 as a film reviewer, and we therefore have some very useful insight as to his views and opinions of numerous films. Interestingly enough, he did not like Hitchcock, who had - it seemed to Greene - an 'inadequate sense of reality'. He had a low opinion of *The Thirty-Nine Steps*. The oft-praised details of Hitchcock's films, Greene claimed, added up to nothing:

" His films consist of a series of small 'amusing' melodramatic situations: the murderer's button dropped on the baccarat board; the strangled organist's hands prolonging the notes in an empty church ... very perfunctorily he builds up to these tricky situations (paying no attention on the way to inconsistencies, loose ends, psychological absurdities) and then drops them: they mean nothing: they lead to nothing."[25]

Greene himself divided his fictions into two categories: entertainments and novels, and in this respect he seems aware of the entertainment value of films. Of course, many of his fictions have been turned into films, and he has written screenplays. [26] He notes with obvious relish the cinema's ability to construct and to project atmosphere, particularly (in those monochrome days) the atmosphere of decay, fear, treachery and things falling apart in general. Writing of the 1935 remake of Liam O'Flaherty's novel, *The Informer*, directed by John Ford and starring Victor McLaglen, Greene said:

"It is superb material for the screen: very few words are needed for this drama; terror is not a subtle sensation: it can be conveyed very much easier by images alone than scruples, guilt, tenderness. You only need the Black and Tan patrols through the Liffey fogs, the watching secretive figures outside the saloons as the drunken informer drifts deeper and deeper with his cronies into the seedy night life of Dublin. Mr. Victor MacLaglen has never given an abler performance, and the film, even if it sometimes underlines its points rather crudely, is a memorable picture of a pitiless war waged without honour on either side in doorways and cellars and gin-shops." (*Spectator*, 11 October 1935)[27]

Graham Greene highlights several qualities which are highly relevant when considering the fiction of John le Carré. One is the generation of atmosphere - the fog which is also emblematic of moral ambiguity. The endless, meaningless conflict (The Troubles in this case, but in le Carré's case, the Cold War) within which human beings and their torments and tensions get drawn into and the way human beings devalue their own high moral conception of themselves and the motives behind their high-principled actions by selling each other. As is so often the case in film noir as a genre, the story is difficult to follow (cf. *The Big Sleep*), but the incomprehensibility of what is going on is part of the sophistication itself as well as being emblematic of the confusions and contradictions of modern life itself.

It seems to me that one of the permanent fascinations of John le Carré's art is the way he has inverted the usual practice, and instead of adapting fiction to film, he has adapted film to fiction.

The Spy Who Came in from the Cold was published in 1963, a year after Ian Fleming's *Dr. No* had been filmed. There was a spate of espionage movies, mostly with a Cold War backdrop, during the 1960s, which was the decade when John le Carré's fiction began to make its unmistakable mark. Among the titles which come most easily to mind are *The Manchurian Candidate* (1962), *From Russia With Love* (1963), *Hot Enough for June* (1963), *Licensed to Kill* (1965), *Goldfinger* (1964), *Charade* (1964), *Thunderball* (1965), *Operation Crossbow* (1965), *Where the Spies Are* (1965), *The Liquidator* (1965), *Our Man Flint* (1965) - (*The Spy Who Came in from the Cold* was released in 1966) - *Torn Curtain* (1966), *Arabesque* (1966), *Funeral in Berlin* (1967), *The Naked Runner* (1967), *Double Man* (1967), *Assignment K* (1968) and *On Her Majesty's Secret Service*(1969). Between 1964 and 1967 our television screens regularly gave us *The Man From U.N.C.L.E.* John le Carré's fiction, then, offered the literary equivalent to the genre of espionage thriller which was very much in vogue. His genius lies in adding ingredients of his own, and working the mixture up in terms of narrative prose fiction which passes muster as 'literature'. That entry in *The Oxford Companion* must not be ignored.

Le Carré imports much from the language and style of popular film in *The Spy Who Came in from the Cold*. It is located in a situation which does not seem to need any explication - the Cold War is simply **there** (like The Troubles in *The Informer* and in much modern television drama set in Ireland) as a backdrop for the melodrama of the foreground. The basic plot mechanism concerns a British professional spy of considerable expertise; he is set up in a situation so that it seems he is finished, then fired and dismissed from the service. This is done to make him an obvious target for recruitment by 'the enemy'. This in turn has been planned so that he may be used to destroy his great opponent and opposite number behind the Iron Curtain, Hans-Dieter Mundt. The narrative tricks are all familiar ones, and they are familiar because we have all seen them many times before in the movies. As Leslie Halliwell tersely observes, it is no more and no less than 'The old undercover yarn with trimmings ...'.[28] But when examined it is clear that many, if not all, the worthwhile qualities (or trimmings, if one insists on Halliwell's phrase) are there on the pages of le Carré's novel. It reads like a film. The exposition in the opening pages is astonishingly cinematic. Le Carré's imagination seems to present itself on the page in the manner of a film; his story unfolds like a movie. It is monochrome. Not much seems to happen. The dialogue is laconic. Details of landscape and location and of character are sparse:

" The American handed Leamas another cup of coffee and said, 'Why don't you go back and sleep? We can ring you if he shows up.'
    Leamas said nothing, just stared through the window of the checkpoint, along the empty street." [29]

Unlike that familiar sense in an English novel that you are at the beginning of something, which will have a middle and, eventually, an end, you seem at the opening of *The Spy Who Came in from the Cold*, suddenly to be **there**, in the middle of things. Films do not open, as novels do. You enter them. You sit in the dark. The credits roll by **and you are there in the action**:

" You can't wait for ever ... he's nine hours over schedule.' 'If you want to go, go. You've been very good,' Leamas added. 'I'll tell Kramer you've been damn good.'

'But how long will you wait?'

'Until he comes.' Leamas walked to the observation window and stood between the two motionless policemen. Their binoculars were trained on the Eastern checkpoint.

'He's waiting for the dark,' Leamas muttered, 'I know he is.'

' This morning you said he'd come across with the work men.' Leamas turned on him.

'Agents aren't aeroplanes. They don't have schedules. He's blown, he's on the run, he's frightened. Mundt's after him, now, at this moment. He's only got one chance. Let him choose his time.'[30]

The detail is very sparse as we come into the midst of the action. The dialogue is very curt, cinematic. The action is present and continuous. The diffculty we have in attempting to understand what is going on is all part of the sophisticated incomprehensibility of the genre, which contributes to its hardboiled and cynical nature. It must have been simple to translate this to the screen. It was not 'written for' the cinema, but it is in the style of a series of films immediately recognizable to the generation which would have seen any of that series of gunmen/spy melodramas directed by Carol Reed in the late 1940s and early 1950s: *Odd Man Out* (1946), *The Third Man* (1949), and *The Man Between* (1953).

The ingredients are immediately recognizable. There is a grainy black-and-white realism, bordering on the harsh and inhuman. The setting is invariably a large urban area - Dublin, Berlin, Vienna, it does not really matter - which is torn apart by some vast inexplicable international or internecine conflict which divides people into goodies and baddies. Moral values are reduced to black-and-white terms. And yet the entire moral ambience is ambiguous. Who is really virtuous? Who is really guilty? Who really wins, in the end? The conflicts and tensions within which the human beings we watch have to play out their pitiful destinies are confusing to those caught within them. We who are watching do not need even to know the whys and wherefores of them. It is enough that we acknowledge that they are there. What made these movies so intoxicating was their atmospheric intrigue, and it is this which John le Carré has so brilliantly transported to the printed page:

" Pushing up the collar of his jacket, Leamas stepped outside in the
icy October wind. He remembered the crowd then. It was something you
forgot inside the hut, this group of puzzled faces. The people changed but
the expressions were the same. It was like the helpless crowd that gathers
round a traffic accident, no one knowing how it happened, whether you
should move the body. Smoke or dust rose through the beam of the arc-
lamps, a constant shifting pall between the margins of light." [31]

Le Carré is at his most efficient and sparkling at this kind of thing,
because it is intensely visual. He has certain images and effects of light
in his imagination as he writes, and it is his gift to be able to translate
these visual impressions into words. It is not simply a matter of lanscape
and description, though, for he is equally brilliant in evoking action. The
scene where Karl finally appears riding his bicycle and is shot before
Leamas's eyes contains some of le Carré's finest writing, because he
makes you see exactly what Leamas sees, as he sees it. You are there, as
it happens:

" The East German fired, quite carefully, away from them, into his
own sector. The first shot seemed to thrust Karl forward, the second to
pull him back. Somehow he was still moving, still on the bicycle, passing
the sentry, and the sentry was still shooting at him. Then he sagged, rolled
to the ground, and they heard quite clearly the clatter of the bike as it fell
..." [32]

He is at his weakest at those very moments at which novelists are
supposed to shine. Le Carré is not convincing when he tries to convey
what his characters are thinking. His prose then becomes laboured and
we sense a straining after the right images and metaphors. The result is
a rather turgid literariness:

" Leamas was not a reflective man and not a particularly philosophical one. He knew he was written off - it was   a fact of life which
he would henceforth live with, as a man must live with cancer or
imprisonment. He knew there was no kind of preparation which could
have bridged the gap between then and now. He met failure as one day
he would probably meet death, with cynical resentment and the courage
of the solitary. He'd lasted longer than most; now he was beaten. It is said
a dog lives as long as its teeth; metaphorically, Leamas's teeth had been
drawn; and it was Mundt who had drawn them." [33]

This is not good writing. It is inelegant and unsure of itself. It lacks clarity and the syntax betrays its basic lack of purpose. It is unmistakably what it is - an Englishman trying to write as Hemingway and not making a very good job of it. Yet the moment le Carré writes visually his prose comes to life in his hands in a way which is almost electrical:

" They walked to her flat through the rain and they might have been anywhere - Berlin, London, any town where paving stones turn to lakes of light in the evening rain, and the traffic shuffles despondently through wet streets." [34] This is the writing of a mind fully and congenially engaged in its subject-matter. The sentences read well because the ideas and images are clear in the writer's mind; le Carré knows what he wants his readers to see and he can reproduce it easefully on the page before you. The whole of his early relationship with Liz is handled with equal brilliance, right up to the moment she leaves him:

" 'Good-bye, Liz,' he said. 'Good-bye,' and then: 'Don't follow me. Not again.' Liz nodded and muttered: 'Like we said.' She was thankful for the biting cold of the street and for the dark which hid her tears." [35]

This is supremely confident prose which knows where it is going. One notices time and again that when le Carré presents action, it is always seen externally, in cinematic terms. This is true even where the real nature of the action is necessarily ambiguous, such as the scene in the grocer's shop when Leamas assaults the shopkeeper. We see what happens as the camera would see it. We hear what is said, we see people's reactions, we seem to see Leamas strike the grocer, but we are not exactly sure what happens. We do not learn the real professional details until we hear what was said in court about the fractured cheek bone and the dislocated jaw. At moments such as these, le Carré's prose leaps into life. It always weakens when he is trying to show what is in a character's mind. It is then the syntax faulters and similes and metaphors become leaden:

" Christ, they're rushing their fences, Leamas thought; it's indecent. He remembered some silly music hall joke - 'This is an offer no respectable girl could accept - and besides, I don't know what it's worth.' Tactically, he reflected, they're right to rush it. I'm on my uppers, prison experience still fresh, social resentment strong. I'm an old horse, I don't need breaking in; I don't have to pretend they've offended my honour as an English gentleman. On the other hand they would expect practical objections. They would expect him to be afraid; for his Service pursued traitors as the eye of God followed Cain across the desert."[36]

The plot structure of *The Spy Who Came in from the Cold* is one that would be familiar to those with a wide experience of movie dramas of the '40s and '50s: good guy set up as bait by dismissal and criminal conviction so as to be snaffled up by the bad guys, thus providing the entrance to the labyrinth where the answer to the problem may be found. But it is also put before us cinematically: the lengthy section which details the steady establishment of the relationship between Leamas and Peters not only looks and reads like cinematic material, but le Carré uses this opportunity for lengthy flashbacks which fill in all kinds of details we need to know about Leamas's past and the espionage operations. [37]

The narrative techniques are all strongly reminiscent of the movies. There is the cross-cutting between what is happening to Liz in London and what happens to Alec Leamas in East Germany. He signs letters he does not fully understand. He begins to fear the whole thing is going wrong. Then he is arrested and comes face to face with Mundt:

"Above him shone the light, large, clinical and fierce. No furniture, just whitewashed walls, quite close all round, and the grey steel door, a smart charcoal grey, the colour you see on clever London houses. There was nothing else. Nothing at all. Nothing to think about, just the savage pain.

He must have lain there hours before they came. It grew hot from the light, he was thirsty but he refused to call out. At last the door opened and Mundt stood there. He knew it was Mundt from the eyes. Smiley had told him about them."[38]

The climax of *The Spy Who Came in from the Cold*, which covers the tribunal, is written in a magnetic style. I do not think le Carré ever surpasses it in any of his other novels. It is entirely gripping from beginning to end. But it is based on a model which the cinema very early in its history found was wholly appropriate to the kind of narrative it could cope with - the trial. The gradual unravelling of the truth of a matter, through the presentation of the case by opposing advocates, the interrogation of witnesses, the presentation of witnesses - all this has become an area of dramatic technique wholly suitable to cinema with its effective use of cross-cutting, reaction shots and unique ability denied to stage drama of focusing attention entirely and directly at its own will. What better witness could we call upon than Leslie Halliwell, who deposed in the

Filmgoer's Companion: 'Courtroom scenes have been the suspenseful saving grace of more films than can be counted; and they also figure in some of the best films ever made.'[39]

The deception and exploitation of Alec Leamas does not dawn on him; it strikes him 'with the terrible clarity of a man too long deceived ...'.[40] At the same moment we too become aware of the whole plot mechanism. All the pieces suddenly make sense, just as in *Citizen Kane* the riddle of 'Rosebud' is resolved in a flash. And once again we must acknowledge the mastery with which the basic lessons and principles of film narrative have been fully absorbed - albeit unconsciously in all probability - by John le Carré, and carried over into narrative prose. Technology and science made new things possible and in turn some of these new and exciting possibilities have been carried over into the craft of the novel. Graham Greene has publicly opined that *The Spy Who Came in from the Cold* is the best spy story he has ever read - and this comment is printed on the back cover of the paperback edition. It is not hyperbole to claim that it is also the best spy story ever written, but it must be acknowledged that the art of the cinema made it possible. It was John le Carré who had the sense to exploit those possibilities. The last fourteen pages of the novel, the chapters 'The Wall' and 'In from the Cold', comprise almost entirely dialogue and visual descriptions of the very bleak location where the final catastrophes occur. Their impact on the imagination, stark and powerful as they are, is entirely the result of their cinematic quality.

John le Carré is the master of this particular genre. We need not seek for those qualities of moral awareness and deep psychological probing, combined with irony and compassion which Dr. F.R. Leavis and his followers have taught us to expect from the novel. If every picture tells a story, not all stories can be told in pictures.

NOTES

1. Marshall McLuhan, 'The Photograph - Brothel Without Walls' in *Understanding Media* (Routledge & Kegan Paul, 1964), p. 204.

2. Susan Sontag, *Under the Sign of Capricorn* (Writers and Readers, 1980), p. 13.

3. Sontag, op. cit., p. 15.

4. Walter Ong, *Orality and Literacy: The Technologising of the Word* (Methuen, 1982), pp. 17ff.

5. John Lyly, *Euphues and his England* (1580; London, Arber Reprints, 1910), p. 225.

6. Miguel Cervantes, *Three Exemplary Novels*, translated by Samuel Putnam (Cassell, 1952), pp. 221-22.

7. Walter Ong, *Rhetoric, Romance and Technology* (Ithaca and London: Cornell University Press, 1971), pp. 284-303. See Keith Selby, *Time and the Novel*, unpublished M.A. dissertation, University of Wales, 1981. *The Rambler*, 31 March 1750. Cf Robert Giddings, *The Tradition of Smollett* (Metheun, 1967), pp. 46ff.

8. See Louis James, *Fiction for the Working Man 1830-1850* (Oxford University Press, 1963), pp. 32ff.

9. See Robert Giddings (ed.), *The Changing World of Charles Dickens* (Vision Press, Barnes & Noble, 1983), pp. 10-16, and John Butt and Kathleen Tillotson, *Dickens at Work* (Methuen, 1970)

10. Louis James, *Print and the People 1819-1851* (Allen Lane, 1976), pp. 83-7.

11. Terry Eagleton, *Criticism and Ideology* (New Left Books, 1976), p. 104.

12. Marshall McLuhan, 'Movies: The Reel World' in *Understanding Media* (Routledge & Kegan Paul, 1964) p. 304.

13. Keith Reader, *The Cinema: A History* (Hodder & Stoughton, 1979), pp. 4-5.

14. See Peter Wollen, 'Cinema and Semiology: Some Points of Contact' in *Readings and Writings: Semiotics and Counter Strategies* (New Left Books, 1982), pp. 3-17.

15. McLuhan, op. cit., p. 305.

16. See Gerald Mast and Marshall Cohen, (eds.), *Film Theory and Criticism* (Oxford University Press, 1979), pp. 394ff.

17. Quoted from Siegfried Kracauer, 'Theory of Film: The Redemption of Physical Reality' (1960) in Mast and Cohen, op. cit., p. 7. Cf. J. Dudley Andrew, *The Major Film Theories* (Oxford University Press, 1976), pp. 106ff.

18. See especially 'Narrative Structures in Fleming' in Umberto Eco, *The Role of the Reader: Explorations in the Semiotics of Texts* (Hutchinson, 1981), pp. 144-72, and Terence Hawkes, *Structuralism and Semiotics* (Methuen, 1977). A useful starting point might be the essay on the 'Structural Analysis of Narratives' by Roland Barthes, reprinted in *Barthes: Selected Writings*, edited by Susan Sontag (Fontana, 1980), pp. 251-95.

19. This is the basis of *montage* as evolved by Eisenstein. See Reader, op. cit., pp. 18-22, and *The Complete Films of Eisenstein*, translated by John Hetherington (Weidenfeld & Nicolson, 1974).

20. For an excellent analysis of Hitchcock's *The Thirty Nine Steps* (1935) see

Donald Spoto, *The Art of Alfred Hitchcock* (W.H. Allen, 1977), pp. 37-43.

21.   See John Russell Taylor, *Hitch: The Life and Work of Alfred Hitchcock* (Faber, 1978), pp. 256, and Spoto, op. cit., pp. 371-75, and Robert Giddings: 'Sound and Vision' in the *Listener*, 17 May 1984.

22.   See Pauline Kael, *The Citizen Kane Book* (Boston: Little Brown, 1972), and Ronald Gottesman (ed.), Focus on 'Citizen Kane' (Englewood Cliffs, New Jersey: Prentice Hall, 1971).

23.   See James Monaco, *How to Read a Film* (Oxford University Press, 1981), pp. 140-91, and *The Moving Picture Book*, op. cit., pp. 46-74.

24.   Significantly enough, neither Alistair MacLean nor Len Deighton merit a place in *The Oxford Companion to English Literature*.

25.   Graham Greene, *The Pleasure Dome: The Collected Film Criticism 1935-40*, edited by John Russell Taylor (Oxford University Press, 1980), p. 2.

26.   *Stamboul Train* (1934); *This Gun for Hire* (1942); *The Ministry of Fear* (1943); *Confidential Agent* (1945); *The Man Within* (1946); *Brighton Rock* (1947); *The Fugitive* (1948); *Fallen Idol* (1948); *The Third Man* (1949); *The Heart of the Matter* (1953); *The End of the Affair* (1955); *The Quiet American* (1958); *Our Man in Havana* (1959); *The Comedians* (1967); *Travels with my Aunt* (1973).

27.   Graham Greene, *The Pleasure Dome*, op. cit., p. 26.

28.   Leslie Halliwell, *Film and Video Guide*, 5th edn. (Granada, 1985), p. 916.

29.   John le Carré, *The Spy Who Came in from the Cold* (1963; Pan Books, 1987), p. 1.

30.   Ibid., p. 1.

31.   Ibid., p. 7.

32.   Ibid., p. 12.

33.   Ibid., p. 13.

34.   Ibid., p. 35.

35.   Ibid., p. 44.

36.   Ibid., p. 67.

37.   See pp. 74-91.

38.   Ibid., p. 163.

39.   Leslie Halliwell, *Halliwell's Filmgoer's Companion* (Granada, 1980), p. 159.

40.   *The Spy Who Came in from the Cold*, op. cit., p. 217.